Mel Bay Presents
100 IRISH TUNES
for Piano Accordion

by David DiGiuseppe

1 2 3 4 5 6 7 8 9 0

Includes common session tunes, with over 20 transcriptions from recordings of Jimmy Keane, Phil Cunningham, Karen Tweed and other famous accordionists. Complete with ornamentation, fingering, left hand notation and chord symbols. Appropriate for any G clef instrument.

CD CONTENTS

1. Master Crowley's / The High Reel / The Old Copper Plate *(reels)* [4:36]
2. Slieve Russel / The Cow That Ate the Blanket / The Eavesdropper *(jigs)* [3:38]
3. The Kerry Reel / John Brennan's *(reels)* [3:22]
4. Cronin's Rambles / The Galway *(hornpipes)* [3:04]
5. Glass of Beer / Galway Rambler / Sportin' Pat *(reels)* [3:00]
6. Snug in a Blanket / A Merry Christmas *(jigs)* [2:41]
7. The Congress Reel / Mary McMahon's *(reels)* [2:37]
8. Jerry Daly's Hornpipe / The Echo *(hornpipes)* [3:05]
9. Lad O'Beirne's / Pigeon on the Gate *(reels)* [2:41]

Note — For instructional purposes, the tunes are played a little slower than usual.

MEL BAY®

© 1999 BY MEL BAY PUBLICATIONS, INC., PACIFIC, MO 63069.
ALL RIGHTS RESERVED. INTERNATIONAL COPYRIGHT SECURED. B.M.I. MADE AND PRINTED IN U.S.A.
No part of this publication may be reproduced in whole or in part, or stored in a retrieval system, or transmitted in any form or by any means, electronic, mechanical, photocopying, recording, or otherwise, without written permission of the publisher.

Visit us on the Web at http://www.melbay.com — E-mail us at email@melbay.com

Table of Contents

The Right Hand 4
The Left Hand 4
Suggestions for Beginners 6
Transcriptions 6
About the Author 7

Apples in Winter - jig 8	Maggie in the Woods - polka 63
The Bag of Spuds - reel 9	Maid Behind the Bar - reel 64
Ballydesmond Polka 10	Maid of Ardagh - polka 65
Behind the Bush in the Garden - jig 11	Mary McMahon's - reel 66
The Bird's Nest - reel 12	Master Crowley's - reel 67
Boys of Blue Hill - polka 13	Matt the Thrasher - reel 68
The Boys of the Lough - reel 14	Maudabawn Chapel - reel 69
The Boys of the Town - jig 15	McDermitt's - reel 70
The Broken Pledge - reel 16	McMahon's - reel 71
Bundle and Go - jig 17	Merrily Kiss the Quaker - jig 72
The Carraroe - jig 18	A Merry Christmas - jig 74
The Cliffs of Moher - jig 19	The Millpond - jig 75
The Concert Reel 20	Miss Monaghan's - reel 76
The Congress Reel 21	The Mullingar Races - reel 77
Cooley's Reel 22	Murphy's - hornpipe 78
The Cow That Ate the Blanket - jig 23	The Musical Priest - reel 79
Cronin's Rambles - hornpipe 24	Nine Points of Roguery - reel 80
Delaney's Drummers - jig 26	O'Keefe's Slide 82
The Dram Shell - reel 28	The Old Copper Plate - reel 83
The Dunmore Lasses - reel 29	Out on the Ocean - jig 84
The Earl's Chair - reel 30	Paddy Clancy's - jig 85
The Eavesdropper - jig 31	Paddy Fahy's Reel 86
The Echo - hornpipe 32	Pigeon on the Gate - reel 87
Fermoy Lasses - reel 33	Pipe on the Hob - jig 88
The Fort of Kincora - polka 34	Pretty Girls of Mayo - reel 89
The Galway - hornpipe 35	The Rakes of Kildare - jig 90
The Galway Rambler - reel 36	Reel 91
Glass of Beer - reel 37	Road to Lisdoonvarna - jig 92
The Golden Keyboard - reel 38	Sally Gardens - reel 93
The Gravel Walk - reel 40	Sean Ryan's - jig 94
Green Forest Jig 42	Sean Ryan's Jig 95
The High Reel 43	Ships are Sailing - reel 96
The Humours of Ballyloughlin - jig 44	Silver Spear - reel 97
The Humours of Tulla - reel 46	The Skylark - reel 98
The Hunter's Purse - reel 47	Slieve Russel - jig 99
Hunting the Boyne - reel 48	Snug in a Blanket - jig 100
Julia Delaney - reel 49	Spike Island Lassies - reel 102
Jerry Daly's Hornpipe 50	Sportin' Pat - reel 104
John Brennan's - reel 51	Star of Munster - reel 106
The Kerry Reel 52	The Steeplechase - reel 108
Killarney Boys of Pleasure - reel 53	Sweet Cup of Tea - reel 109
The Kinard Polka 54	Tamlin - reel 110
Knocknagow - reel 55	Tar Road to Sligo - jig 111
Knotted Cord - reel 56	Tatter Jack Walsh - jig 112
Lad O'Beirne's - reel 57	Tom Doherty's - reel 113
Lark on the Strand - jig 58	Trip to Athlone - jig 114
Larry Redican's - slip jig 59	Trip To Durrow - reel 115
Leitrim Fancy - jig 60	The White Petticoat - jig 116
The Limerick Lasses - reel 61	Willie Coleman's - jig 117
The Lonesome Jig 62	The Wise Maid - reel 118

The Right Hand

Right-hand fingering is suggested for all tunes. A number placed over a note indicates the finger to be used (thumb is #1, little finger is #5). Hand should stay in position when no number appears. For example, if a "1" appears over a C note, it is implied that the second finger sits over the D, third finger over the E, etc. Fingering notation will indicate the next position change.

Fingering is not indicated for passages which are executed earlier in the tune. Use the same fingering as previously shown.

The Left Hand

There are two standard fingering positions for the left hand to choose from:

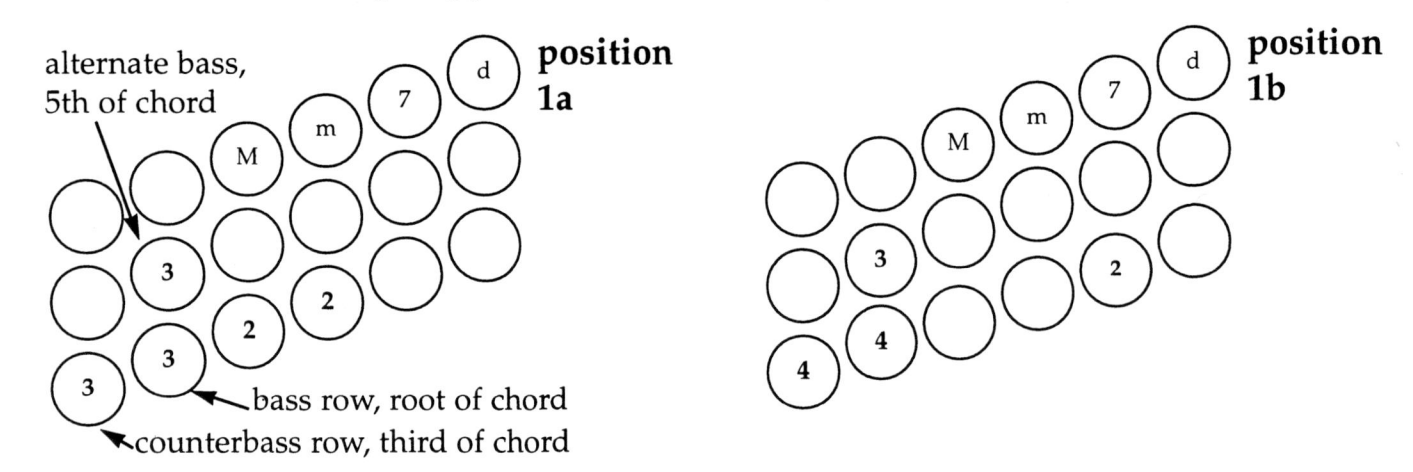

position 1a
alternate bass, 5th of chord
bass row, root of chord
counterbass row, third of chord

position 1b

1a) 3rd finger on bass row (root of chord)
 2nd finger on major chord
 2nd finger on minor chord
 3rd finger on alternate bass (next bass note up – the fifth of the chord)
 3rd finger on counterbass row (the 3rd of the chord)
1b) 4th finger on bass row when playing seventh chord
 4th finger on counterbass row when playing seventh chord
 2nd finger on seventh chord

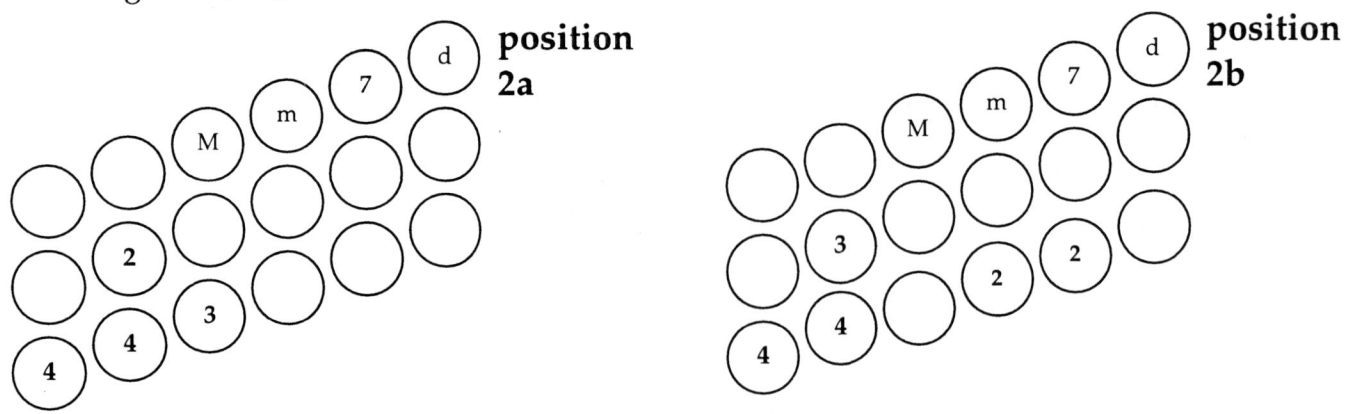

position 2a

position 2b

2a) 4th finger on bass row
 3rd finger on major chord
 2nd finger on alternate bass when playing major chord
 4th finger on counter bass row
2b) 2nd finger on minor and seventh chord
 3rd finger on alternate bass when playing minor or seventh chord

(Note – my personal preference is position 2.)

Left hand of the 120 bass accordion

✖ = double sharp

Suggestions for Beginners

Proper practice habits and good playing technique are inseparable. When you approach a new tune, PRACTICE SLOWLY! There is nothing gained from playing a piece fast and incorrectly. Practice each hand separately until both parts are played well. Simplify the tune by eliminating grace notes and ornaments. Keep shoulders, arms and hands relaxed.

The easier tunes in this collection are: *Ballydesmond Polka, The Galway, The Kinard Polka, Lark on the Strand, Leitrim Fancy, Maggie in the Woods, Maid of Ardagh, O'Keefe's Slide, Paddy Clancy's, Road to Lisdoonvarna* and *Tatter Jack Walsh*.

Transcriptions

Included are a number of tunes transcribed from recordings of musicians playing keyboard accordion, Irish button box or concertina. I have chosen to include the latter two because of their likeness to the keyboard accordion; all are similar sounding, free reed instruments on which ornamentation is approached in a similar fashion.

On keyboard accordion
- Jimmy Keane
    - *Hunting the Boyne* from The Green Fields of America, "Live in Concert" (Green Linnet, CSIF 1096)
    - *Larry Redican's Slip Jig* from Moloney, O'Connell and Keane, "Kilkelly" (Green Linnet, SIF 1072)
- Phil Cunningham, *The Limerick Lasses* from "Relativity" (Green Linnet, GLCD 1059)
- Alan Kelly, *Matt the Thrasher, Pretty Girls of Mayo* from "Out of the Blue" (Kells Music, KM-9511)
- Ian Lowthian, *The Dram Shell* from Catriona Macdonald, Ian Lowthian, "opus blue"
    (Acoustic Radio, ARAD CD 103)
- Karen Tweed
    - *The Humours of Tulla* from "The Silver Spire" (Dave Mallinson Publications, DMPCD9402)
    - *The Old Copper Plate* from "Drops of Springwater" (Dave Mallinson Publications, DMPC9401)
- John Williams, *The Lonesome Jig* from "John Williams" (Green Linnet, GLCD 1157)

On button box
- Joe Burke, *The Fort of Kincora* from "The Tailor's Choice" (Green Linnet, SIF 1045)
- Jackie Daly, *The Bag of Spuds* from Patrick Street, "All in Good Time" (Green Linnet, CSIF 1125)
- Joe Derrane, *The White Petticoat* from "Give Us Another" (Green Linnet, GLCD 1149)
- Tom Doherty, *Sweet Cup of Tea* from "Take the Bull by the Horns" (Green Linnet, CSIF 1131)
- James Keane, *Knocknagow* from "That's the Spirit" (Green Linnet, GLCD 1138)
- Billy McComiskey, *Tom Doherty's* from "Trian" (Flying Fish, FF 70586)
- Paddy O'Brien (of Minneapolis, MN), *The Bird's Nest* from "Stranger at the Gate"
    (Green Linnet, GLCD 1091)
- Martin O'Connor, *Delaney's Drummers* from "The Connachtman's Rambles"
    (Mulligan Music, LUN 027)
- Johnny O'Leary, *Boys of Blue Hill* from "Johnny O'Leary of Sliabh Luachra: Dance Music from the
    Cork–Kerry Border" (The Lilliput Press)
- Sharon Shannon, *Bundle and Go* from "Sharon Shannon" (Philo, C PH 1153)
- John Whelan, *Trip to Athlone* from "From the Heart" (Oenoke Records, OR 0001)
- Tony MacMahon, *Reel* from Noel Hill, Tony MacMahon, "I gCnoc na Grai" (Gael–Linn CEF 114)

On concertina
- Chris Sherburn, *The Concert Reel* from Chris Sherburn, Denny Bartley, "Last Night's Fun!"
    (Sound Out Music, SOM 002)
- Noel Hill, *Reel* from Noel Hill, Tony MacMahon, "I gCnoc na Grai" (Gael–Linn CEF 114)
- John Williams, *The Lonesome Jig* from "John Williams" (Green Linnet, GLCD 1157)

About the Author

Photo by: Lorraine Tipaldi

David DiGiuseppe's musical career began at the tender age of three in the local barber shop, where he was often lifted onto a chair and encouraged to sing his favorite songs. At the impressionable age of eight, he was taking accordion lessons, becoming a model student at Petteruti's School of Music in Providence, Rhode Island. By the age of twelve, the accordion was in the closet and Beatles' tunes could be heard emanating from his guitar.

In 1984, Mr. DiGiuseppe "rediscovered" the accordion and its role in folk music. He has since become an accomplished accordionist, performing Celtic and American traditional music. In addition, he plays for New England-style contra dances.

Mr. DiGiuseppe has performed professionally since 1978, both as a soloist and with numerous bands. He is a versatile singer, accordionist, mandolinist and Irish cittern player, adept at diverse musical styles.

Mr. DiGiuseppe is featured on a number of recordings. His release *Welcome to Heaven...* (Wizmak Productions, Wingdale, New York) highlights his extraordinary accordion playing on music from Celtic, Parisian and American traditions. Reviewer John O'Regan of Limerick, Ireland writes, "A player of immense talent and vision, DiGiuseppe is a musician worth encountering."

http://www.mindspring.com/~daviddg

Apples in Winter

The Bag of Spuds

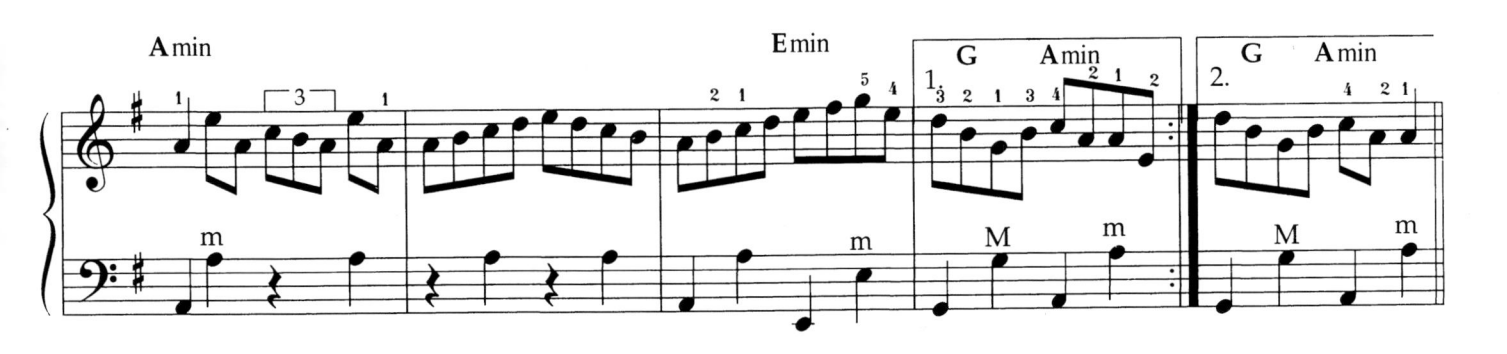

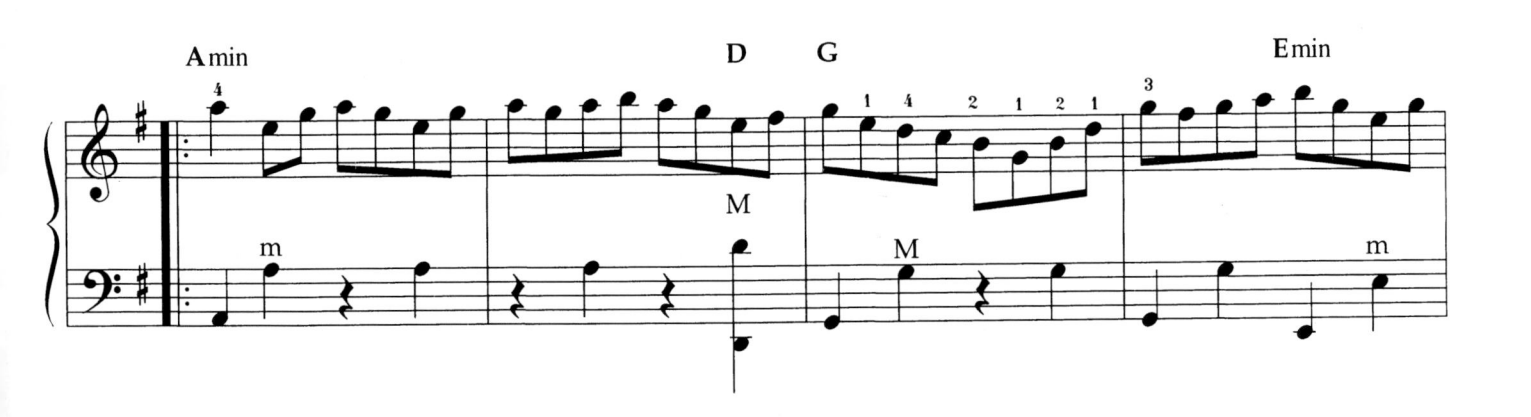

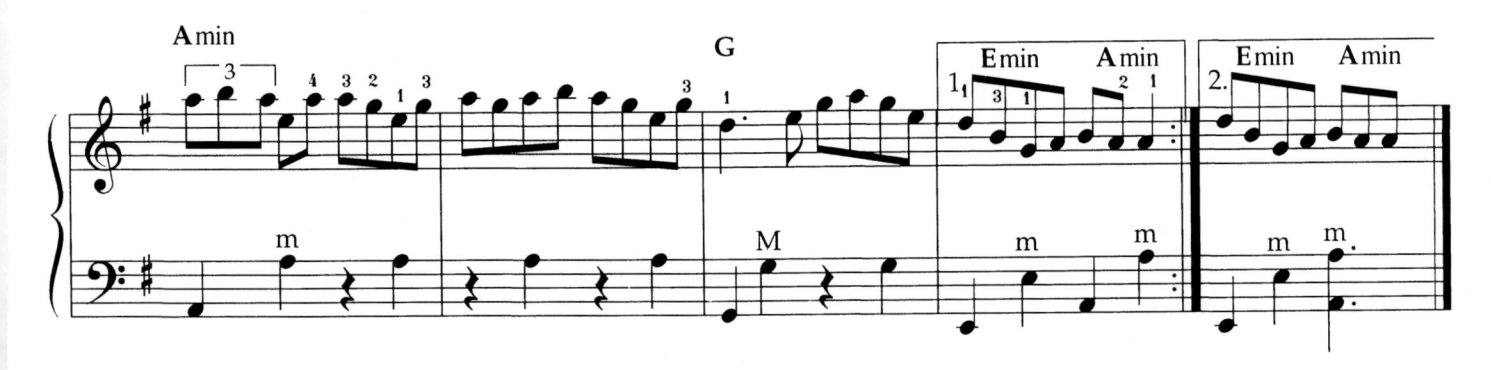

reel
as played by Jackie Daly

Chords based on guitar playing of Arty McGlynn.

arr. © Jackie Daly. All Rights Reserved. Used by Permission.

Ballydesmond Polka

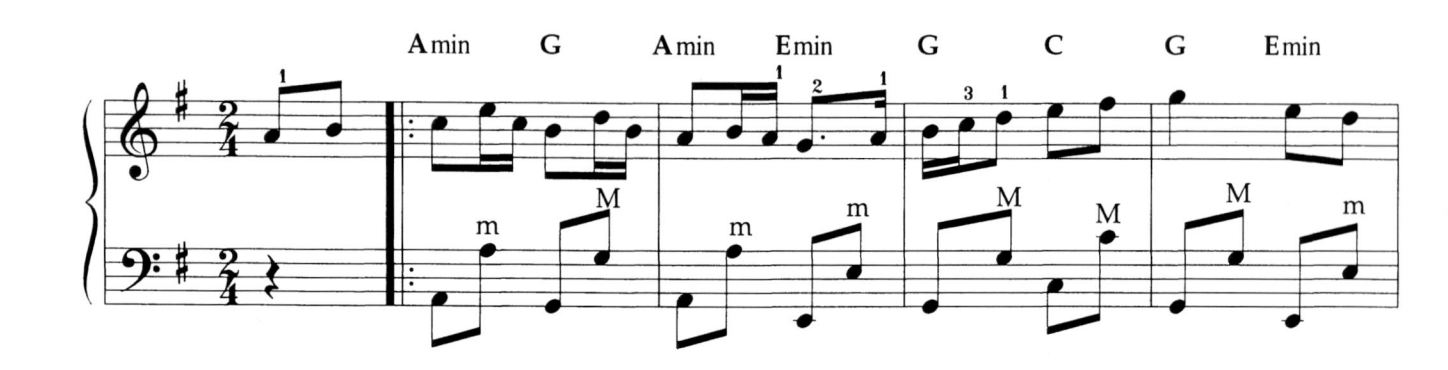

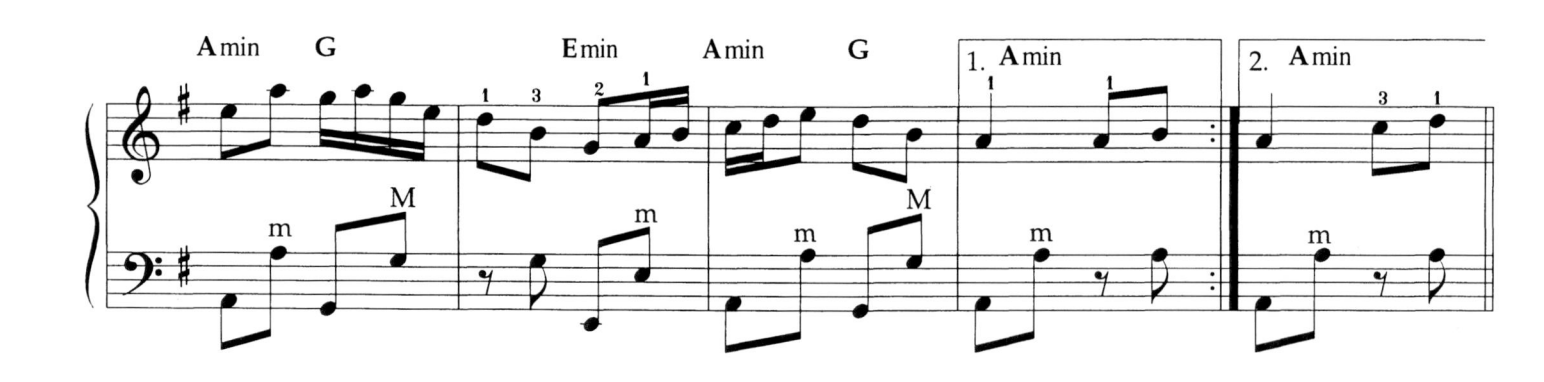

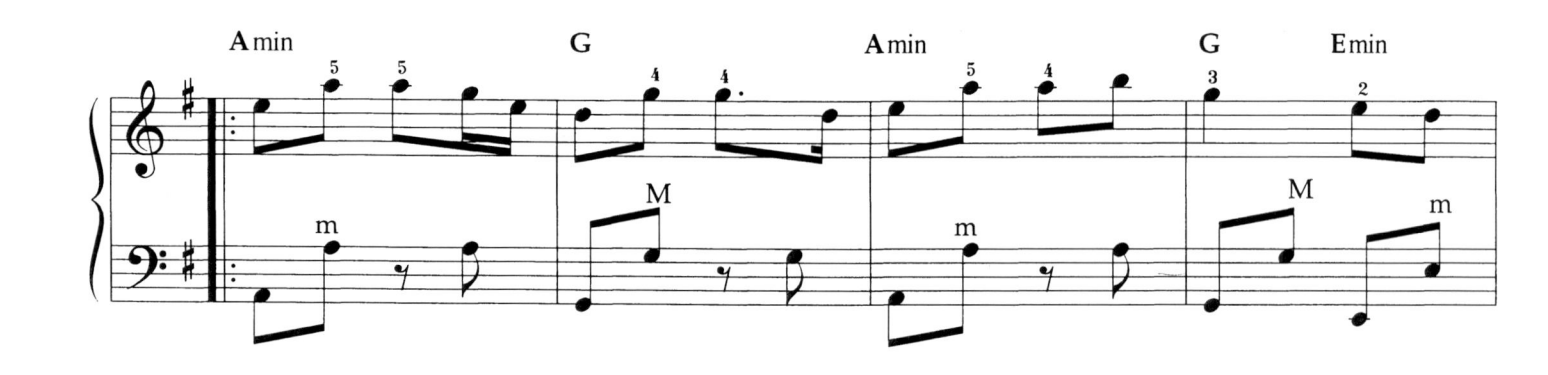

arr. © 1999 Mel Bay® Publications, Inc. All Rights Reserved.

Behind the Bush in the Garden

The Bird's Nest

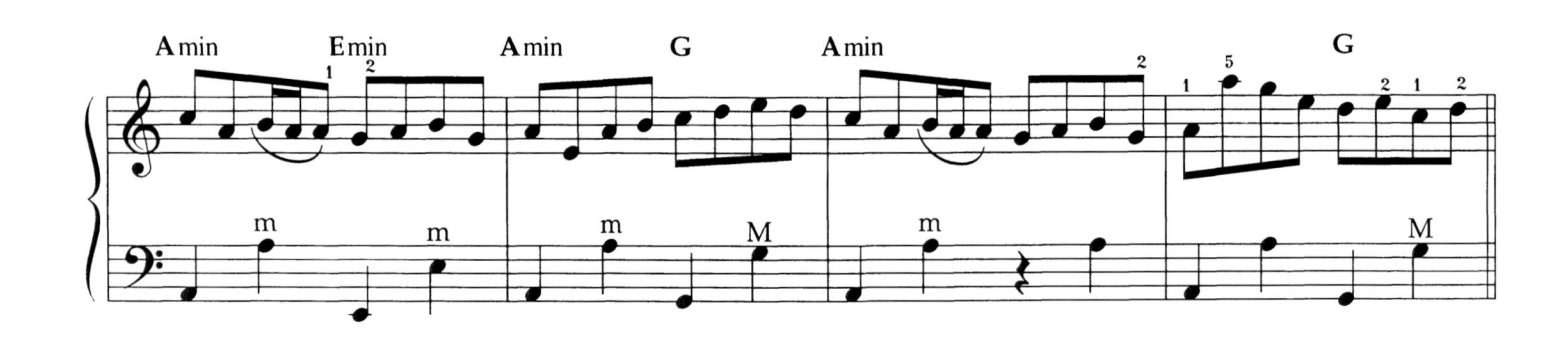

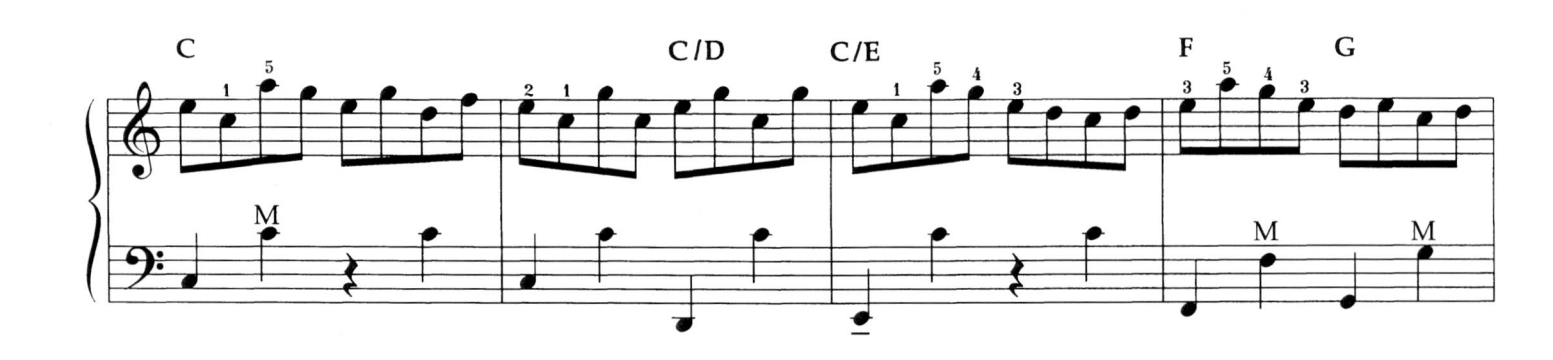

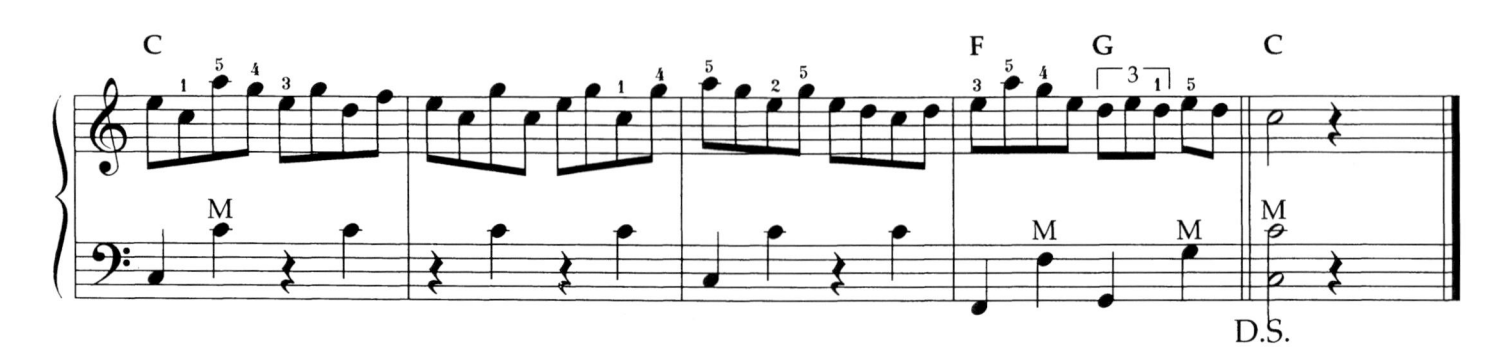

reel arrangement by Paddy O'Brien*

Chords based on piano playing of Daithi Sproule   *Paddy O'Brien of Minneapolis, MN

arr. © Paddy O'Brien. All Rights Reserved. Used by Permission.

Boys of Blue Hill

hornpipe, played with syncopated eighth notes

as played by Johnny O'Leary

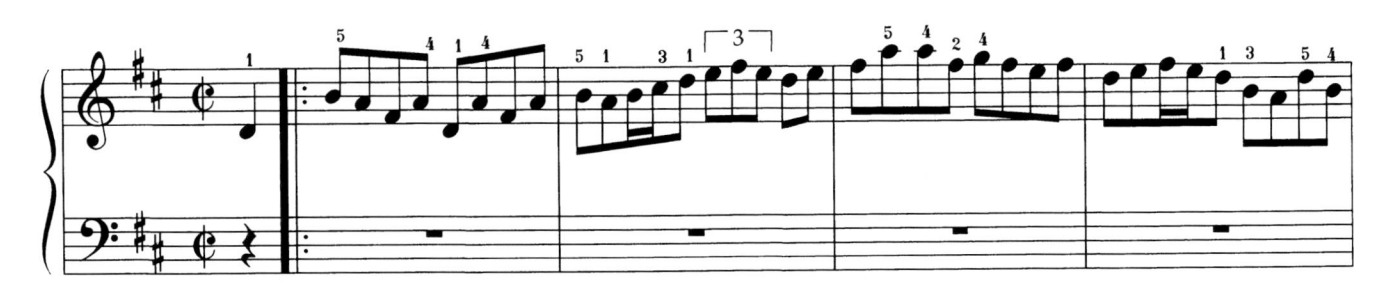

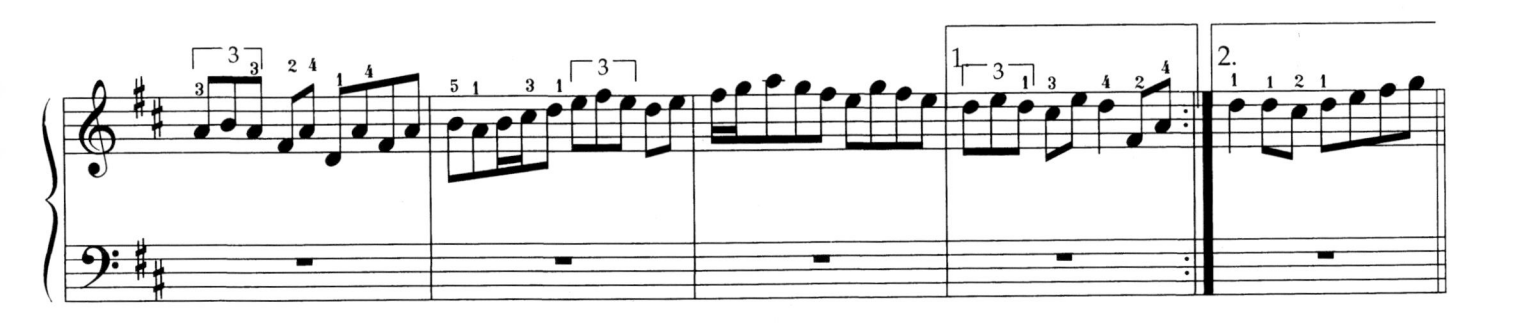

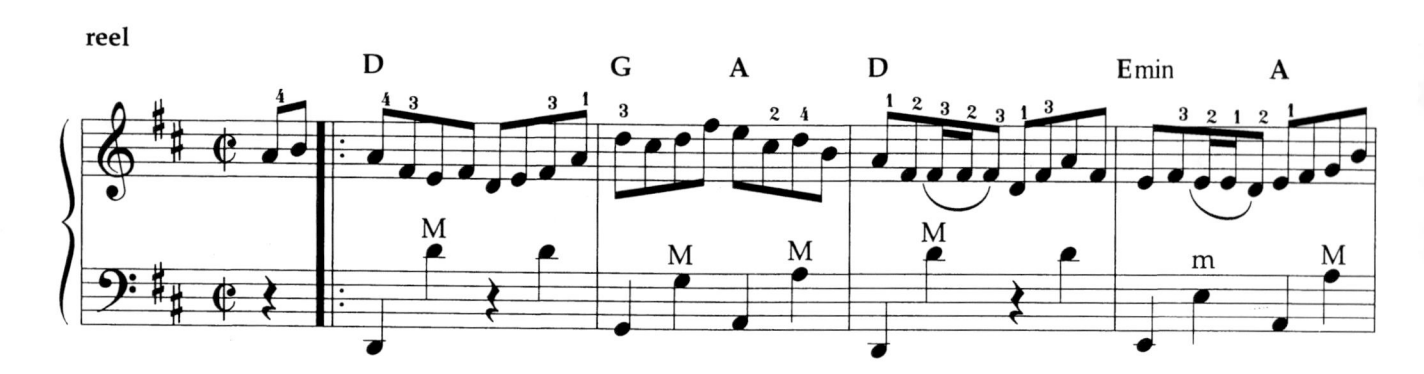

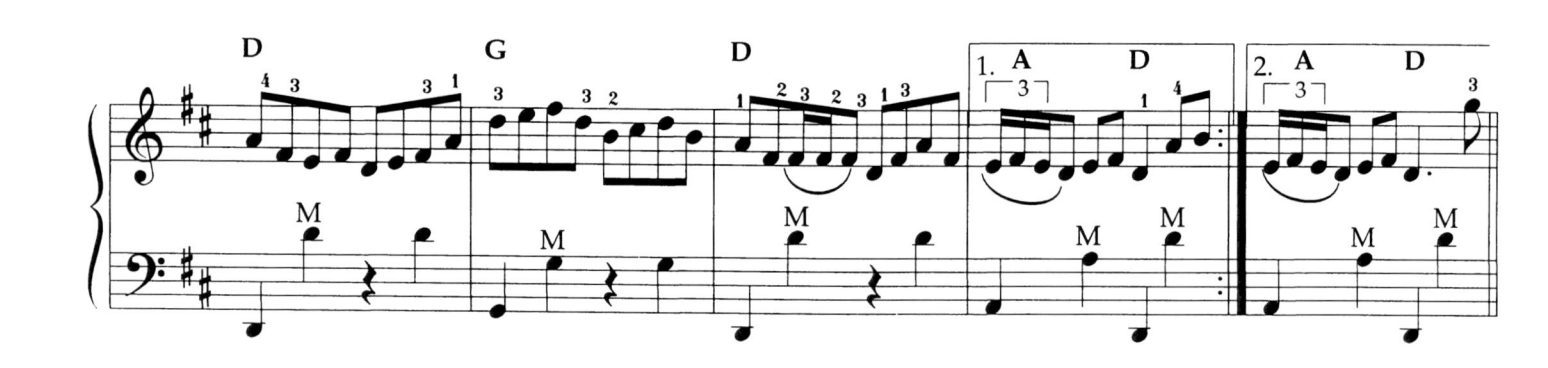

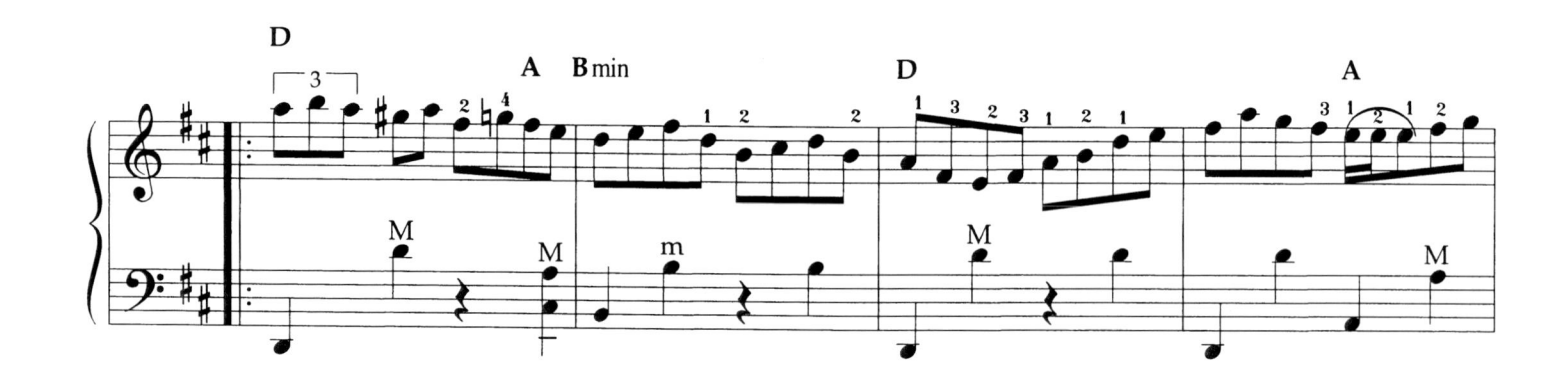

The Boys of the Lough

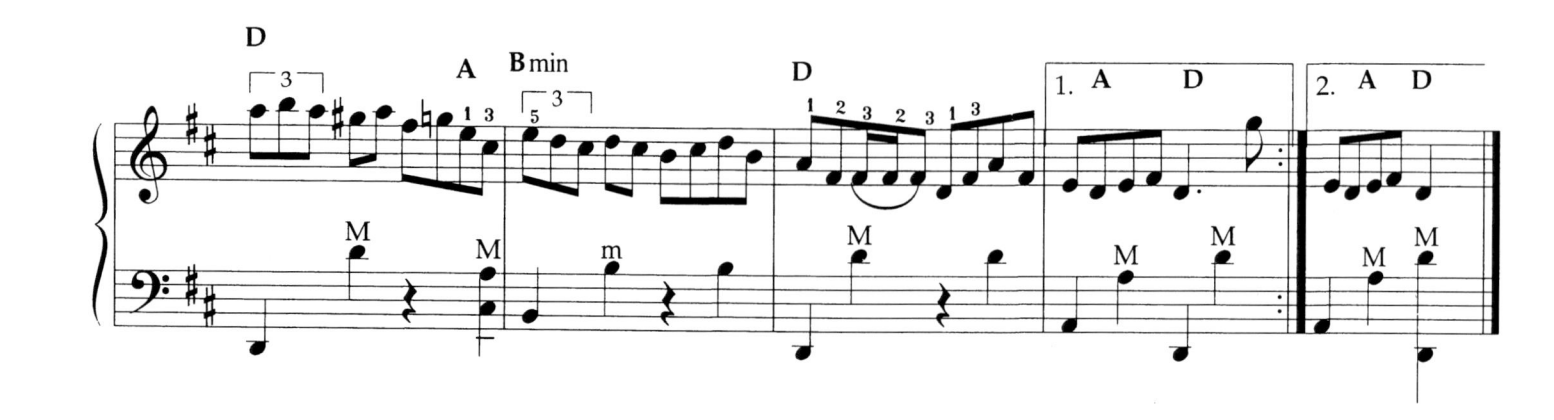

The Boys of the Town

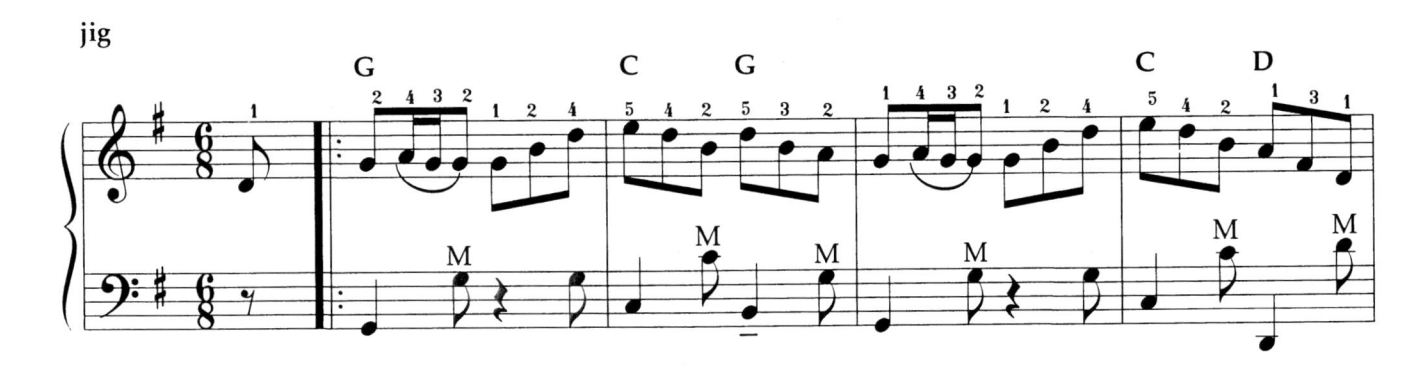

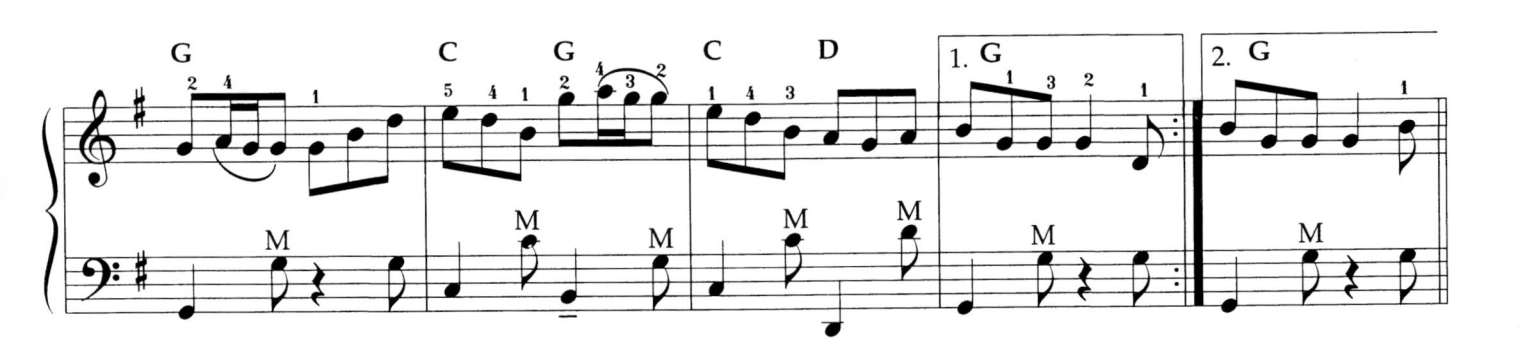

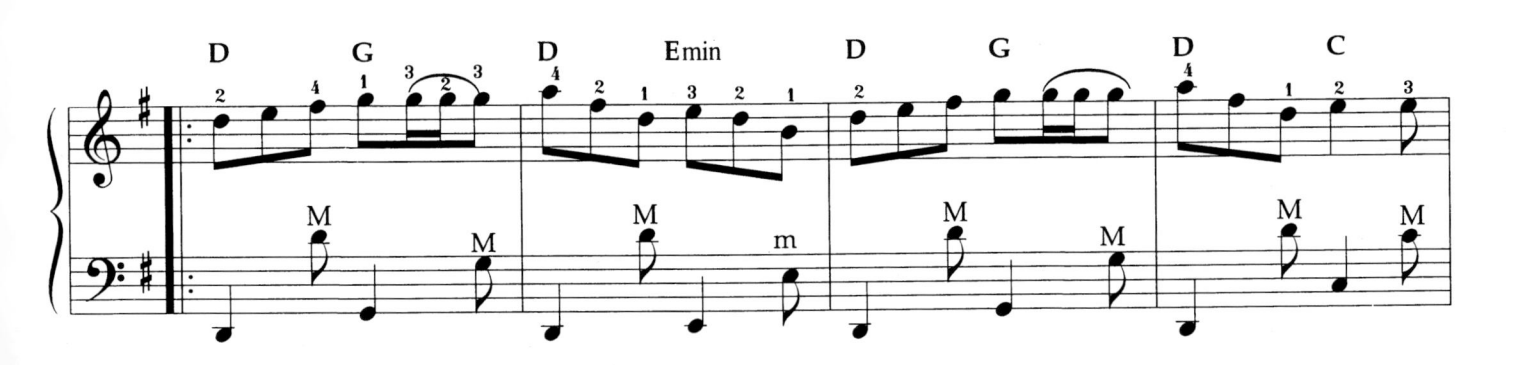

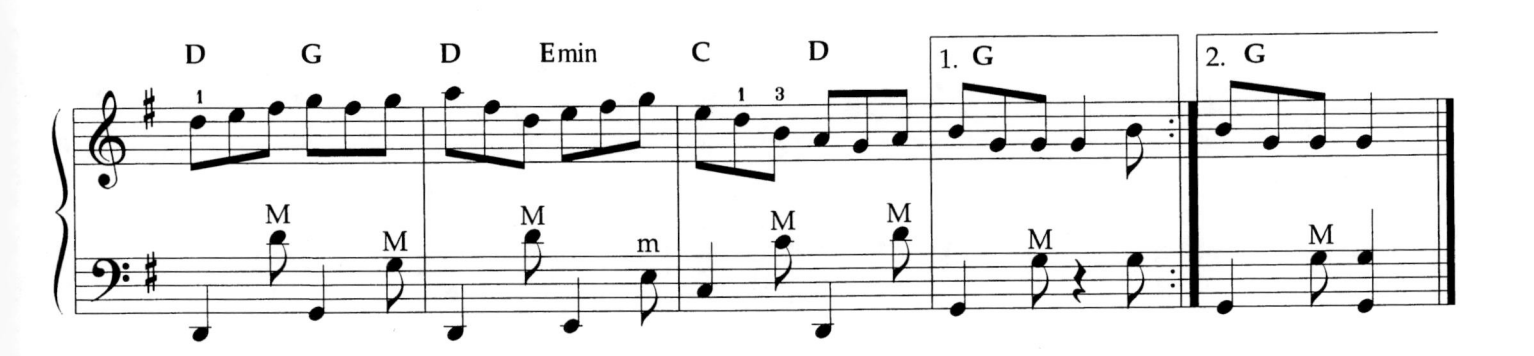

The Broken Pledge

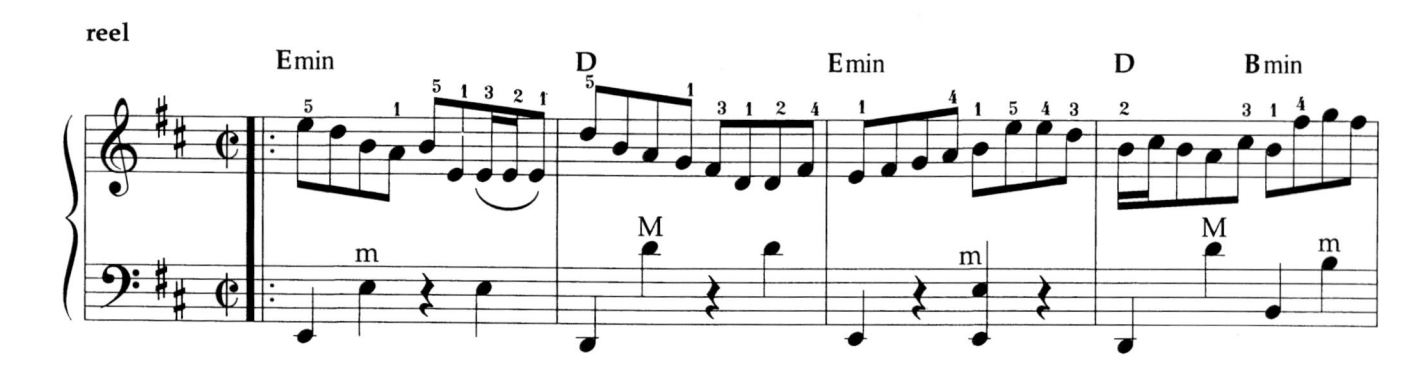

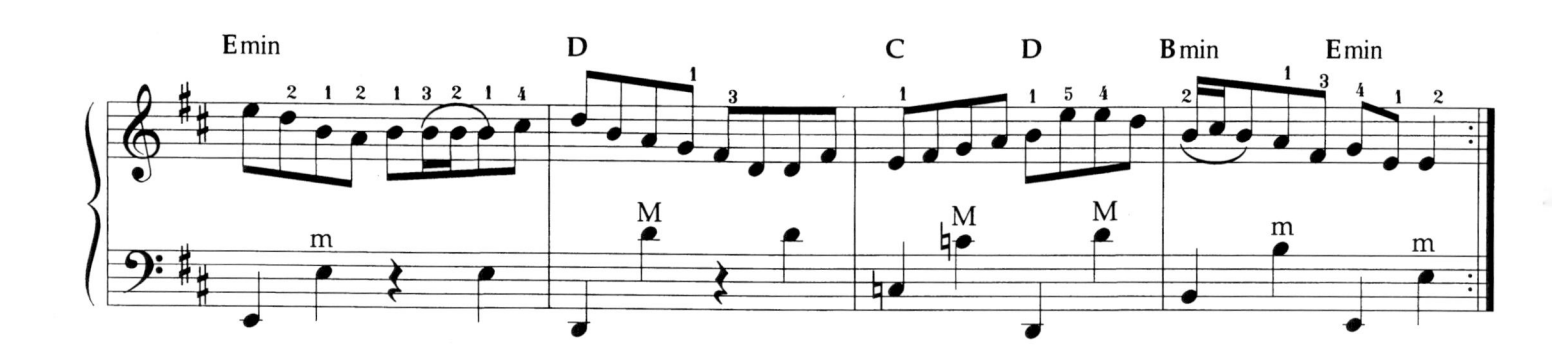

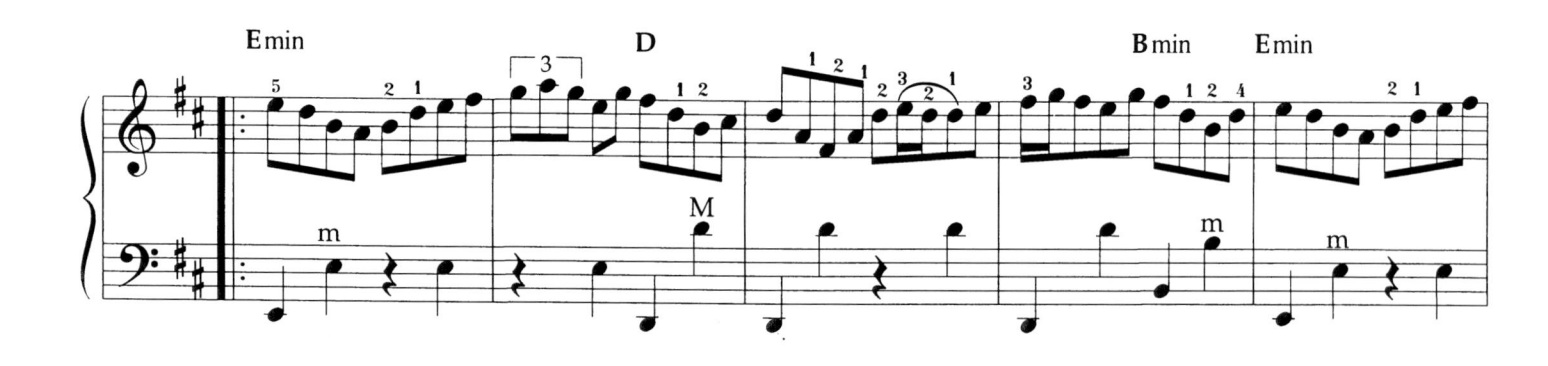

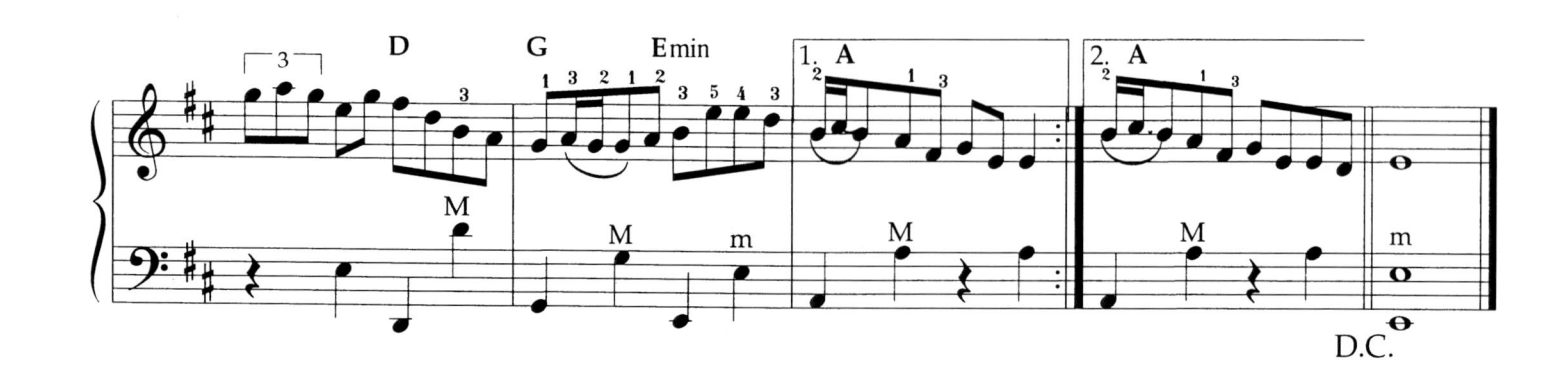

reel

arr. © 1999 Mel Bay® Publications, Inc. All Rights Reserved.

Bundle and Go

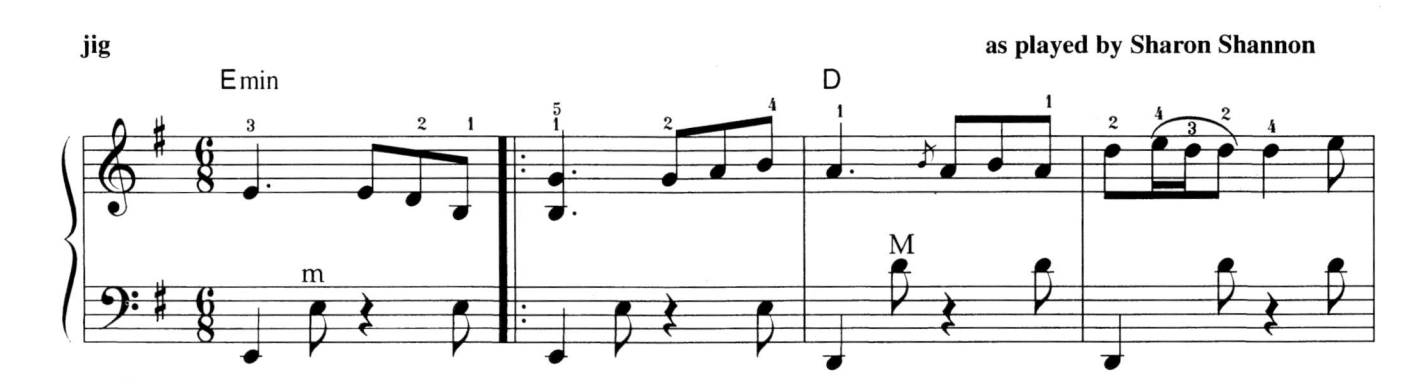

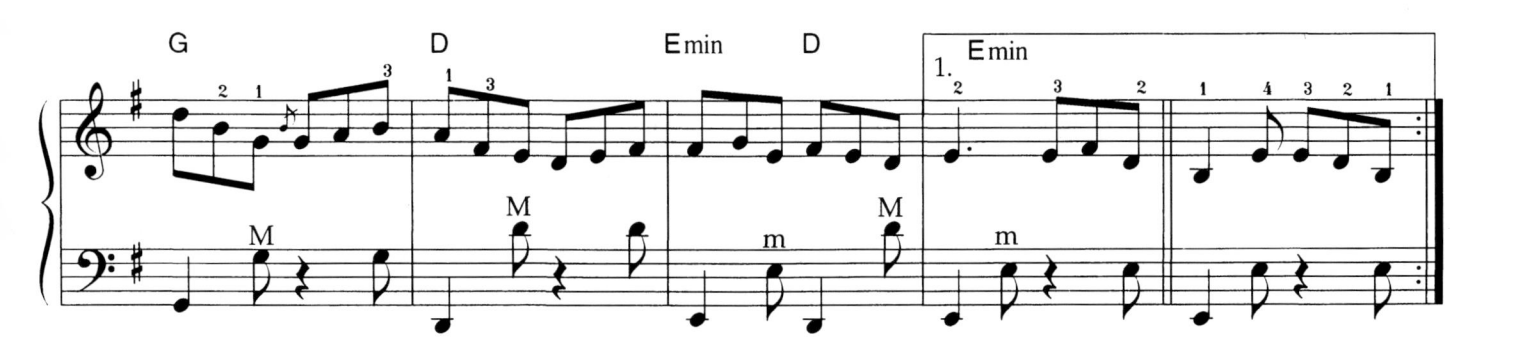

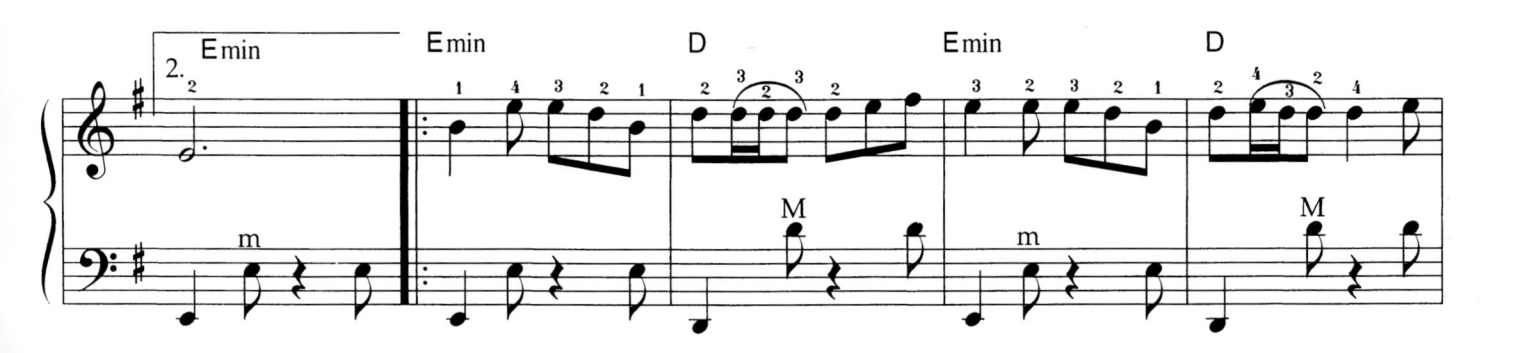

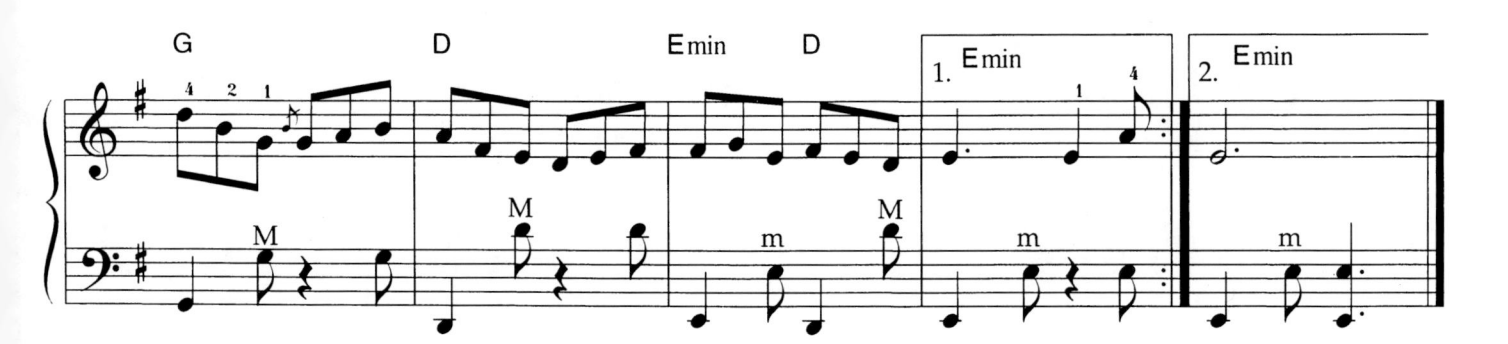

jig
as played by **Sharon Shannon**

Chords based on bouzouki playing of Donal Lunny

arr. © Sharon Shannon. All Rights Reserved. Used by Permission.

The Carraroe

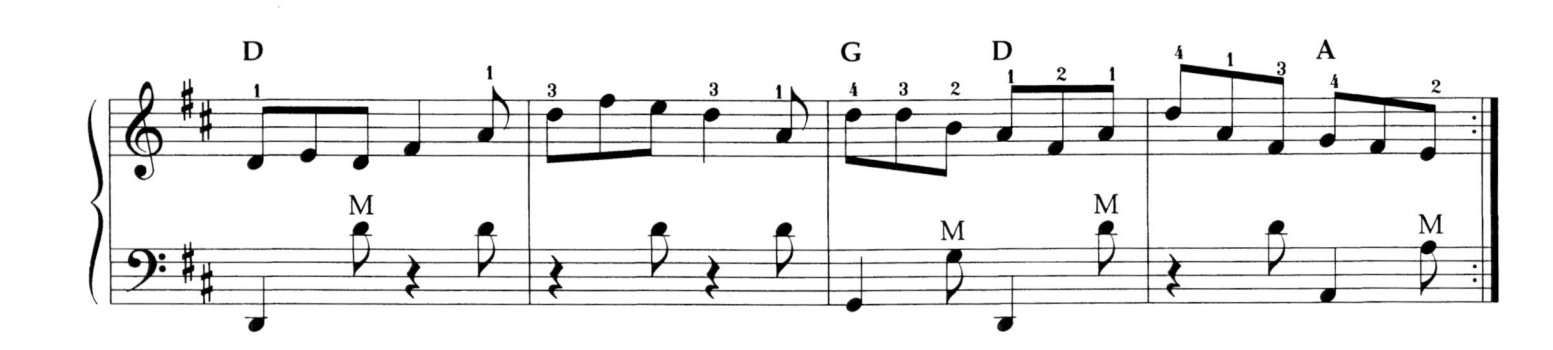

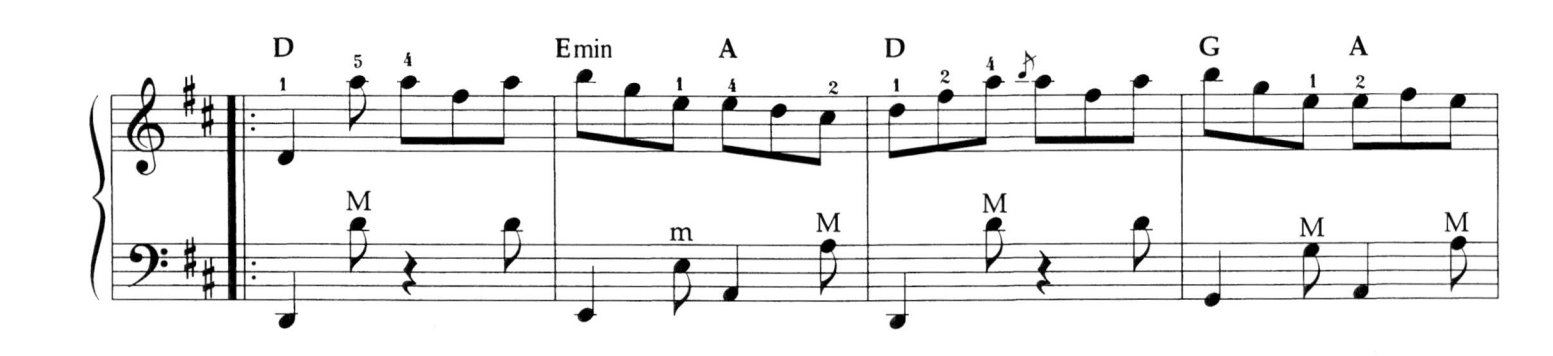

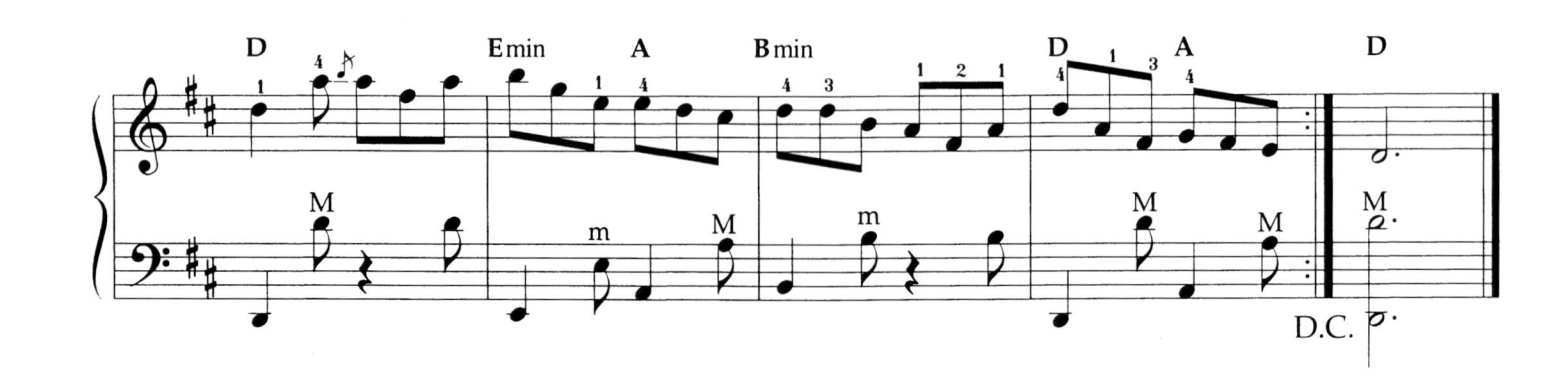

The Cliffs of Moher

The Concert Reel

as played by Chris Sherburn

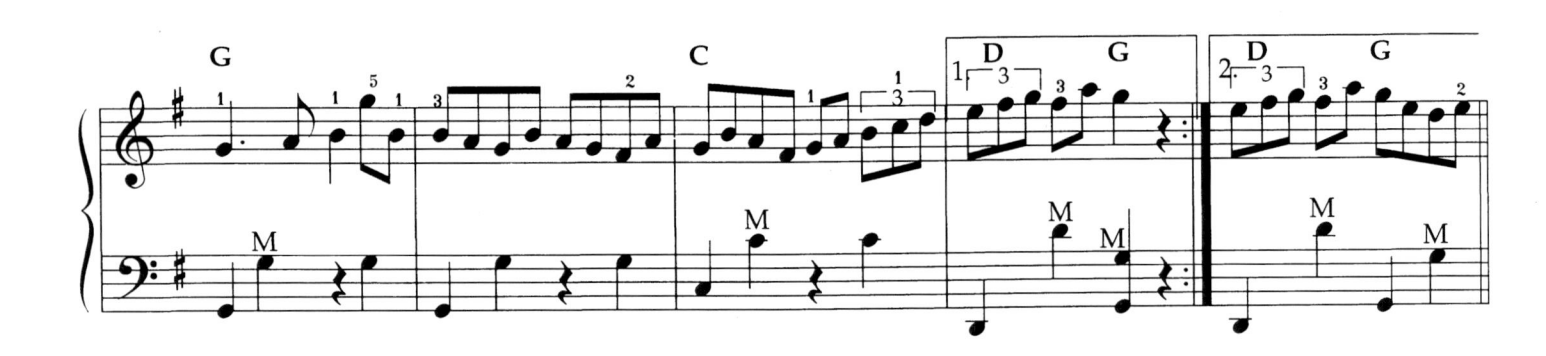

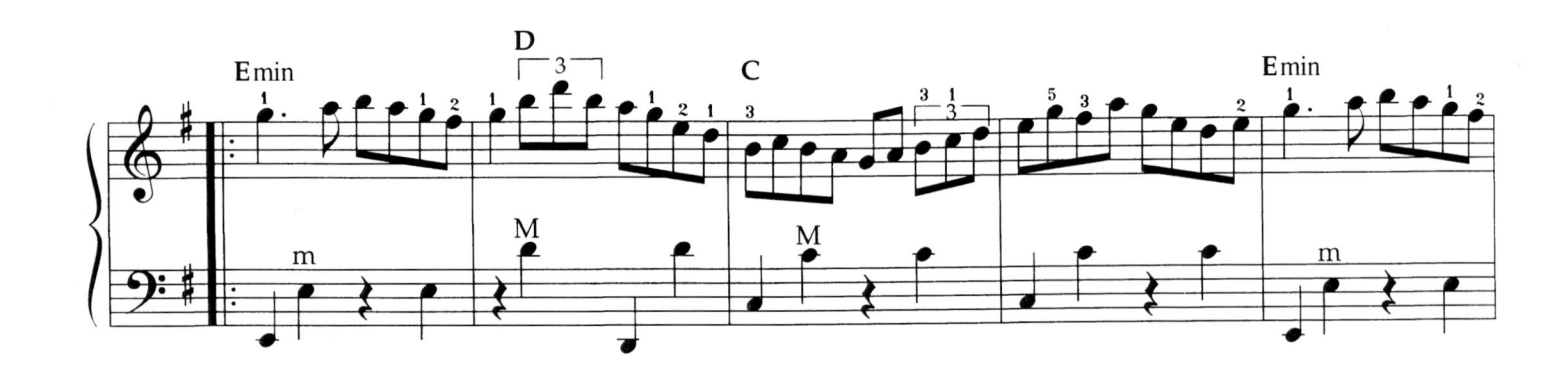

chords based on guitar playing of Denny Bartley

arr. © Chris Sherburn. All Rights Reserved. Used by Permission.

The Congress Reel

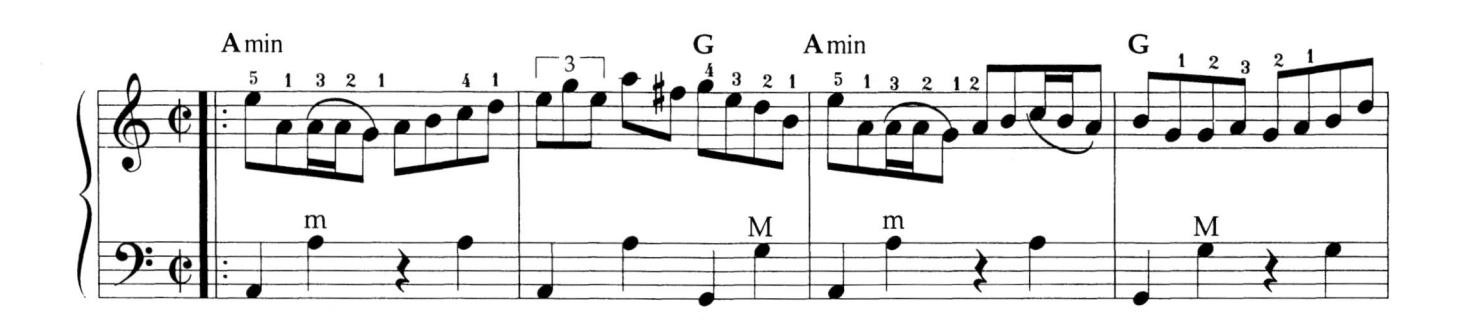

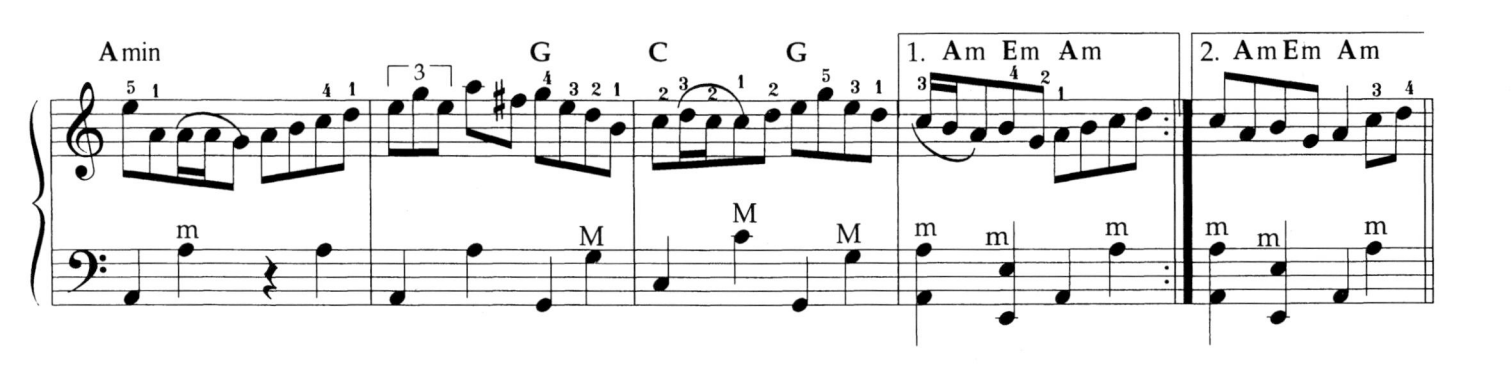

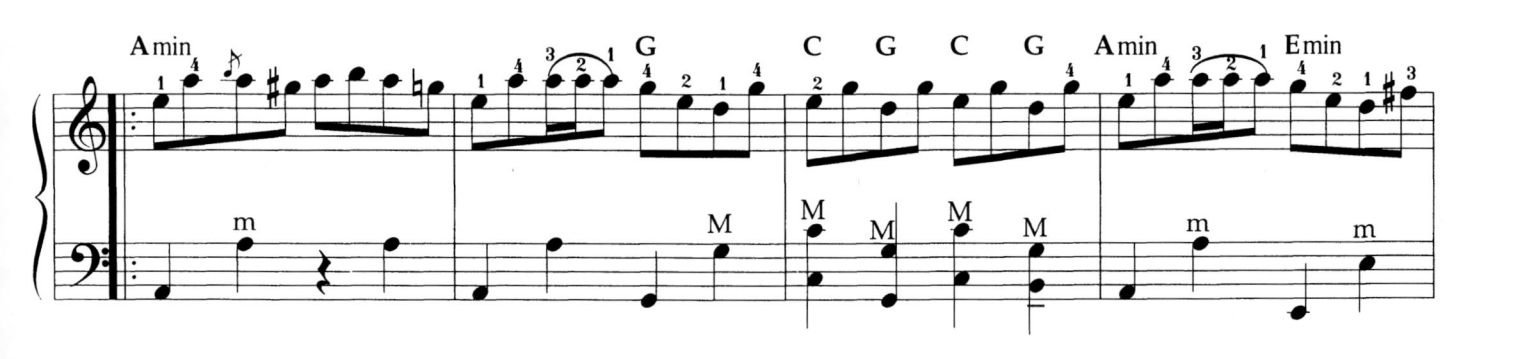

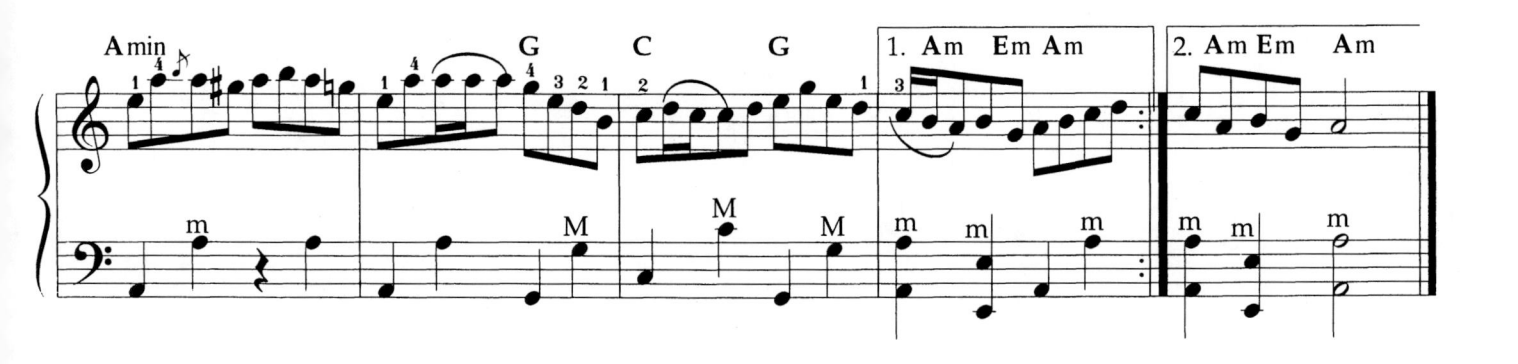

arr. © 1999 Mel Bay® Publications, Inc. All Rights Reserved.

Cooley's Reel

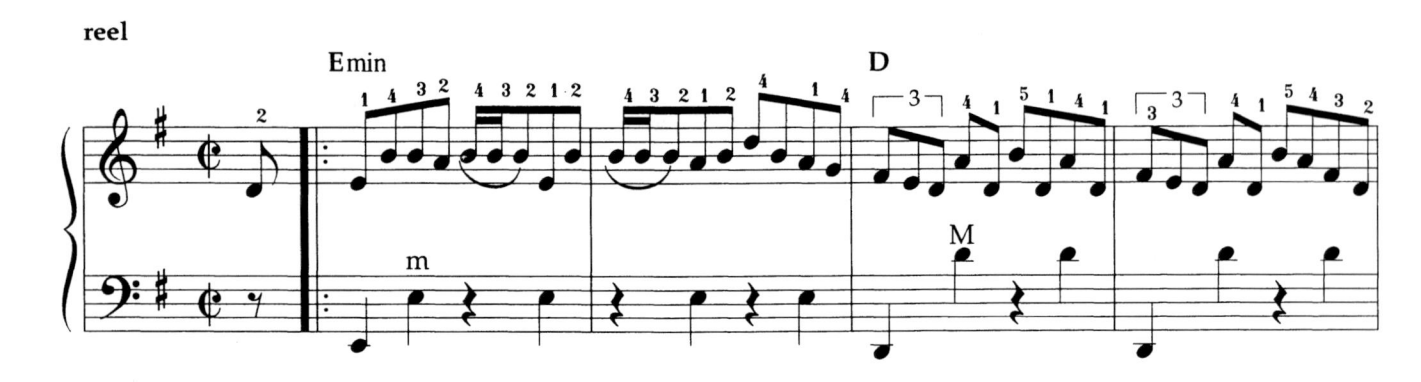

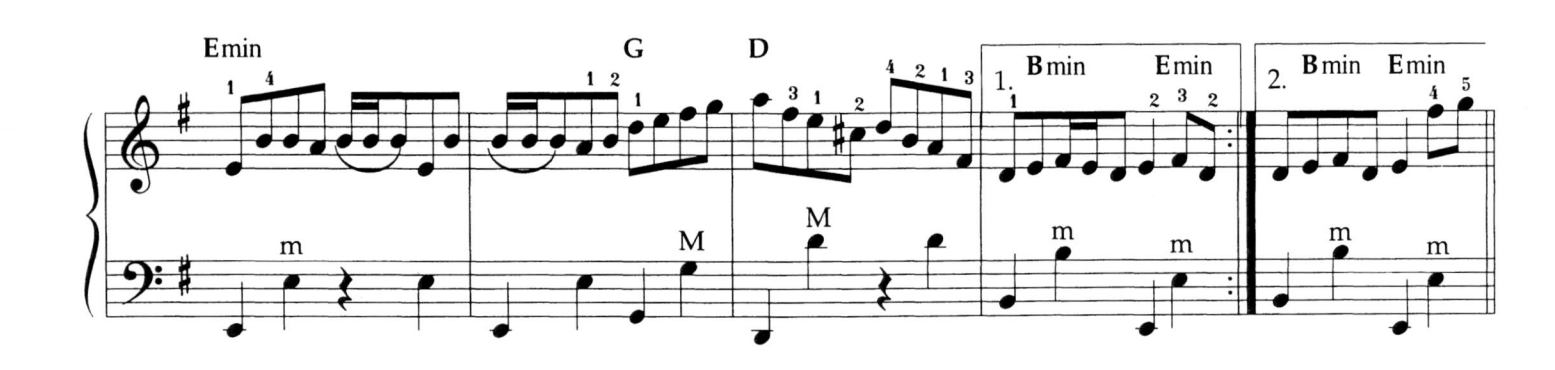

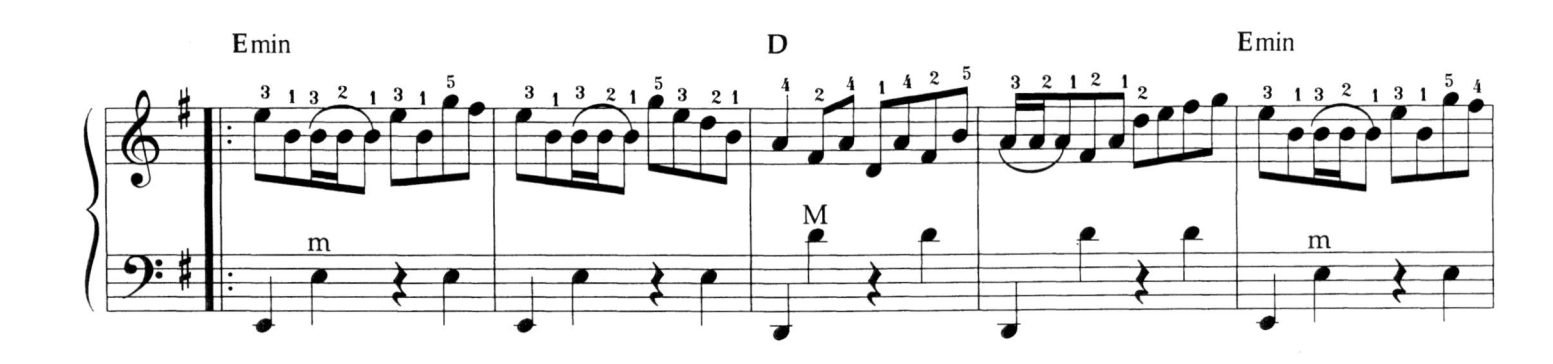

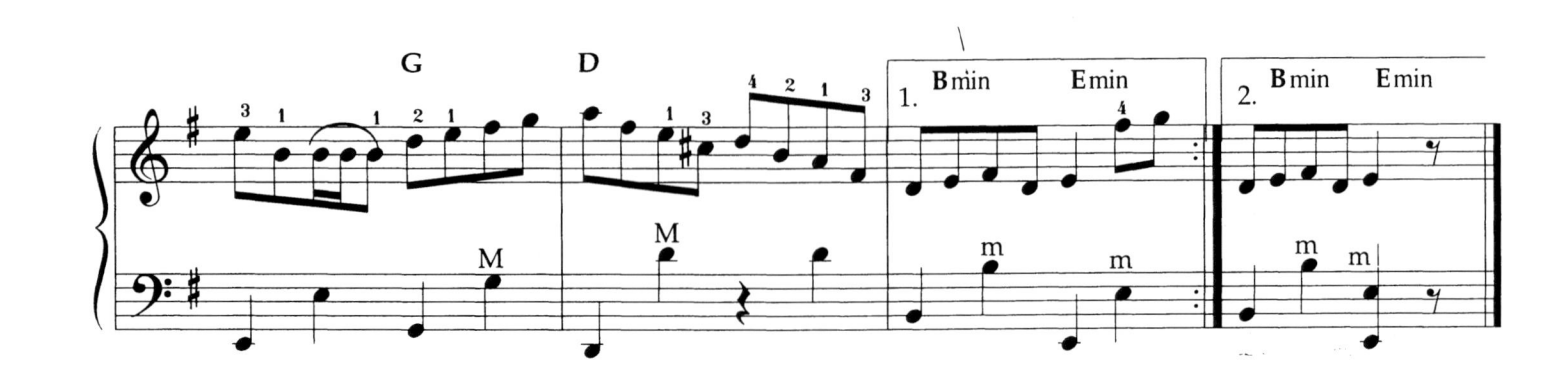

The Cow That Ate the Blanket

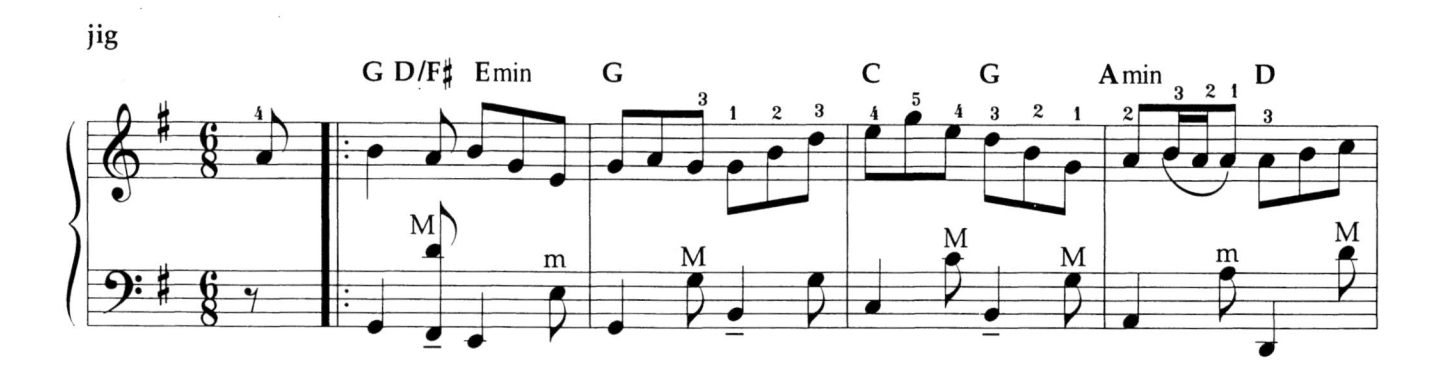

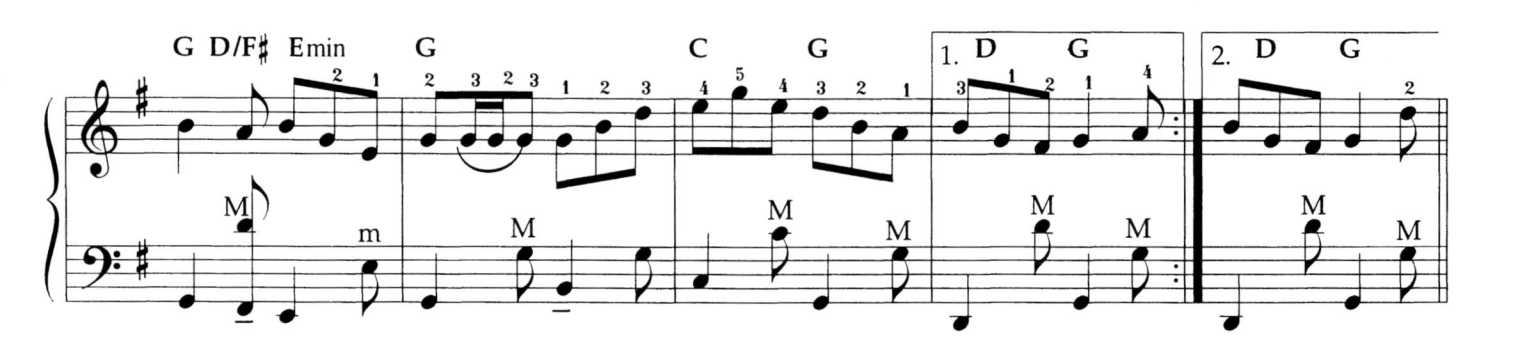

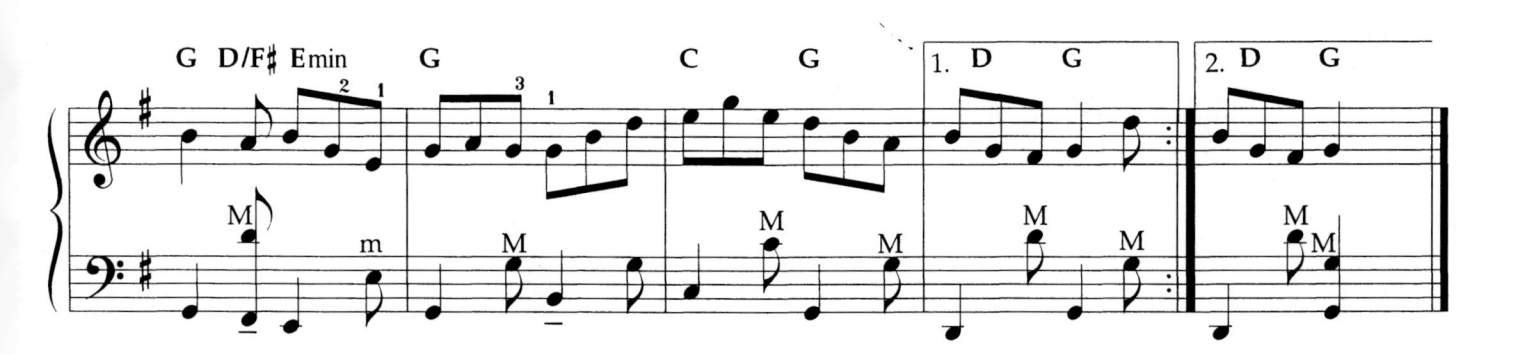

Cronin's Rambles

hornpipe, played with syncopated eighth notes

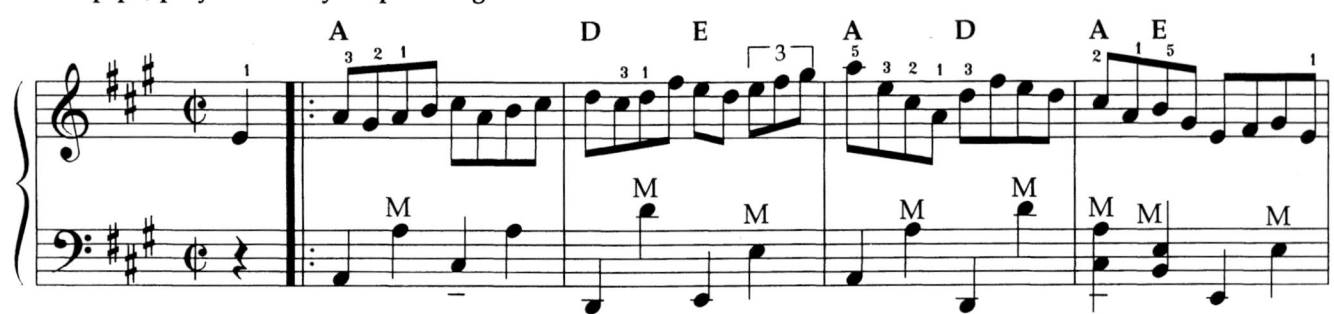

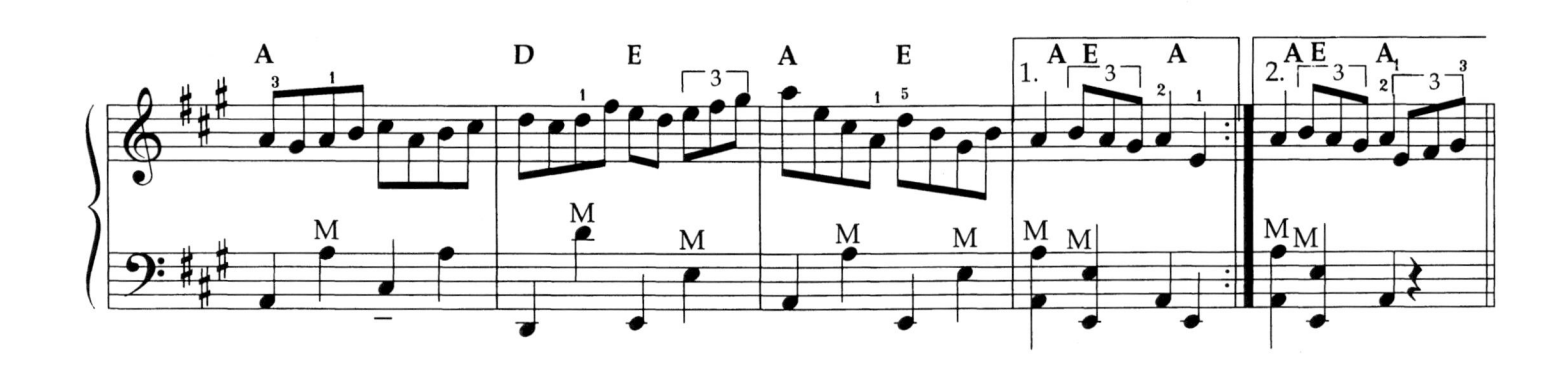

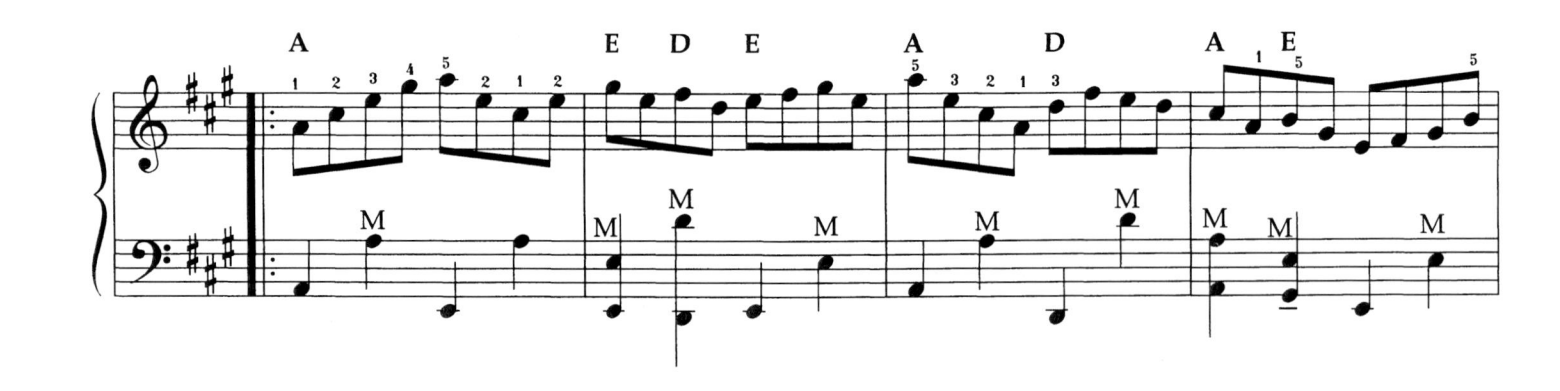

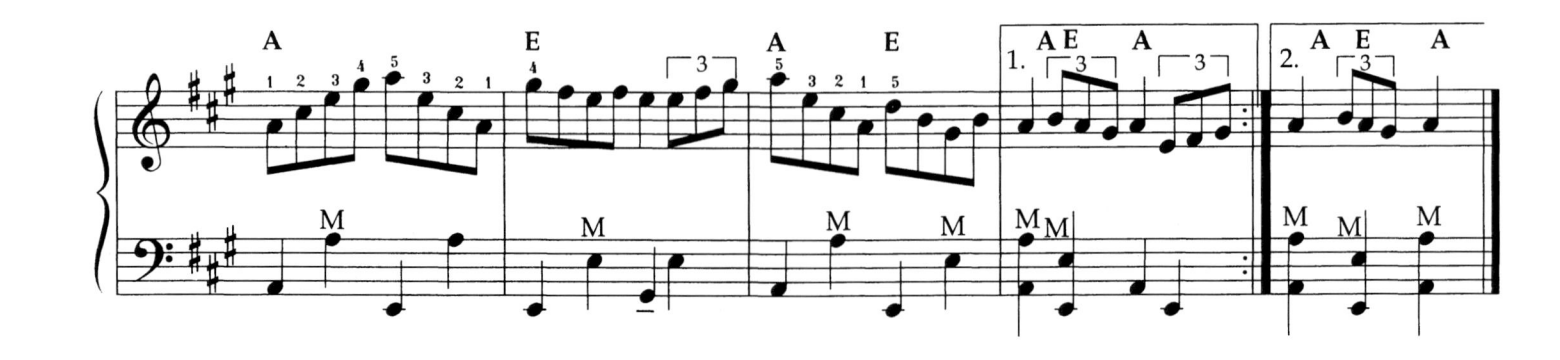

*This page has been
left blank to avoid
awkward page turns*

Delaney's Drummers

jig

as played by Martin O'Connor

27

The Dram Shell
(The Damsel)

reel
arrangement by Ian Lowthian

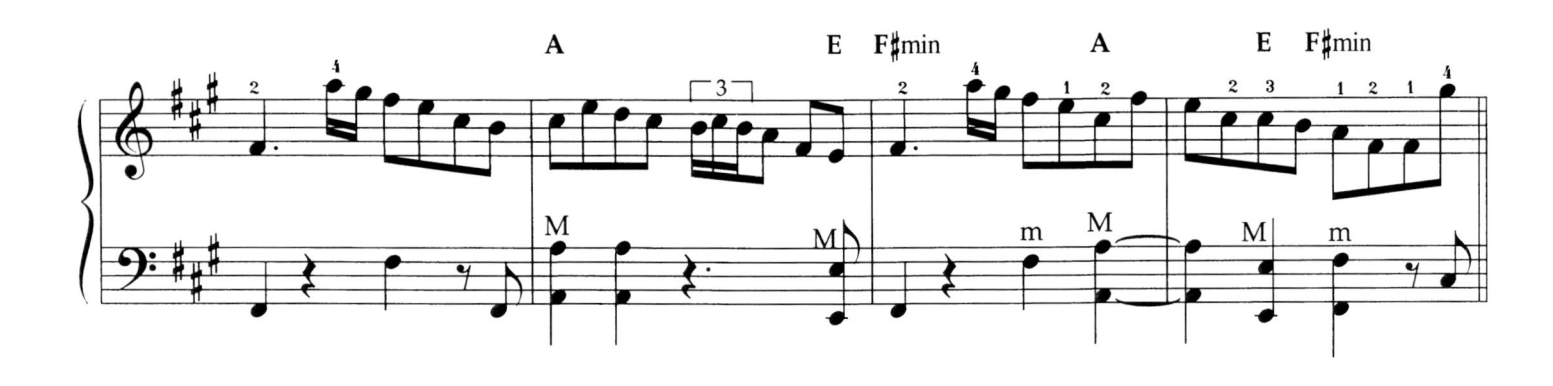

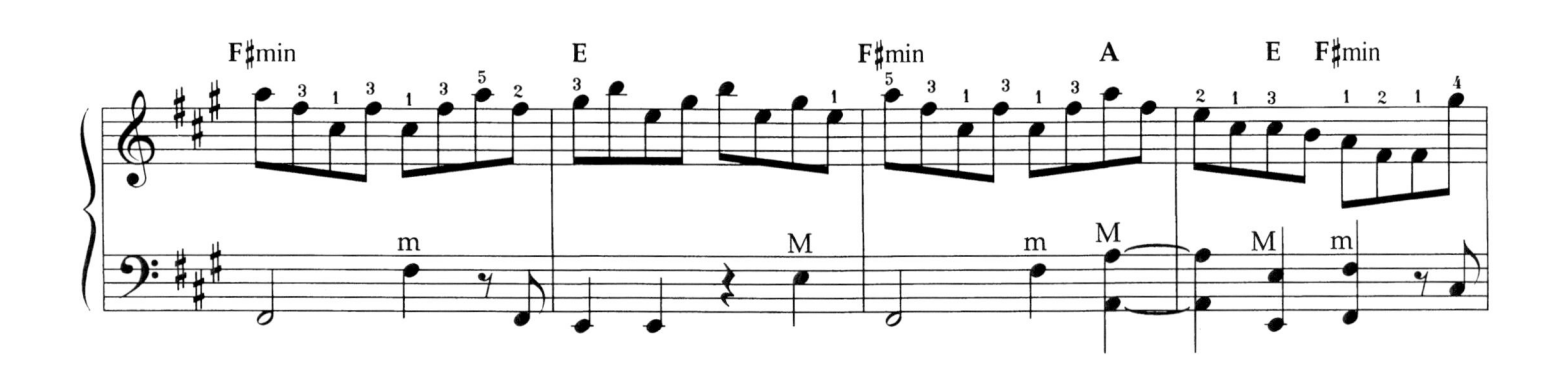

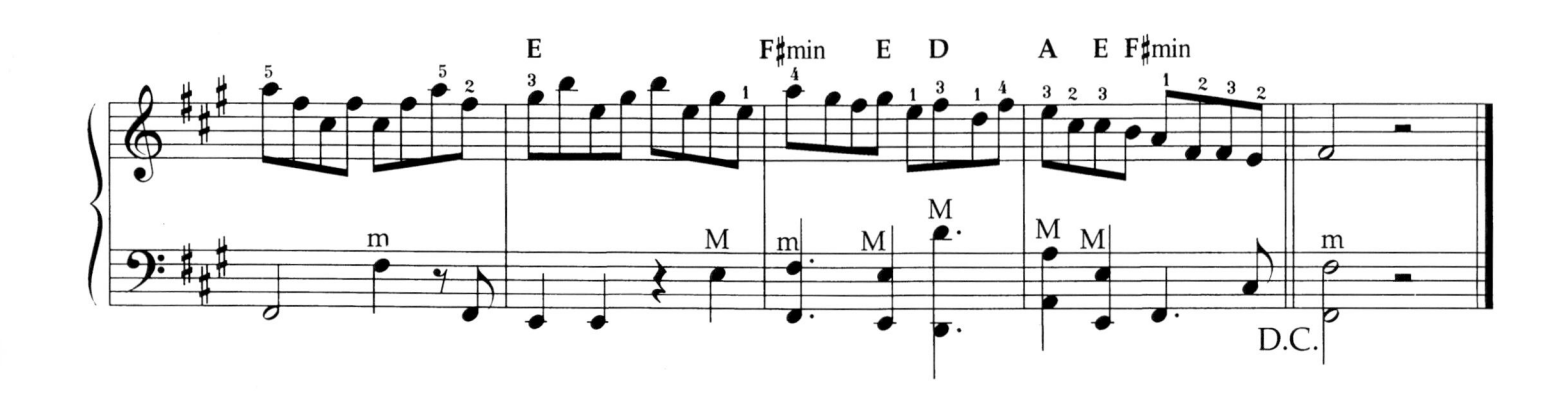

arr. © Ian Lowthian. All Rights Reserved. Used by Permission.

The Dunmore Lasses

optional ornaments for measures 1 and 5

The Earl's Chair

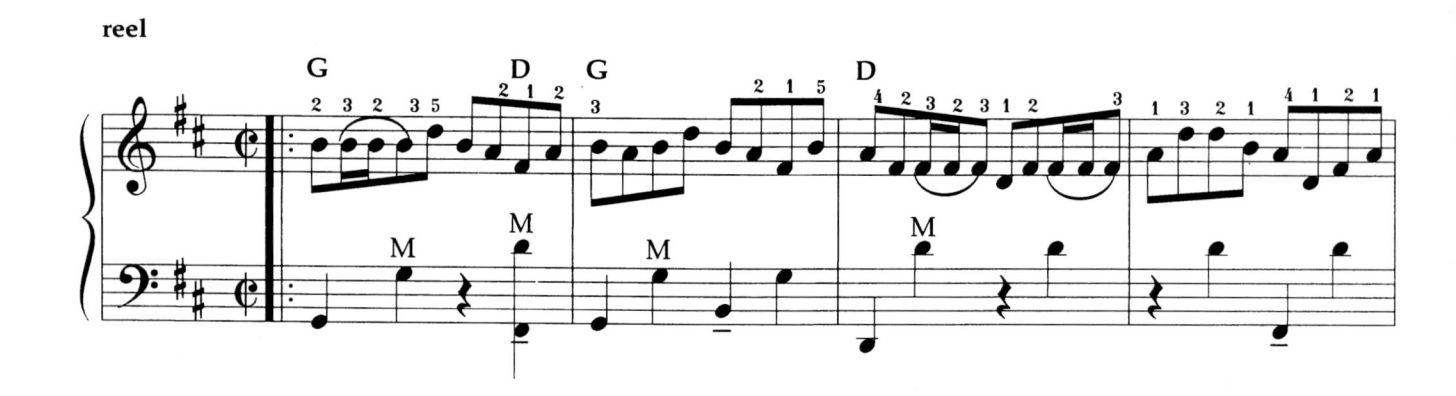

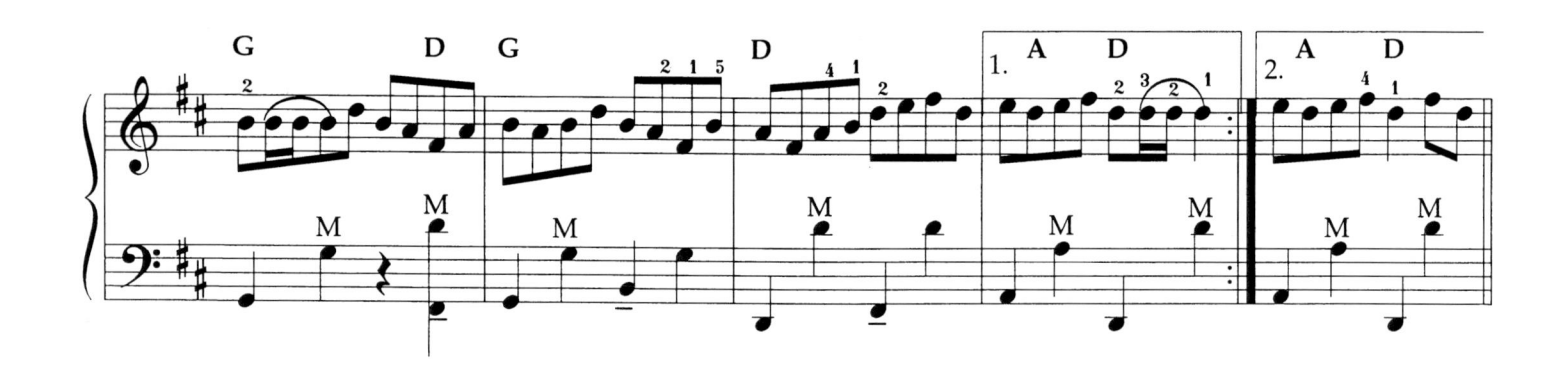

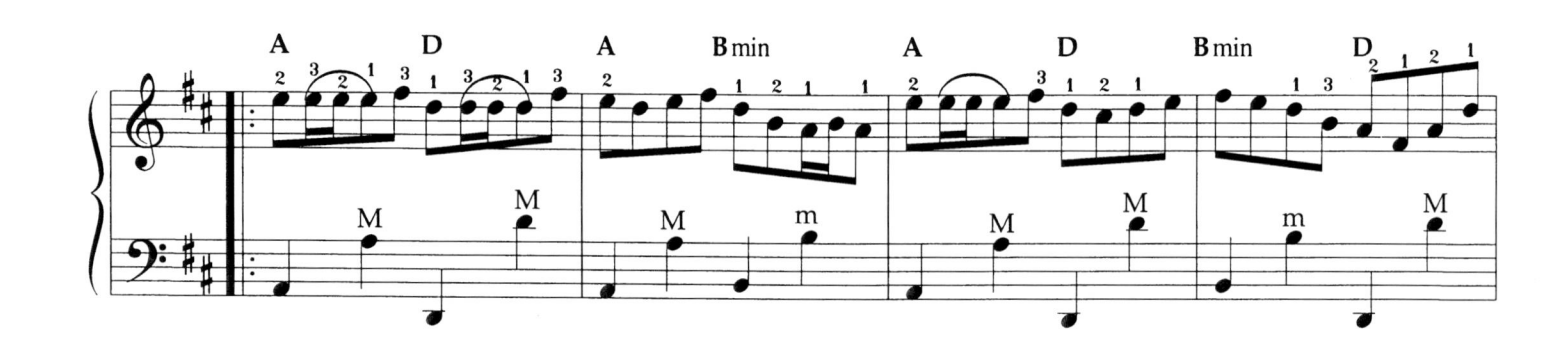

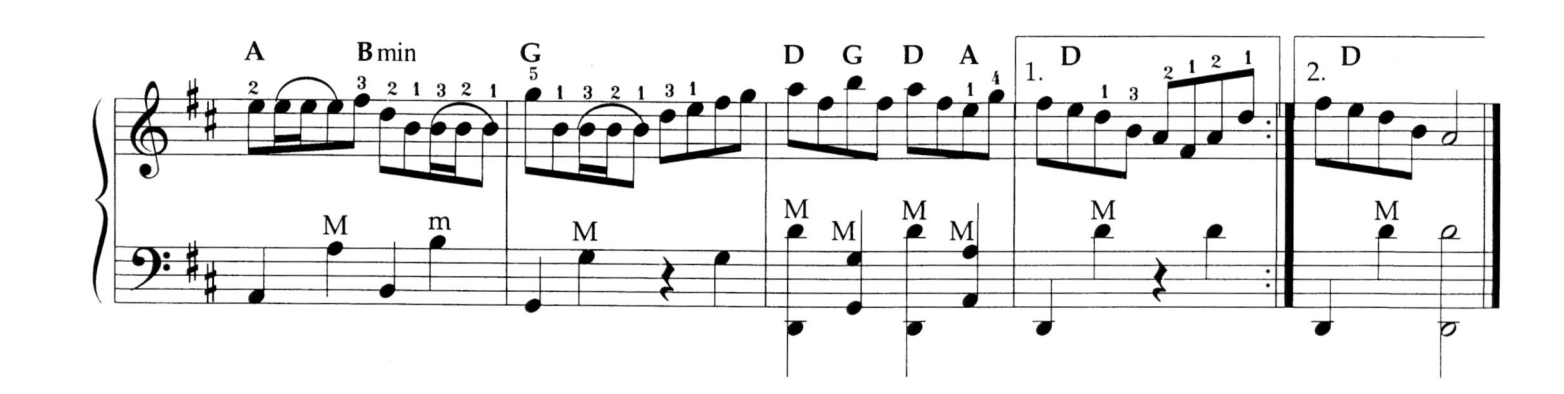

The Eavesdropper

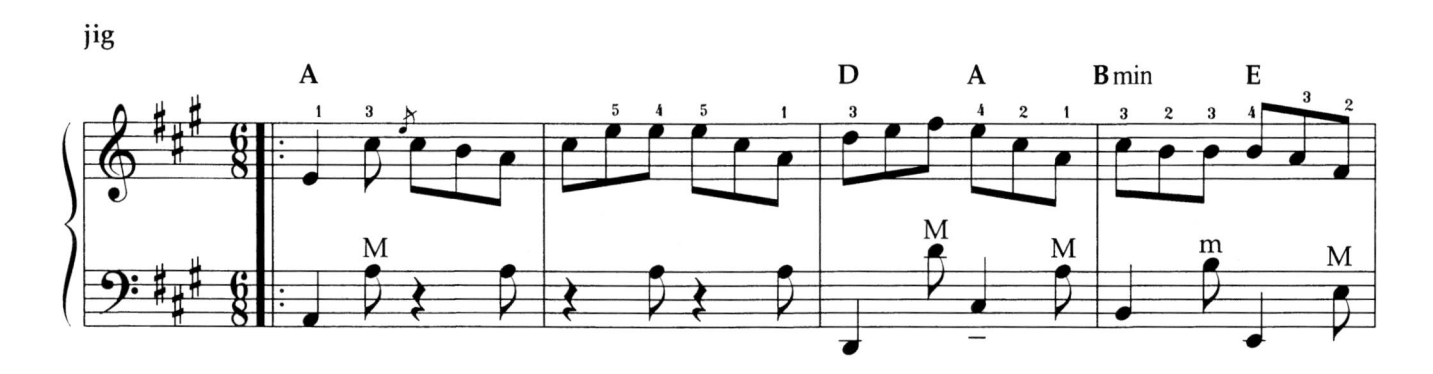

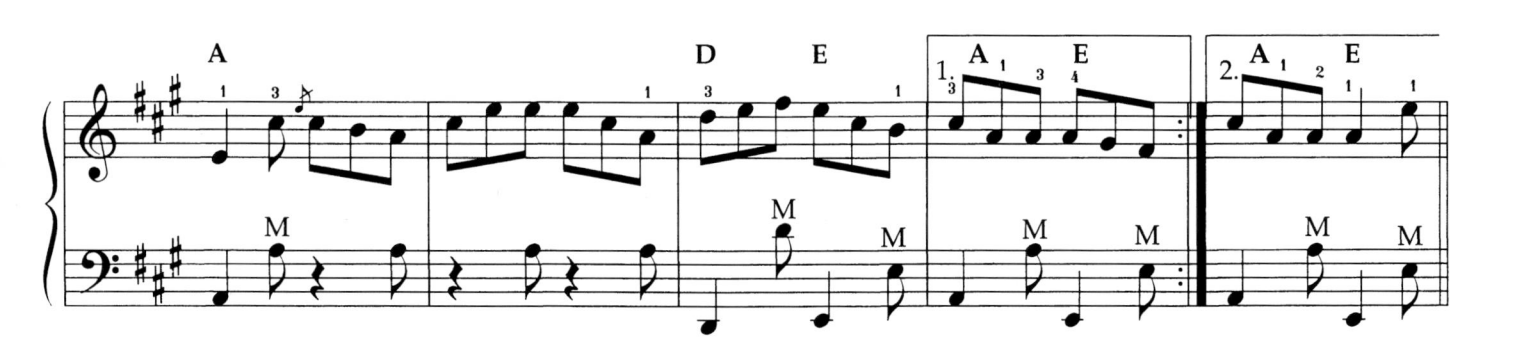

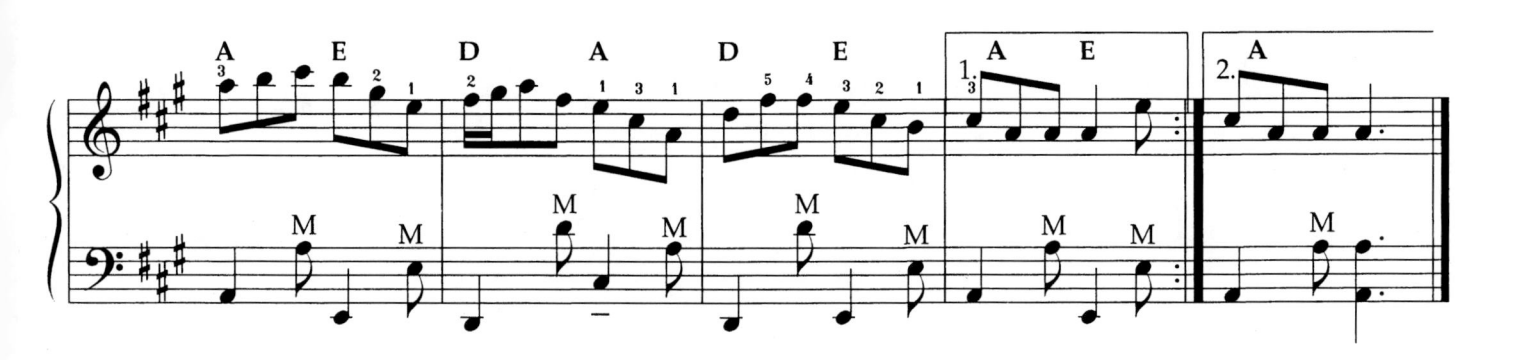

jig

The Echo

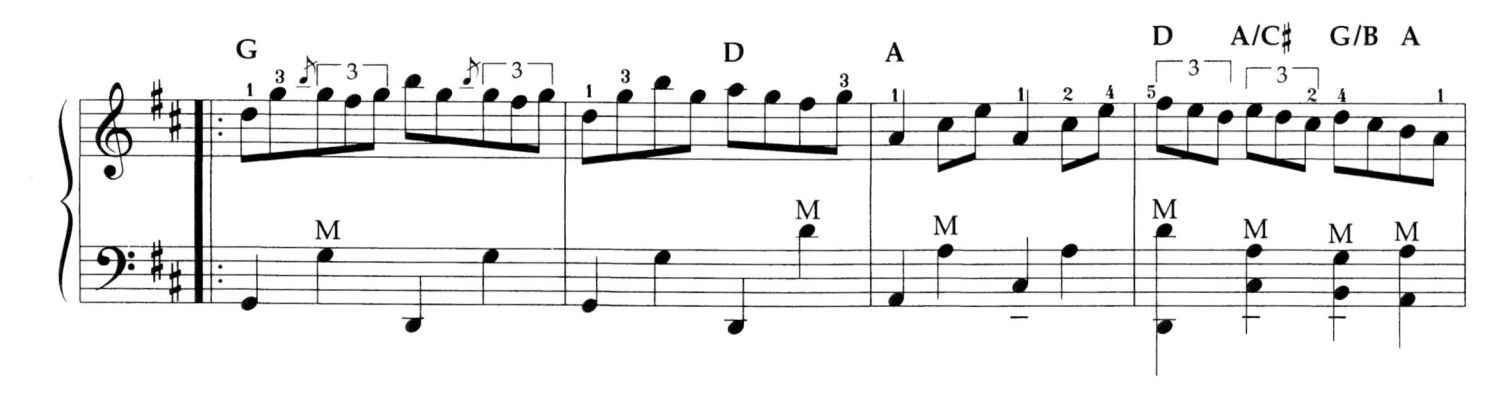

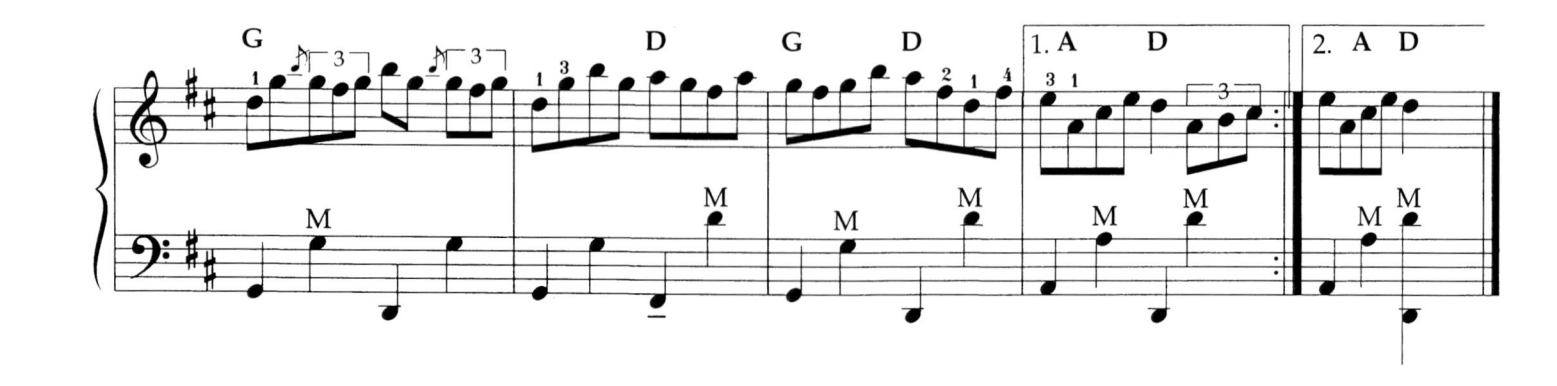

hornpipe, played with syncopated eighth notes

Fermoy Lasses

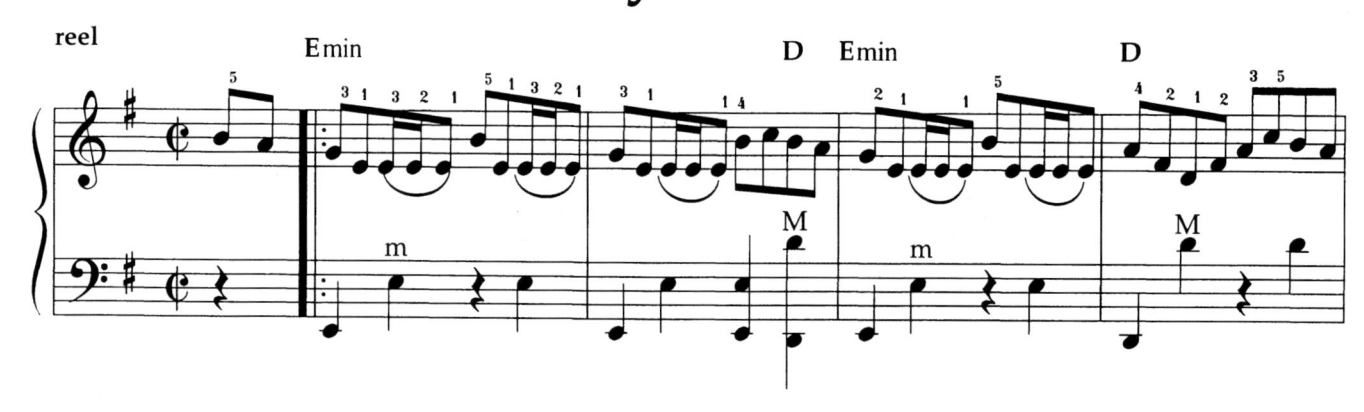

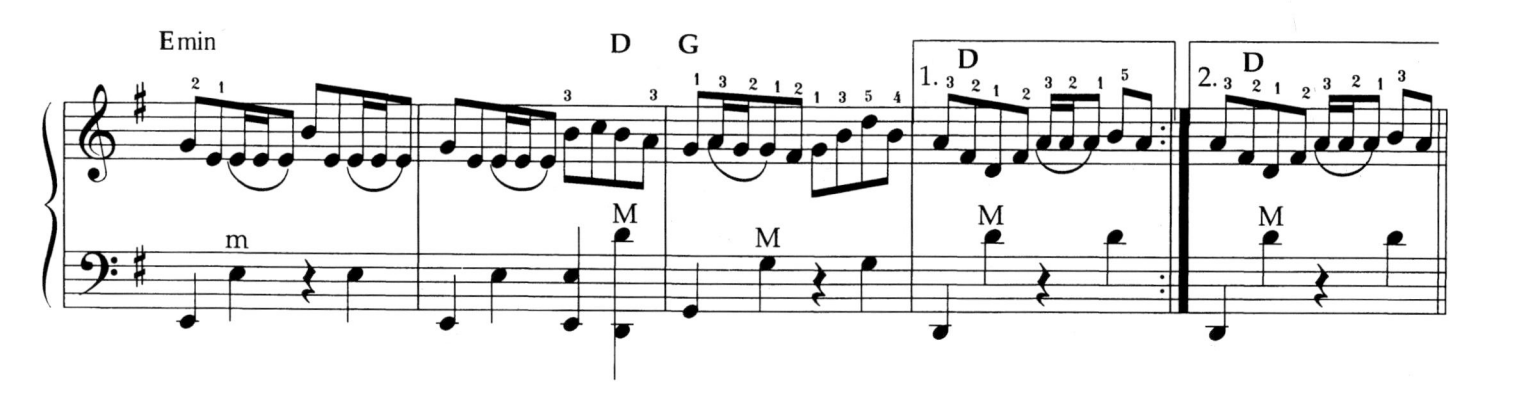

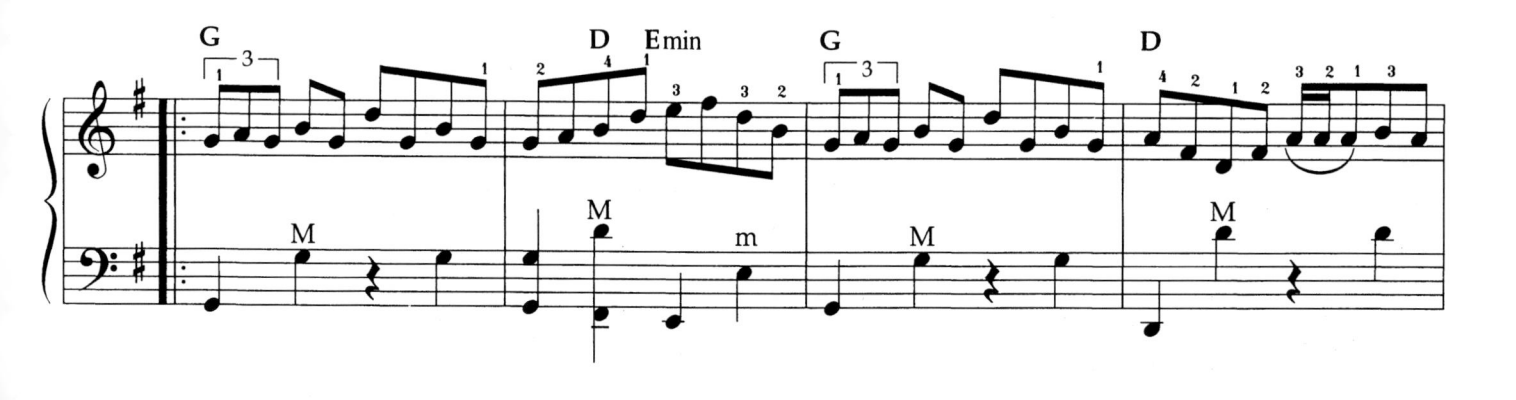

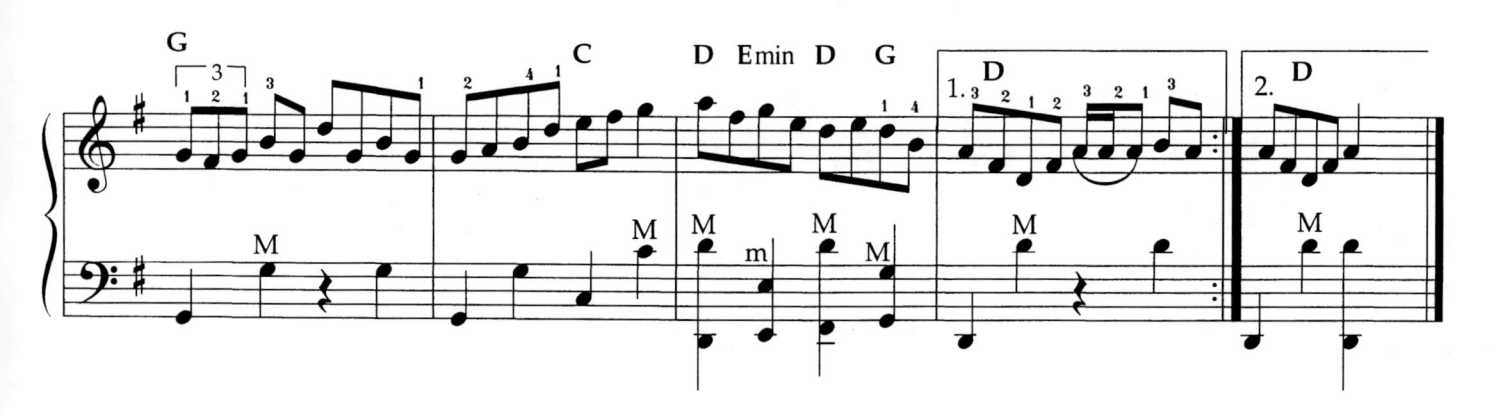

The Fort of Kincora

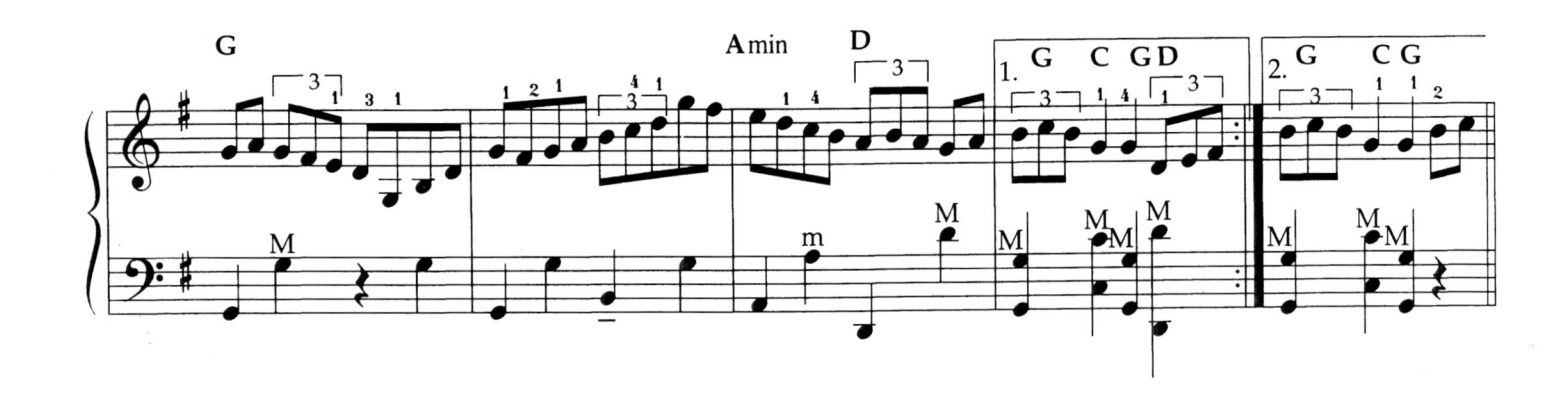

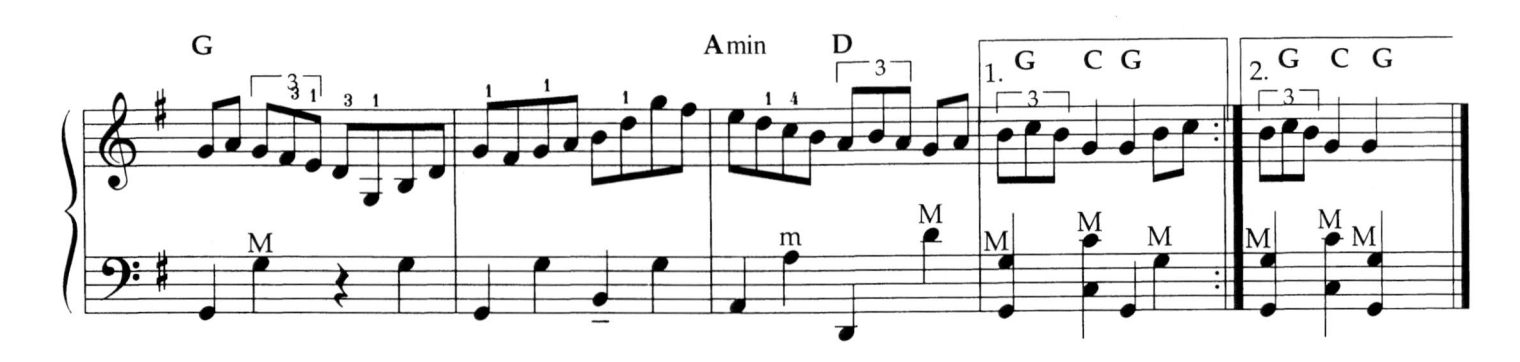

hornpipe, played with syncopated eighth notes

arrangement by Joe Burke

Chords based on harp playing of Maire Ni Chathasaigh.

arr. © Joe Burke. All Rights Reserved. Used by Permission.

The Galway

Hornpipe, played with syncopated eighth notes

arr. © 1999 Mel Bay® Publications, Inc. All Rights Reserved.

The Galway Rambler

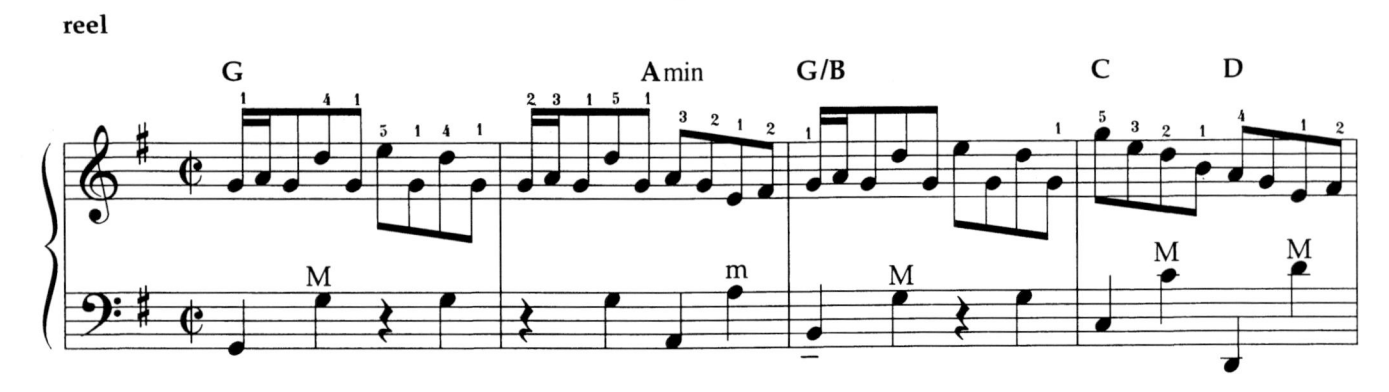

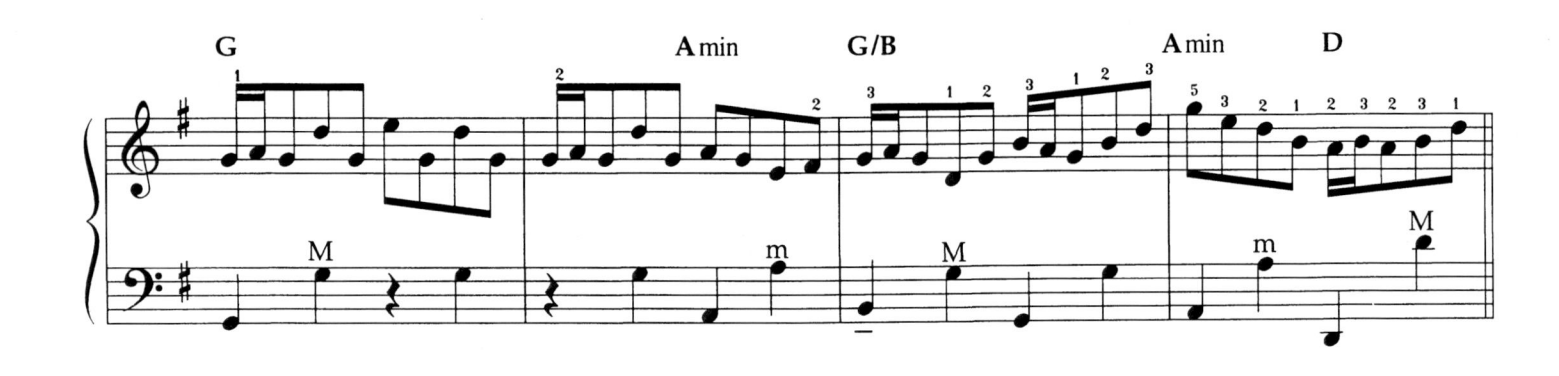

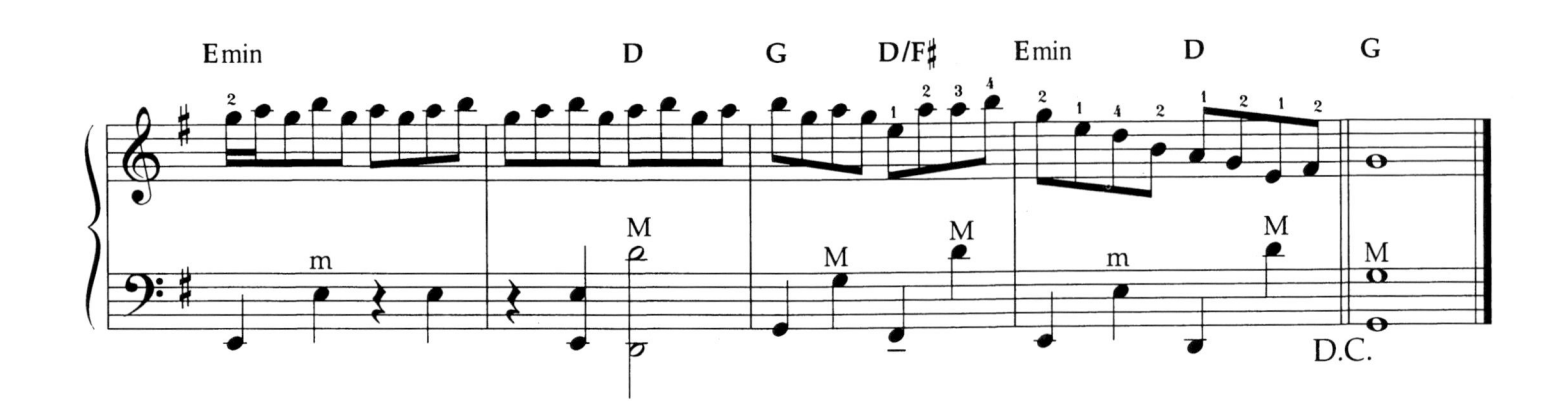

Glass of Beer

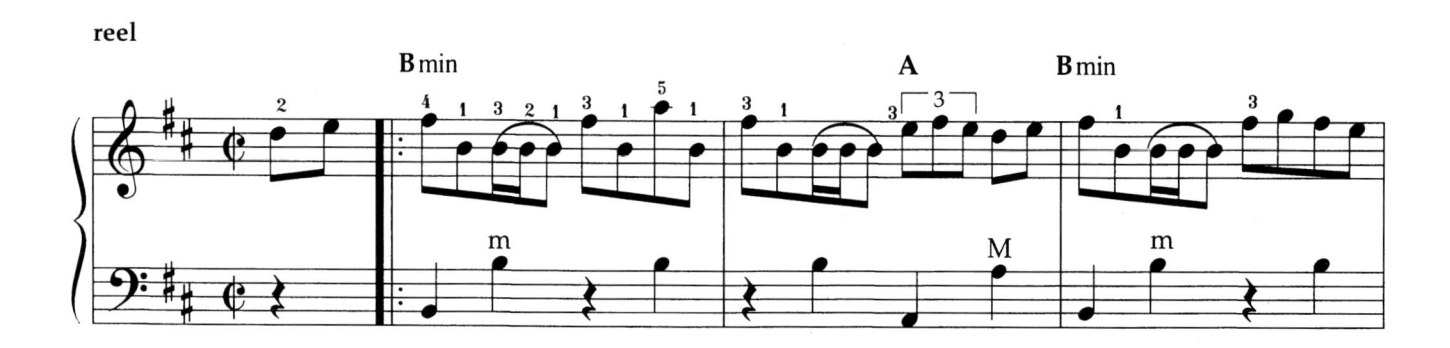

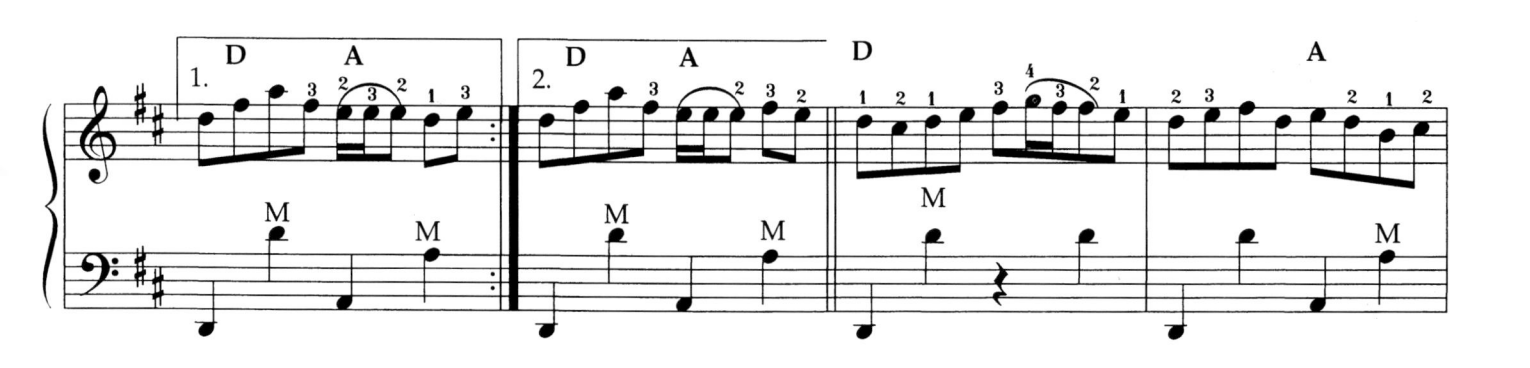

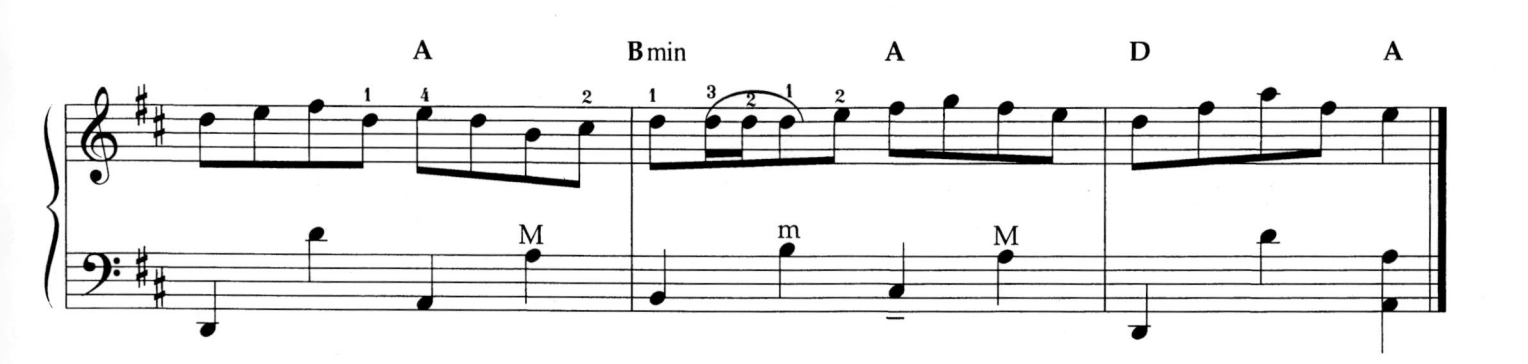

reel

The Golden Keyboard

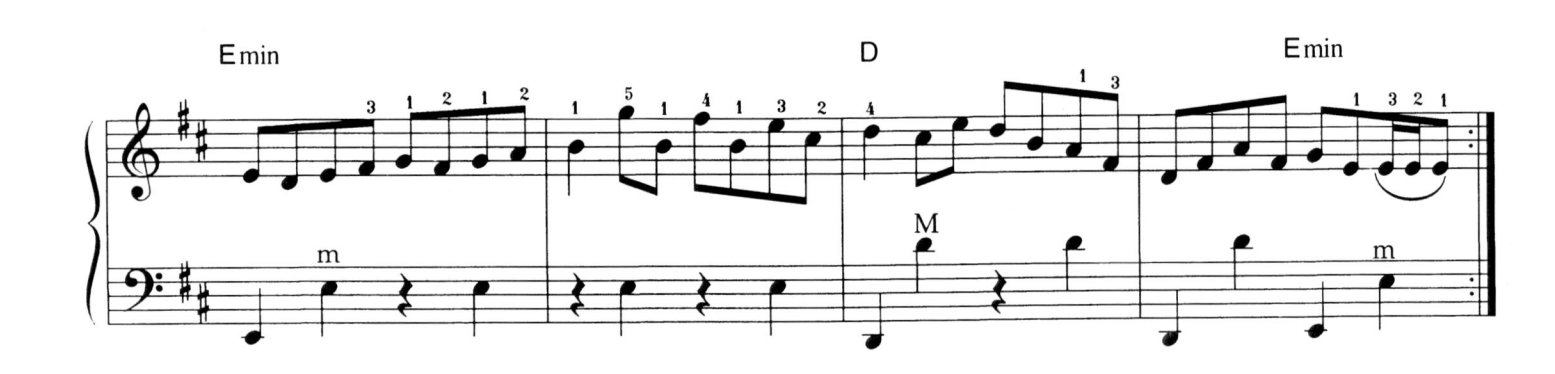

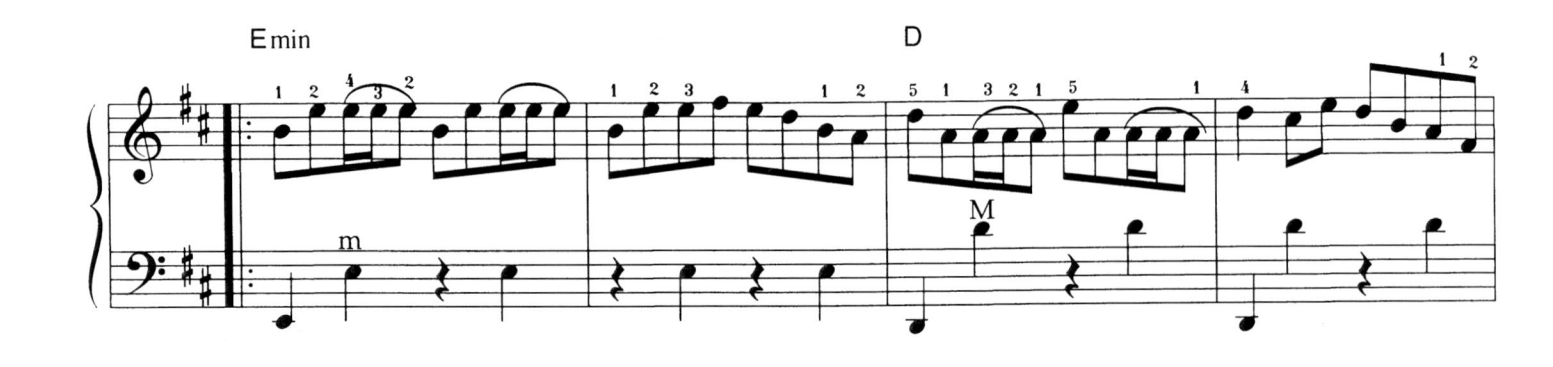

reel   Martin Mulhaire

© Martin Mulhaire. All Rights Reserved. Used by Permission.

*This page has been
left blank to avoid
awkward page turns*

The Gravel Walk

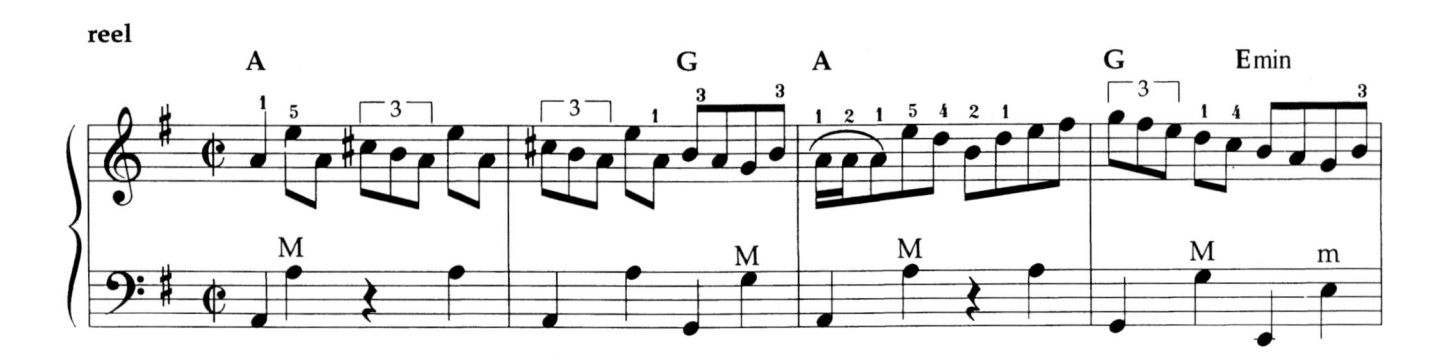

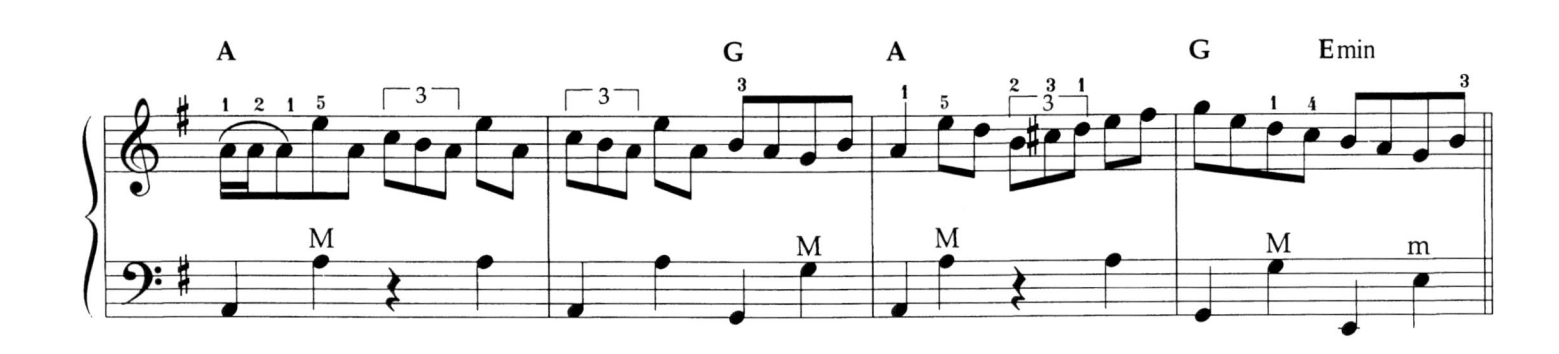

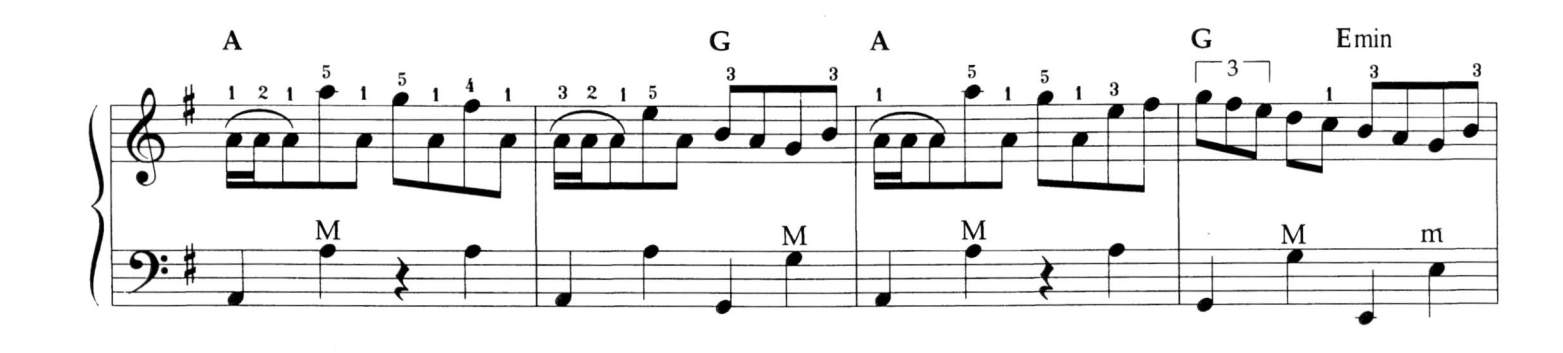

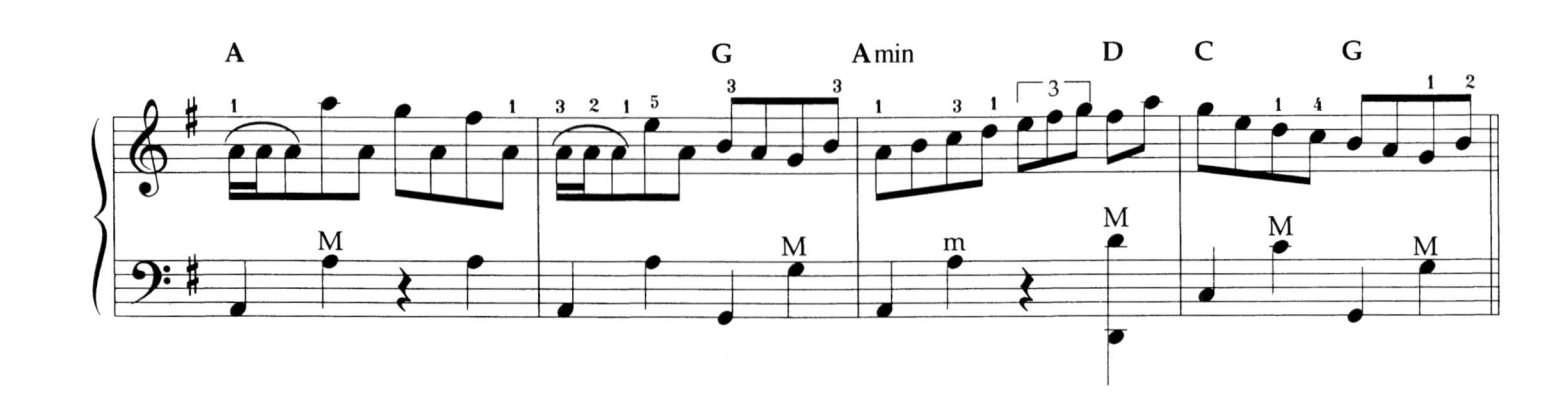

Amin
G
Amin
G
Emin
Amin
G
F
Emin
G
C
G
C
G
C
G
1.
Amin
Emin
G
2.
Amin
G
Emin
Amin
D.C.

Green Forest Jig

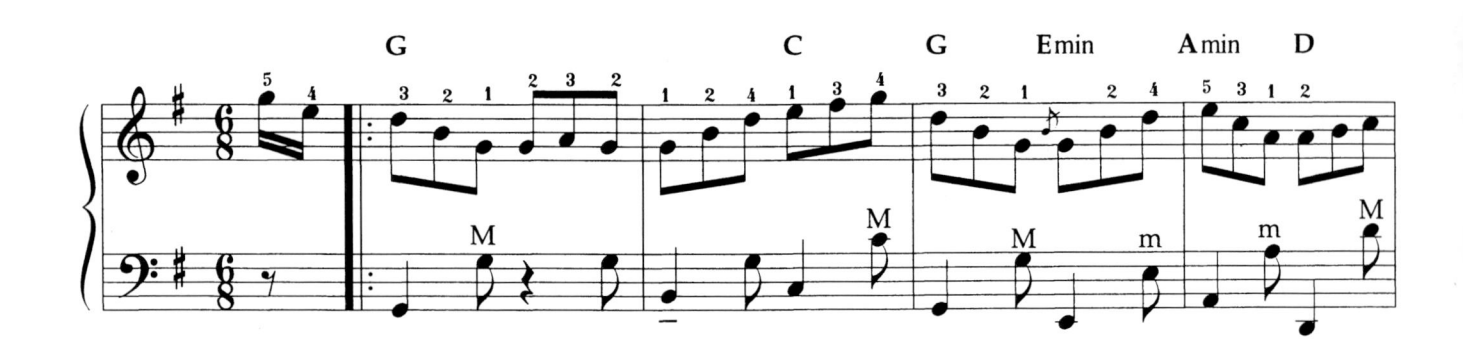

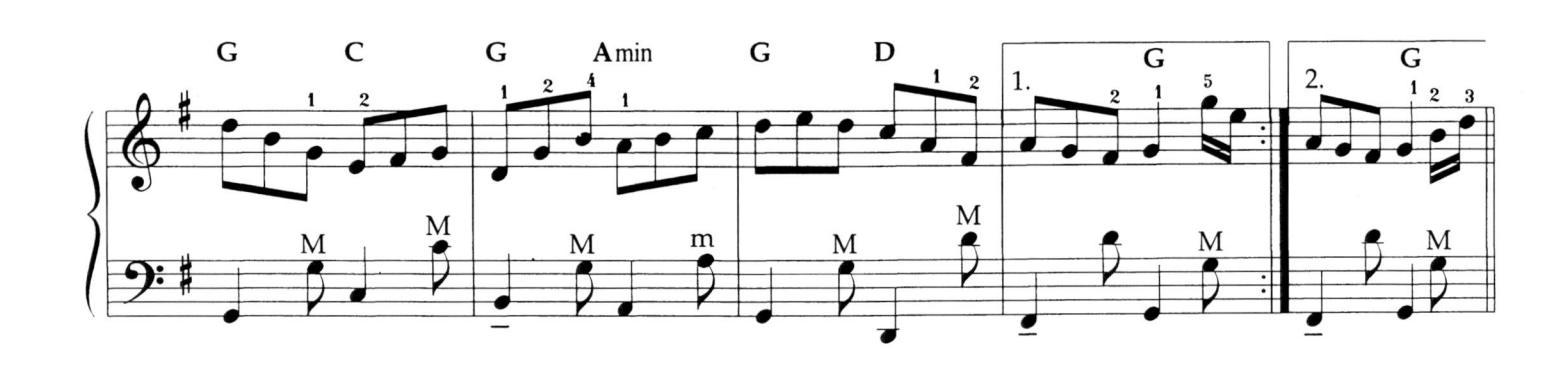

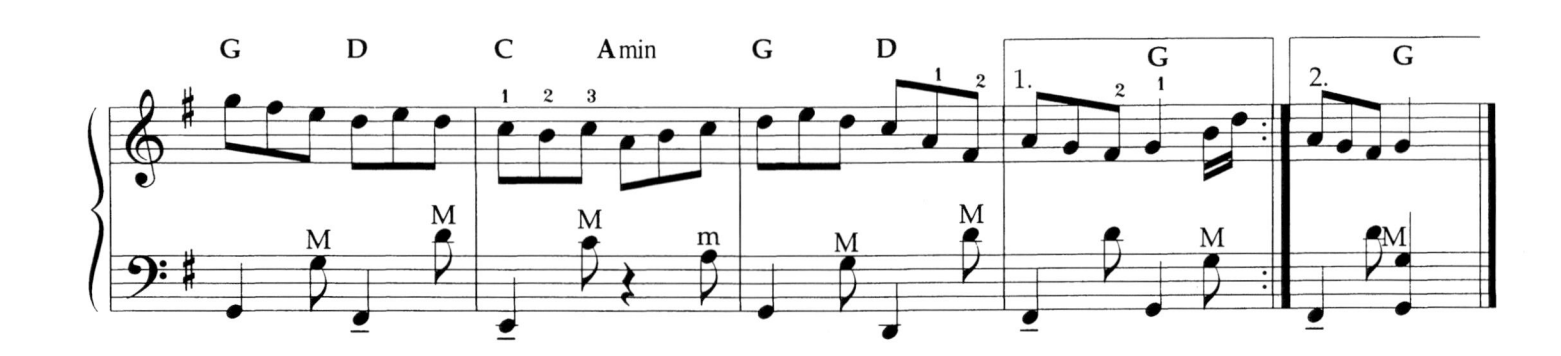

The High Reel
(Duffy the Dancer)

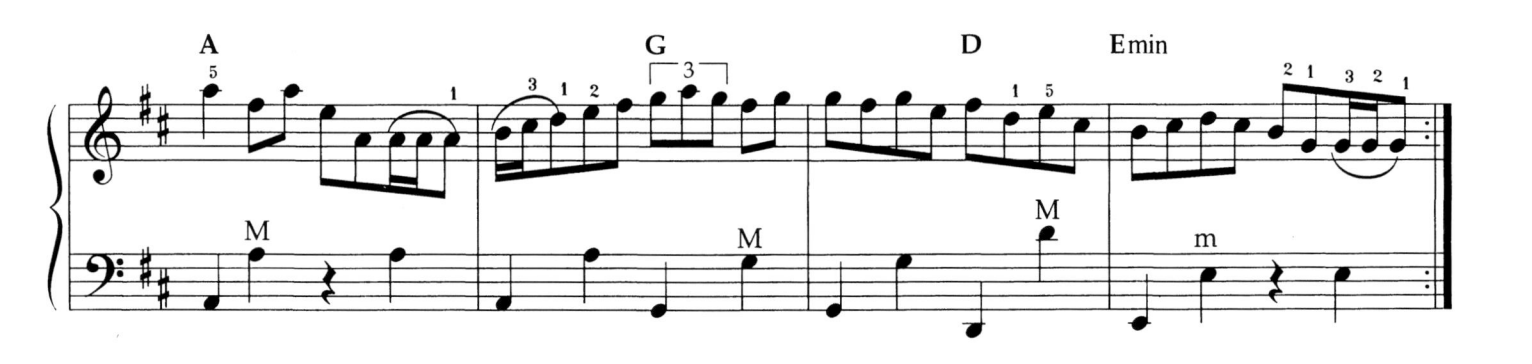

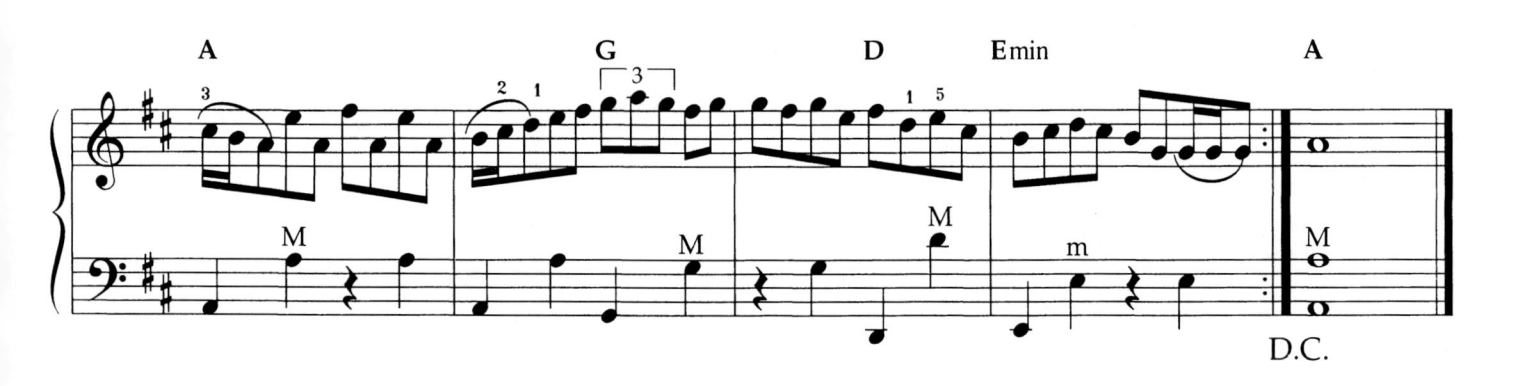

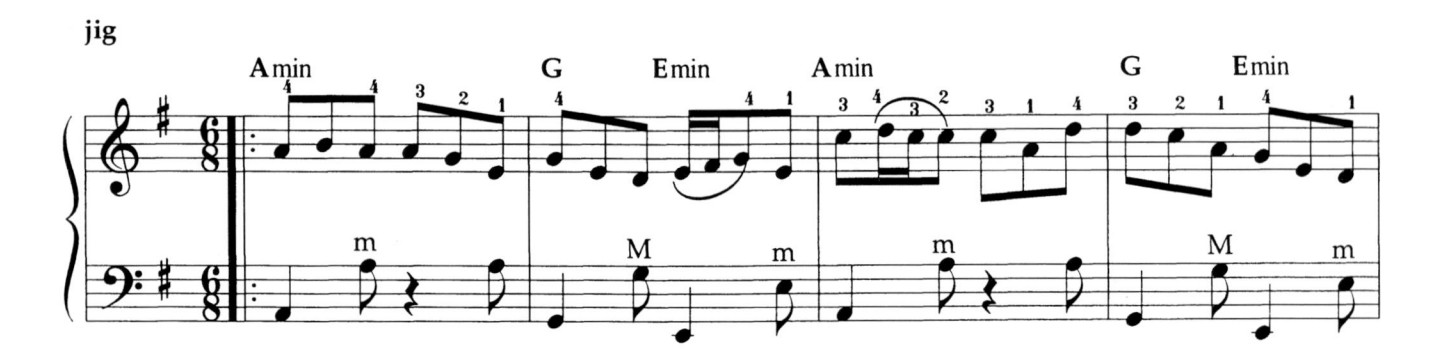

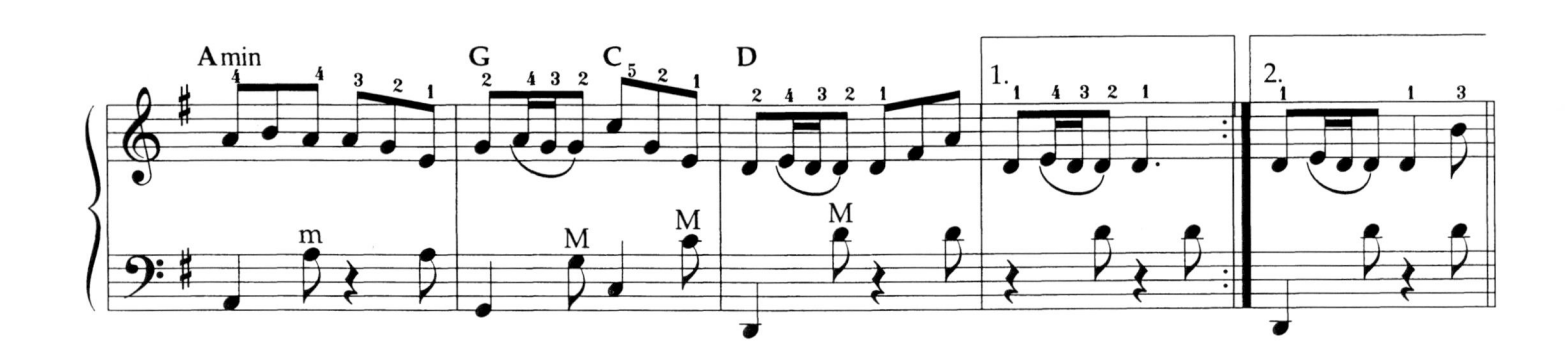

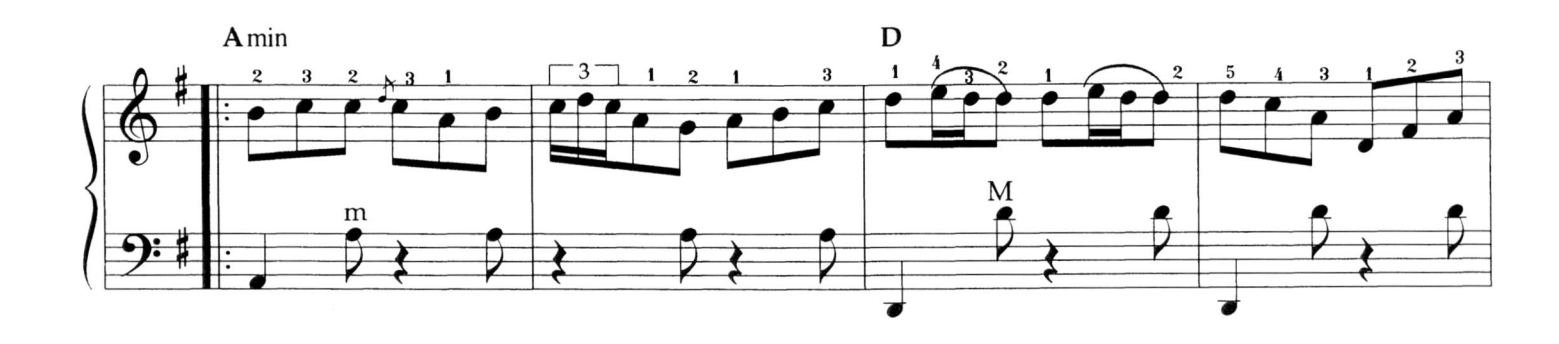

The Humours of Ballyloughlin

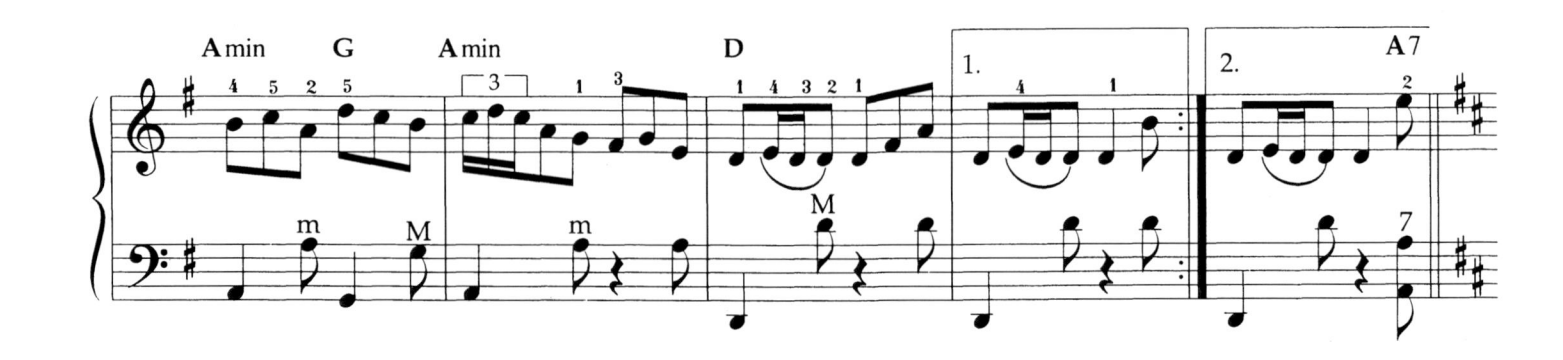

D Emin D/F♯ G A
M m M M M
D Emin D/F♯ G A G/B 1. A/C♯ D 2. A/C♯ D
M m M M M M M M M M
D C A
M M M
D C D 1. A D 2. A D
M M M M M M M

The Humours of Tulla

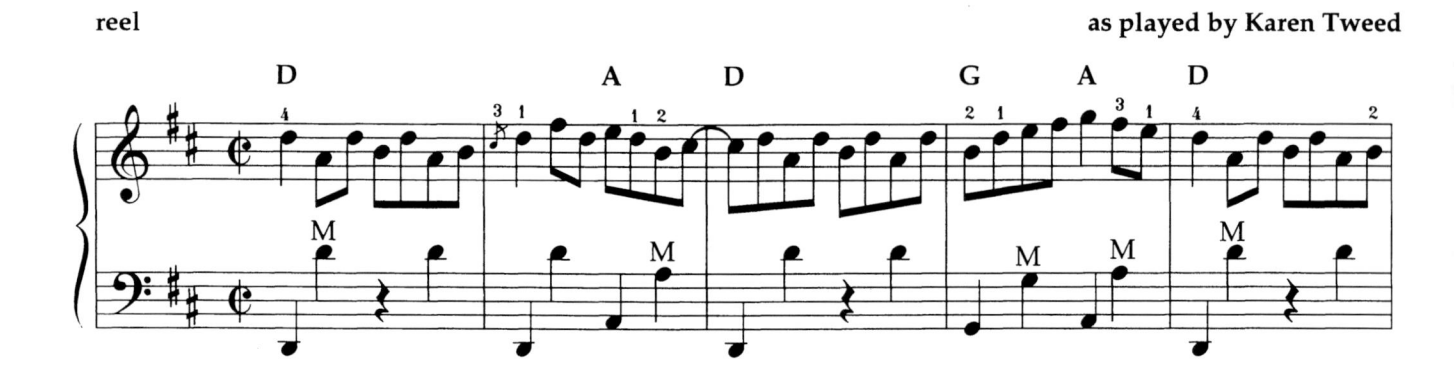

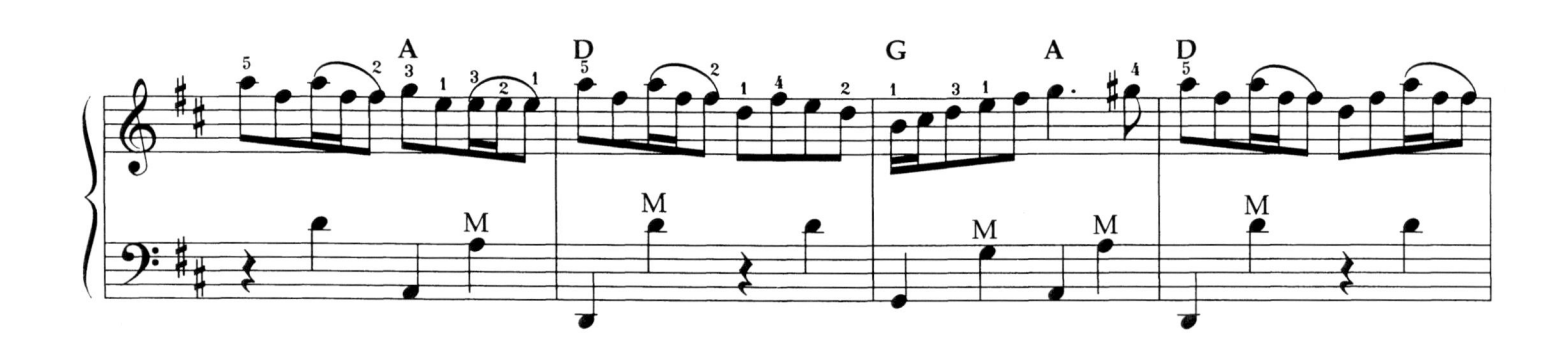

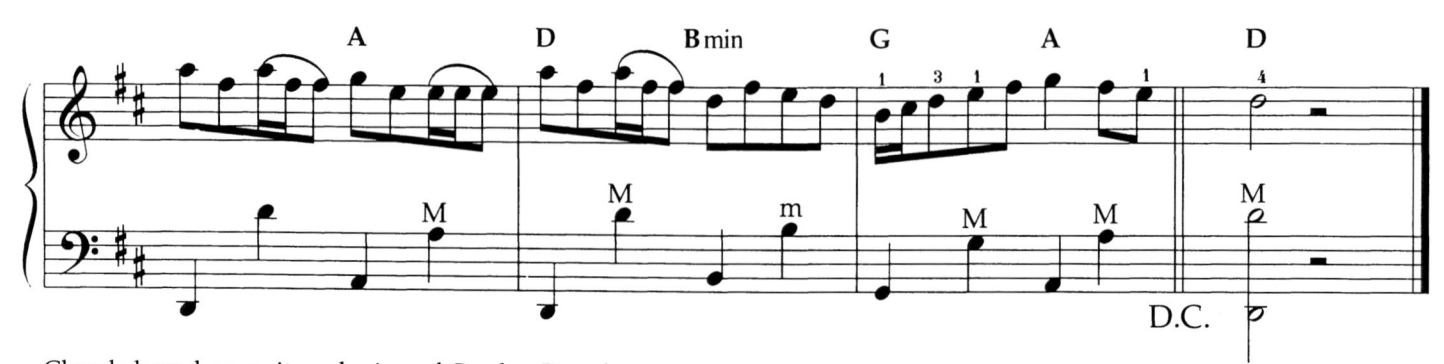

reel
as played by Karen Tweed

Chords based on guitar playing of Gordon Tyrral

arr. © Dave Mallison Publications. All Rights Reserved. Used by Permission.

The Hunter's Purse

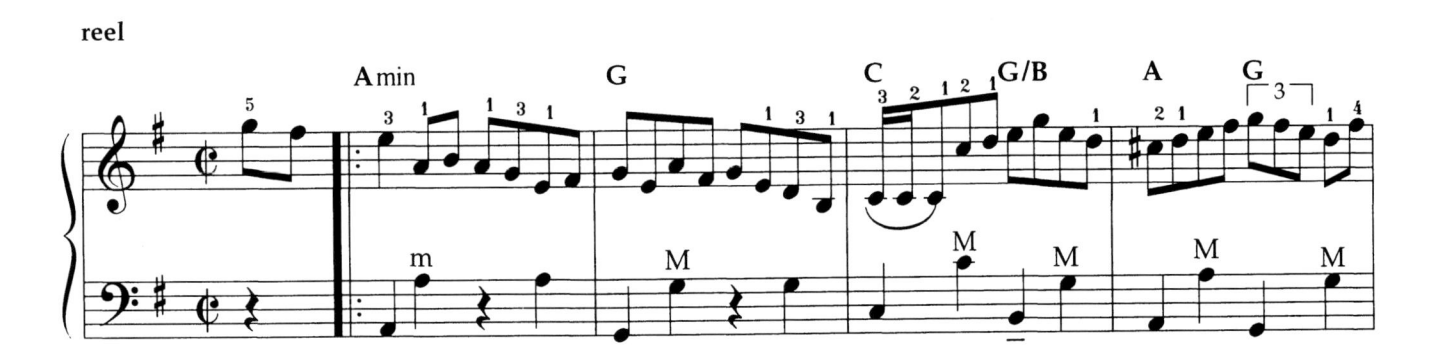

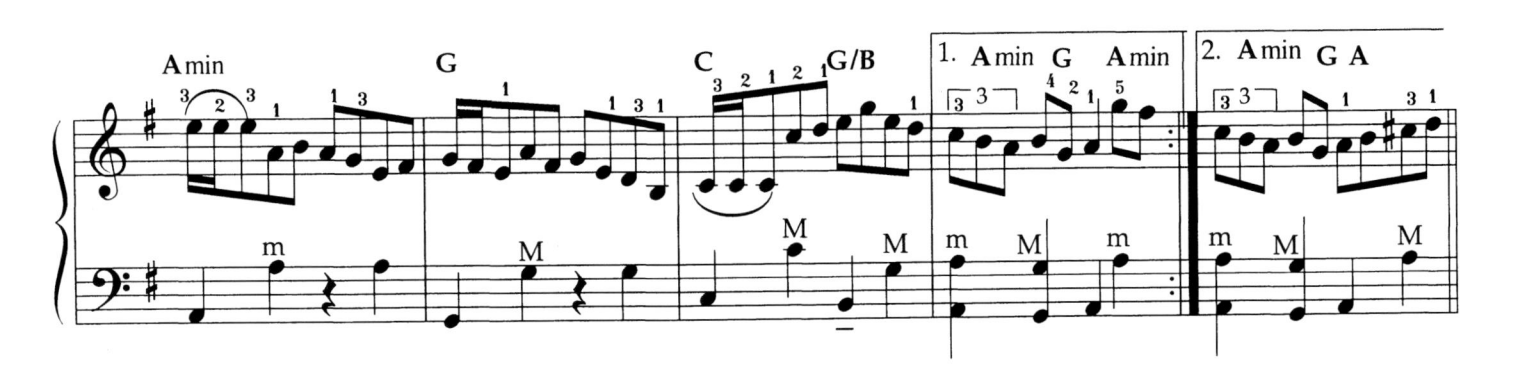

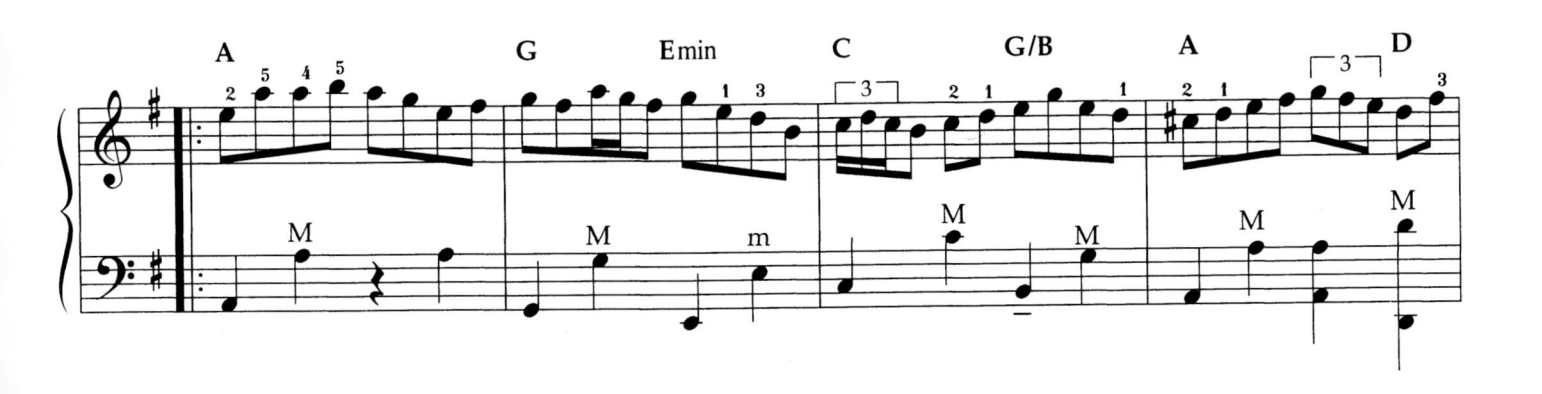

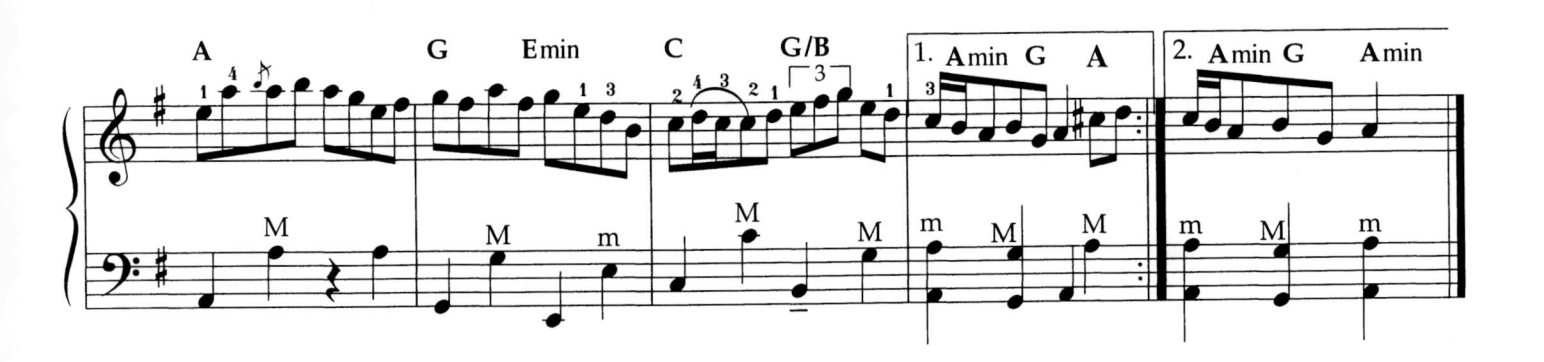

Hunting the Boyne

reel, played with syncopated eighth notes

composed and arranged by Jimmy Keane

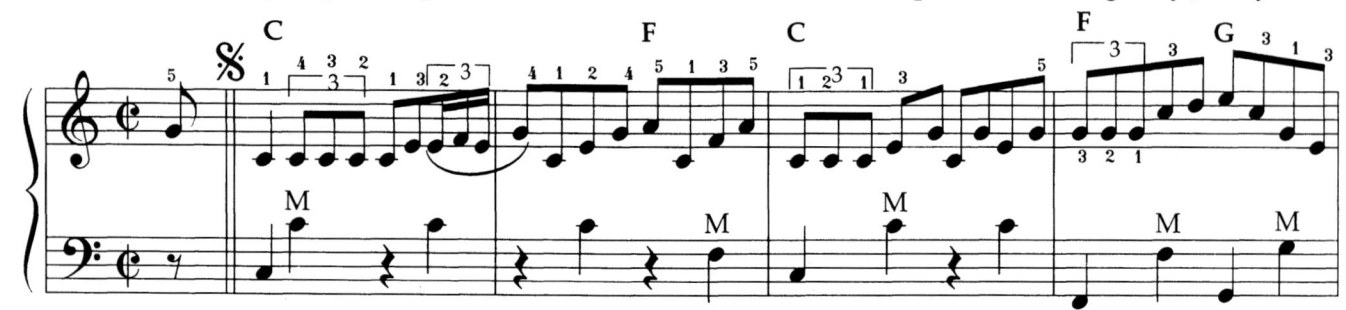

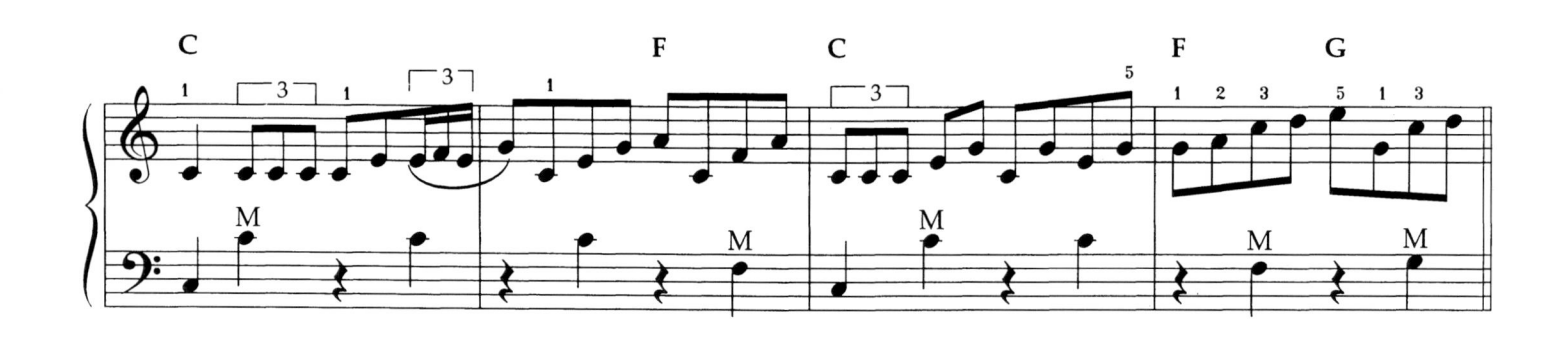

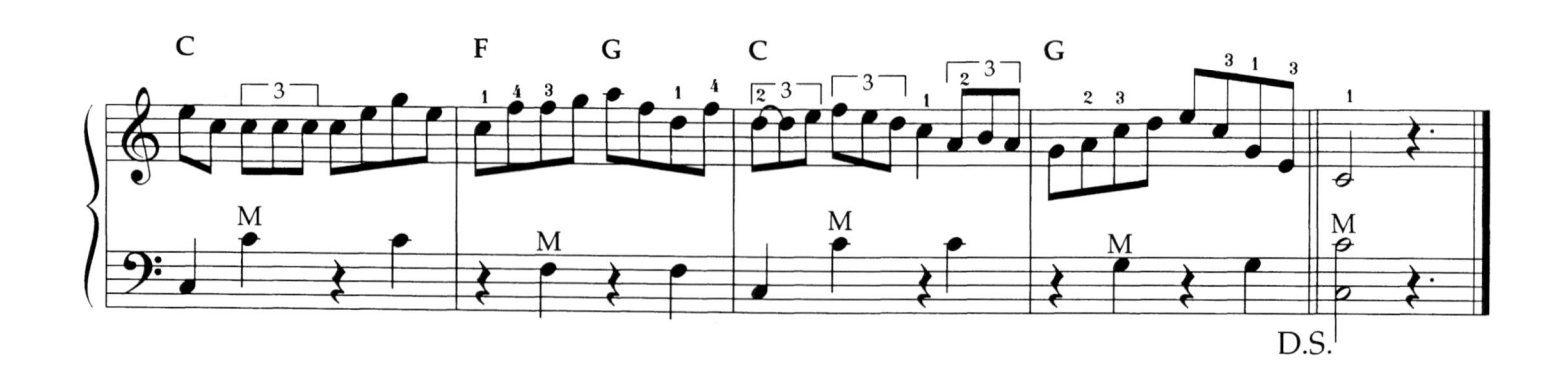

Julia Delaney

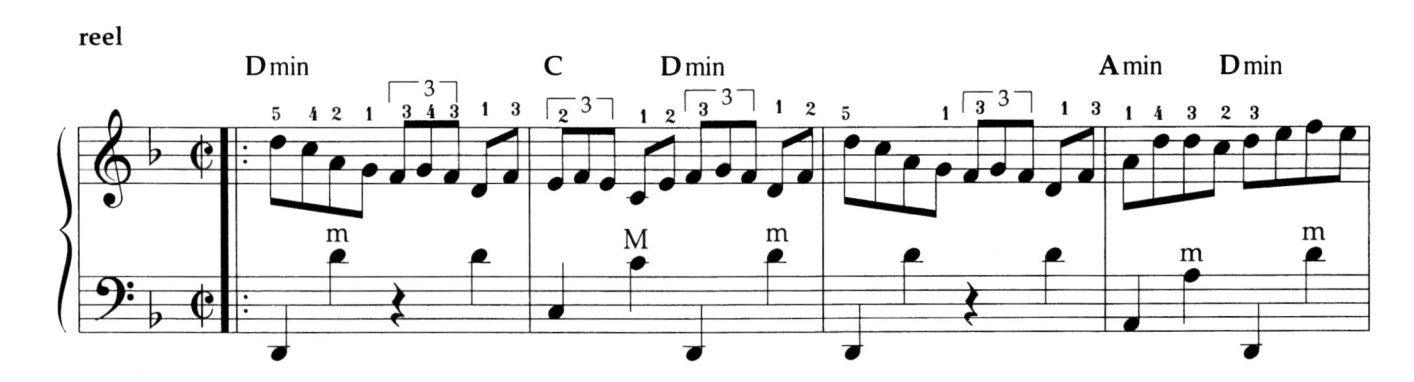

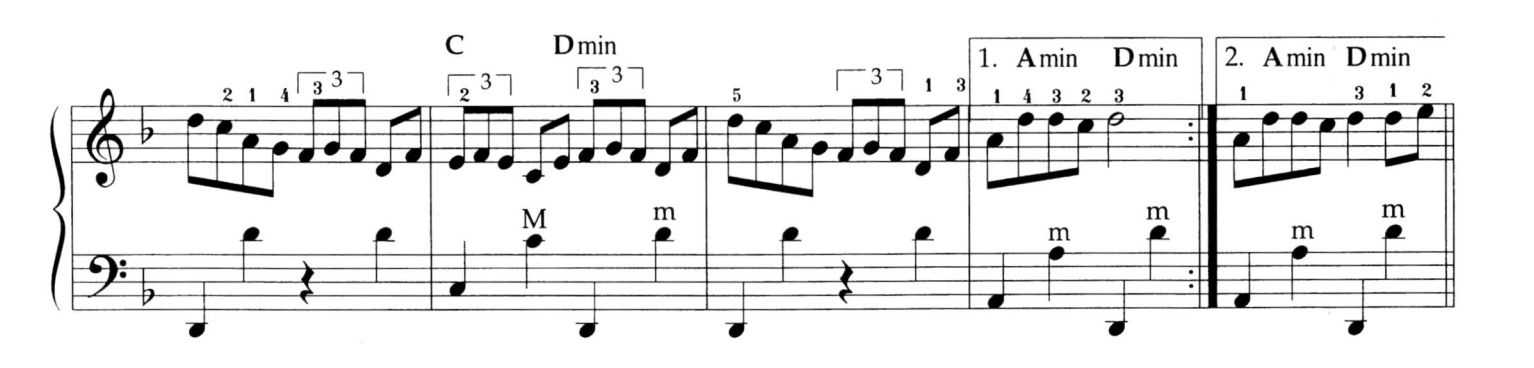

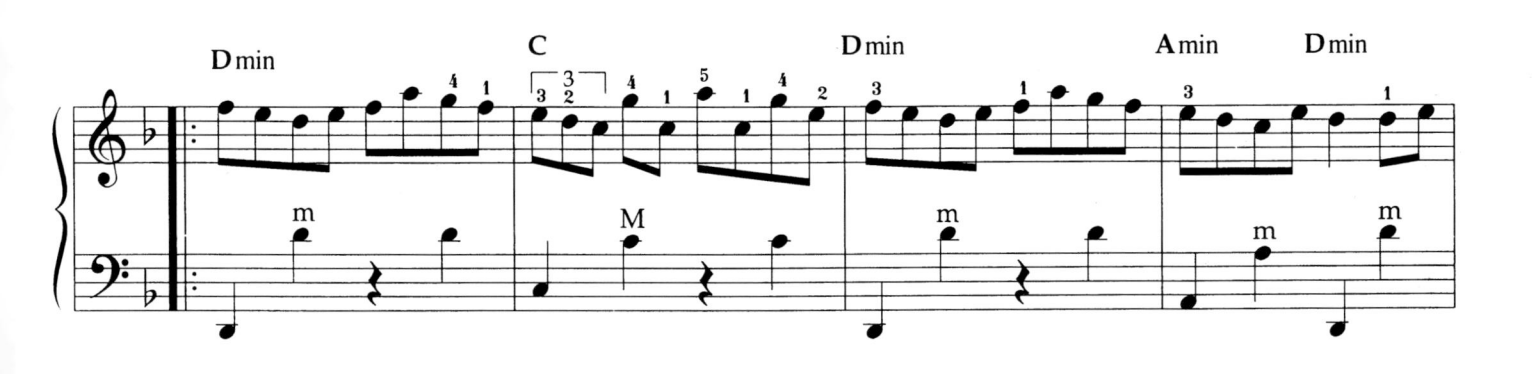

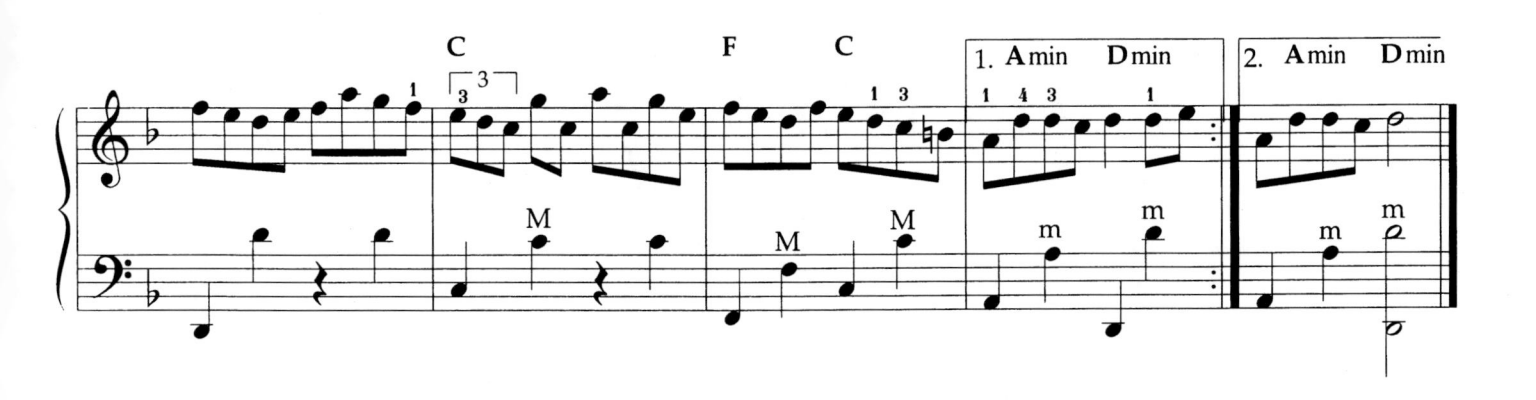

Jerry Daly's Hornpipe

played with syncopated eighth notes

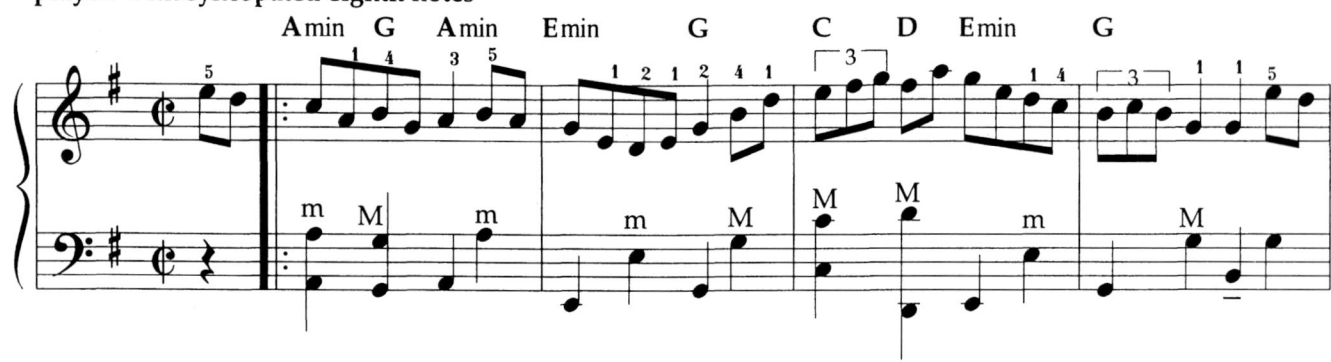

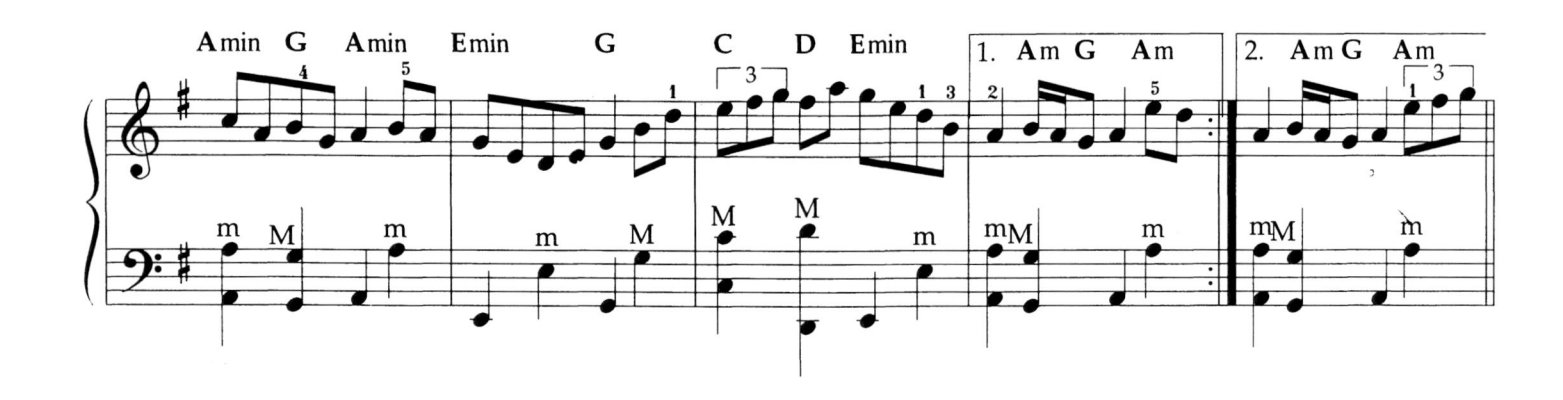

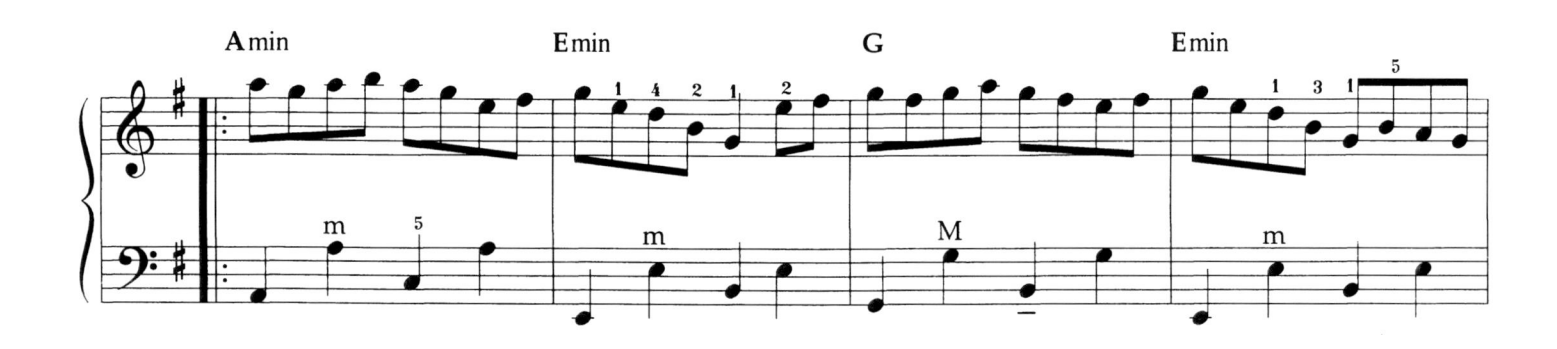

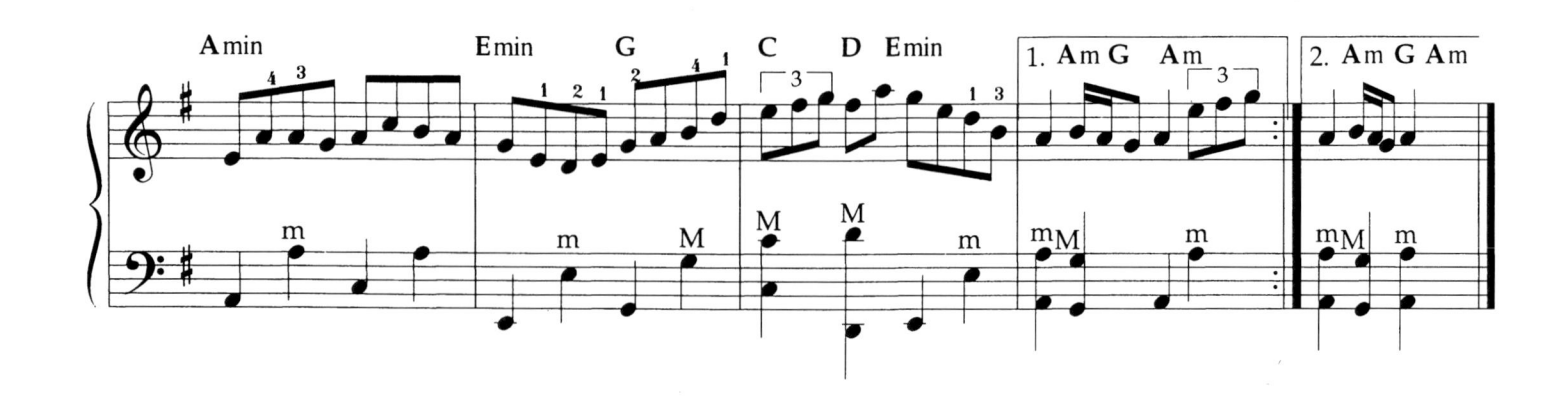

John Brennan's

The Kerry Reel
(The Green Fields of Rosbeigh)

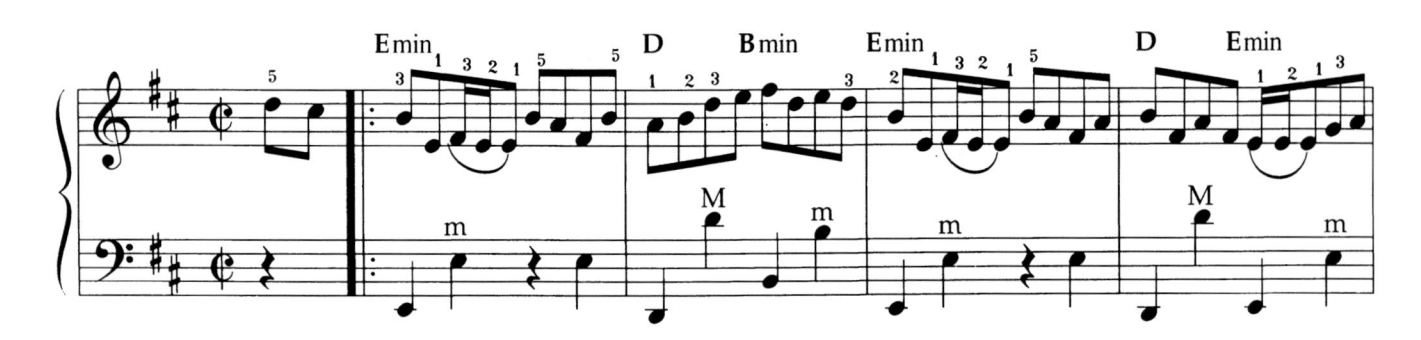

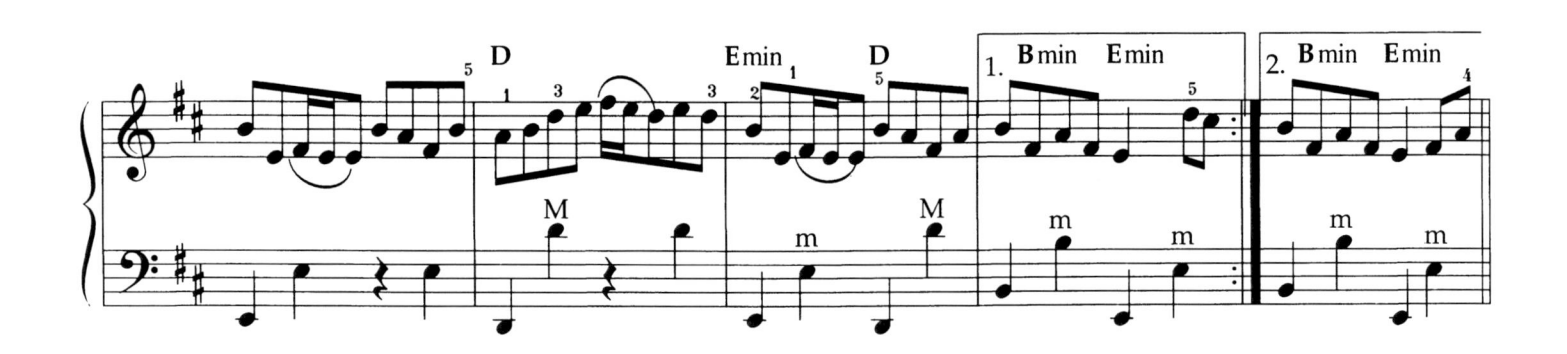

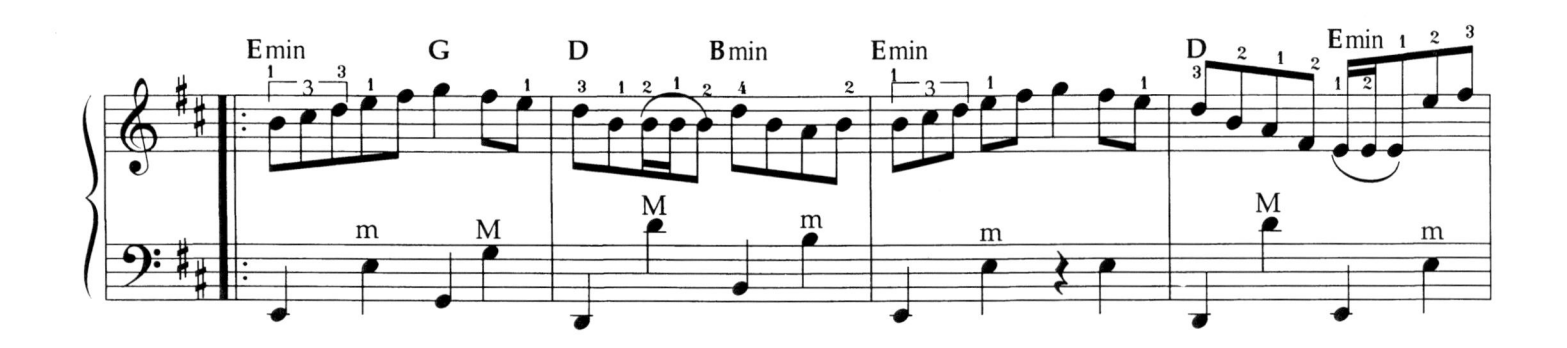

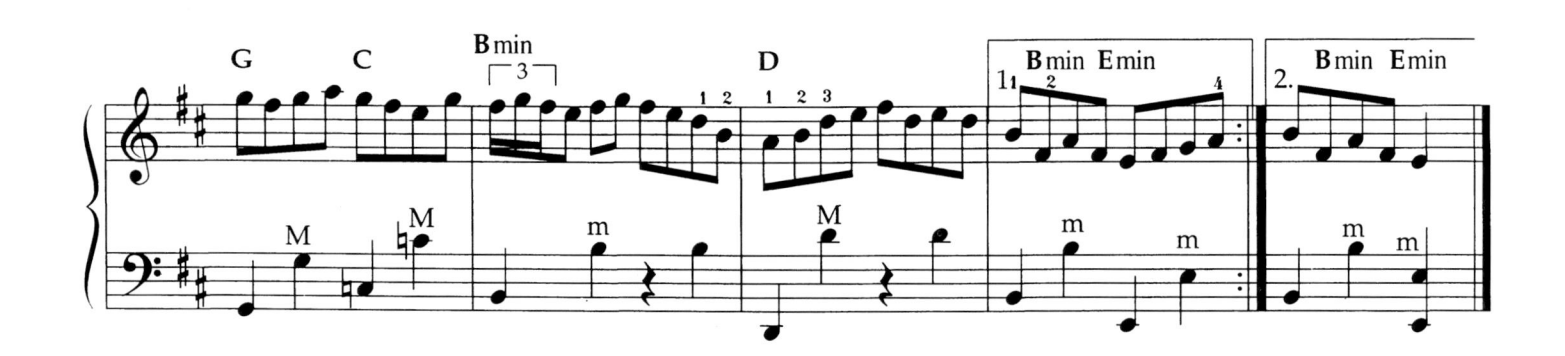

Killarney Boys of Pleasure

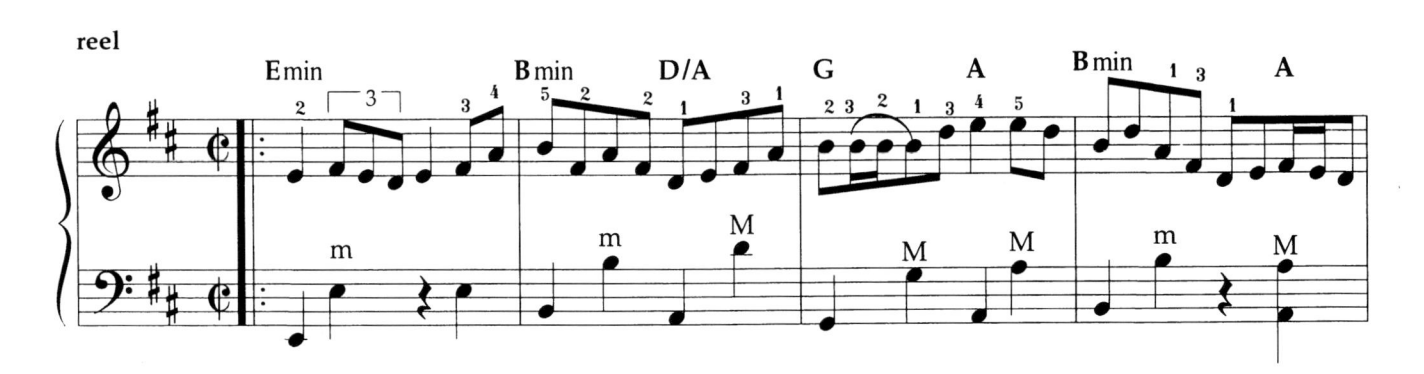

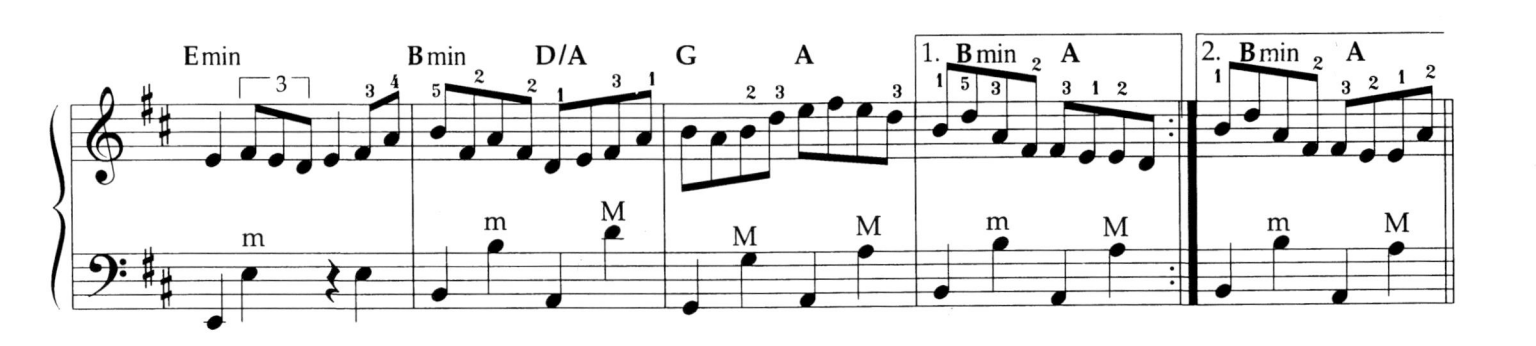

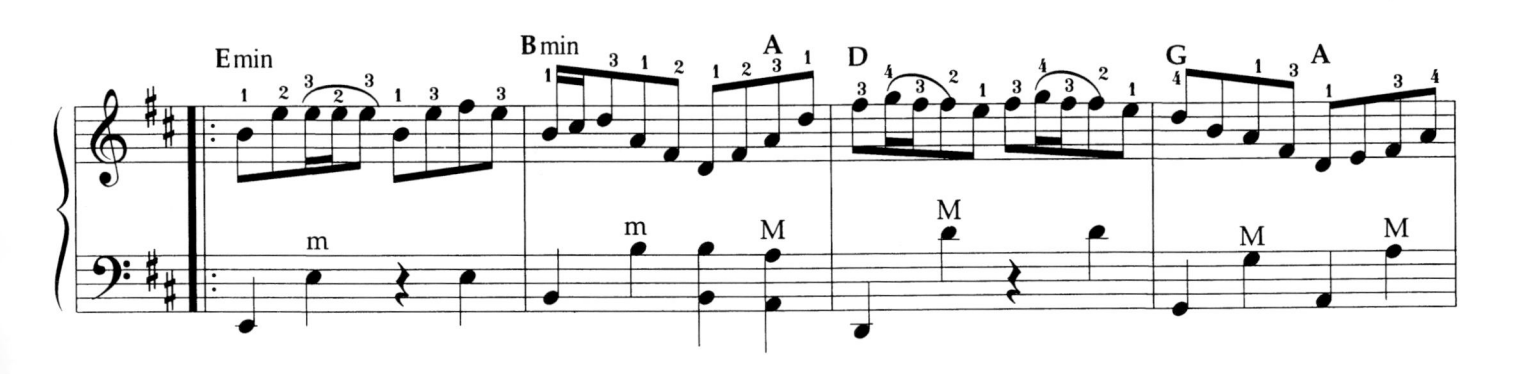

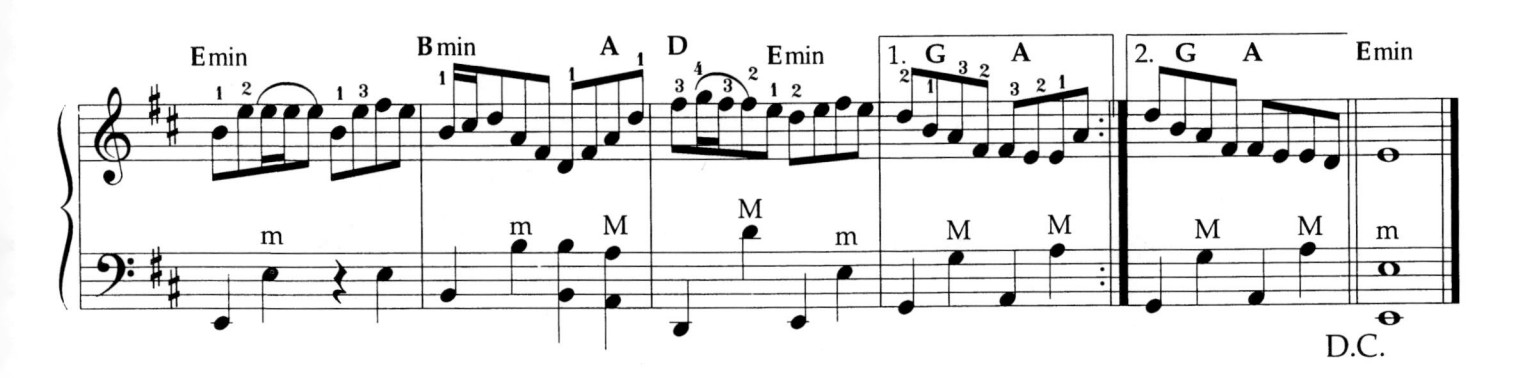

The Kinard Polka

arr. © 1999 Mel Bay® Publications, Inc. All Rights Reserved.

Knocknagow

reel, played with syncopated eighth notes

arrangement by James Keane

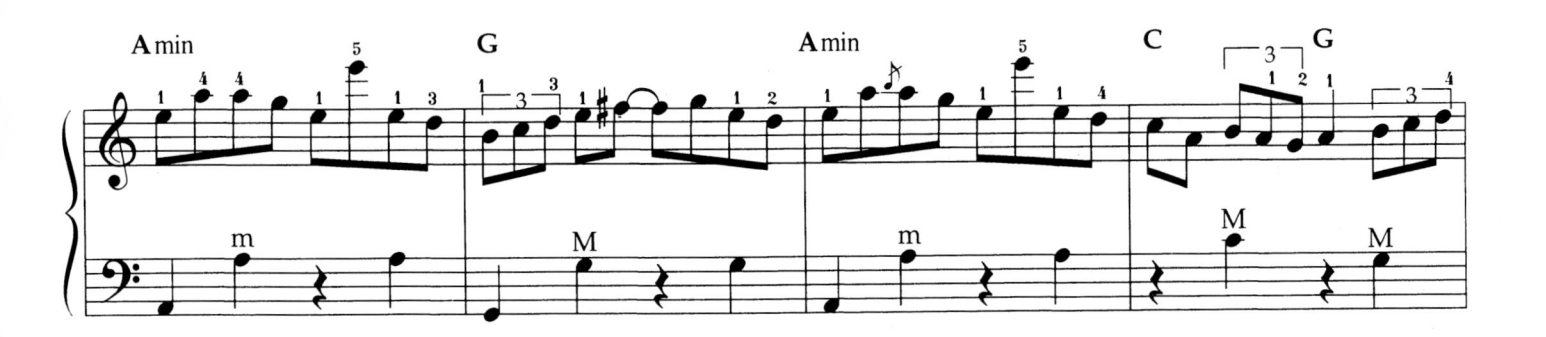

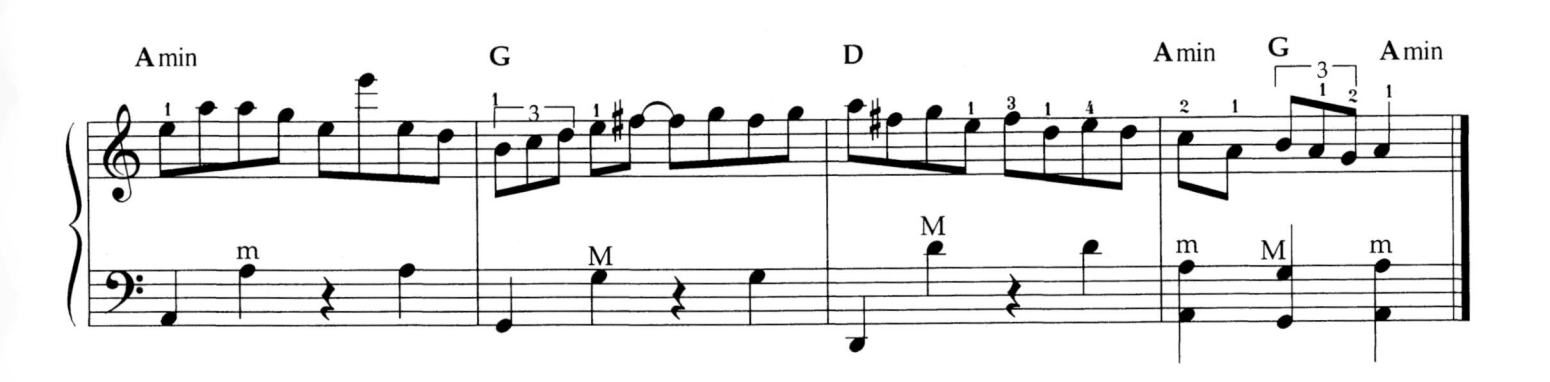

Knotted Cord

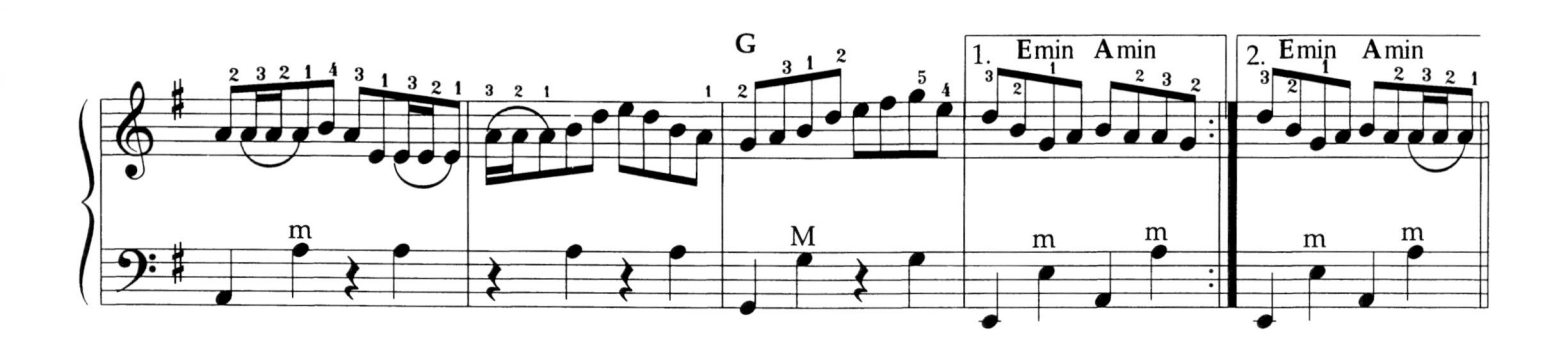

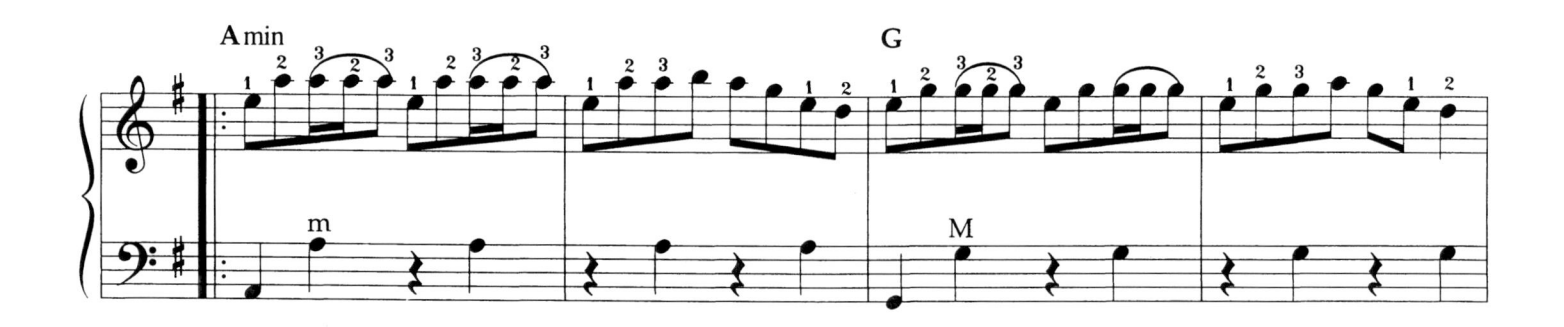

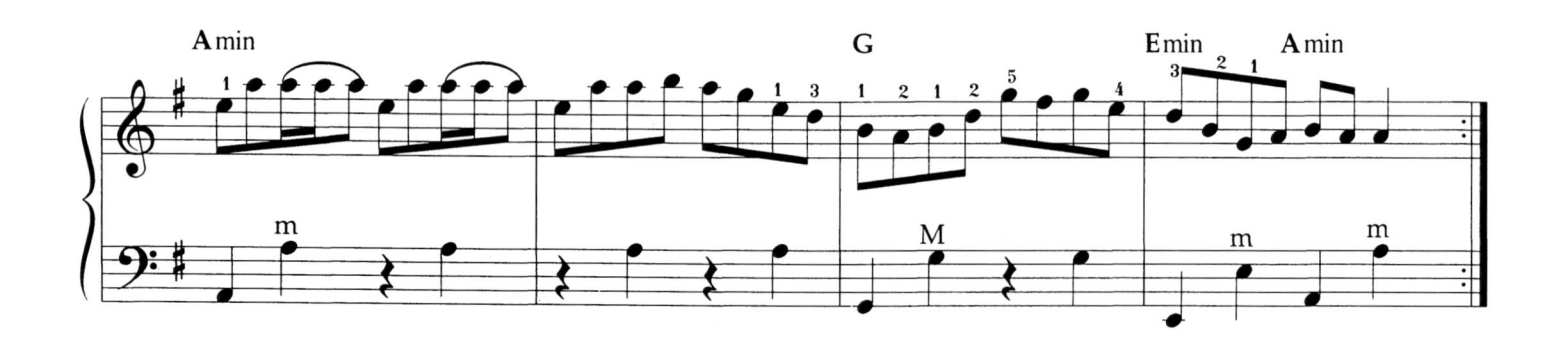

Lad O'Beirne's

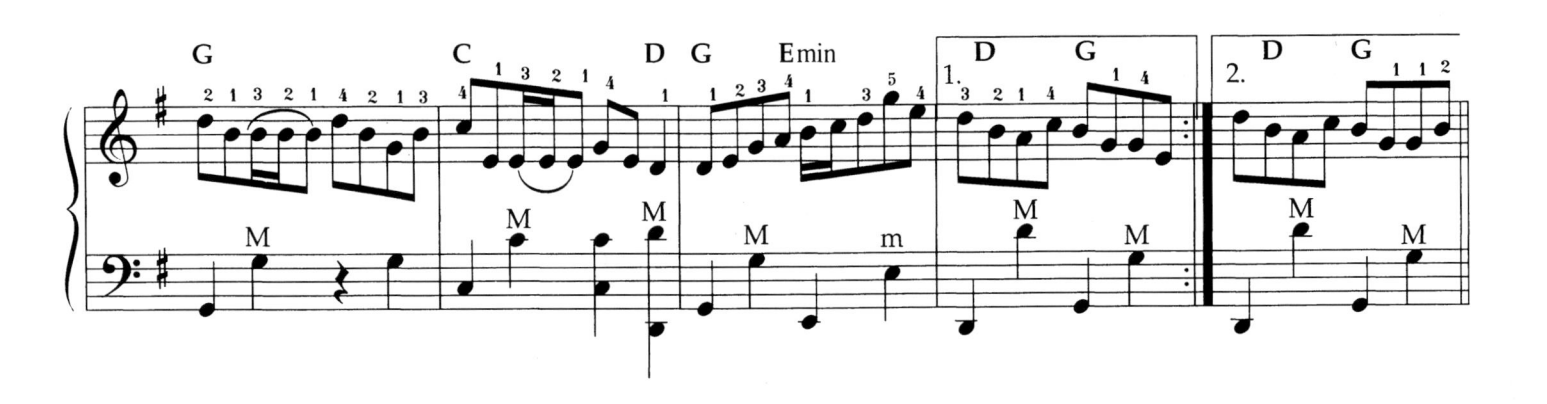

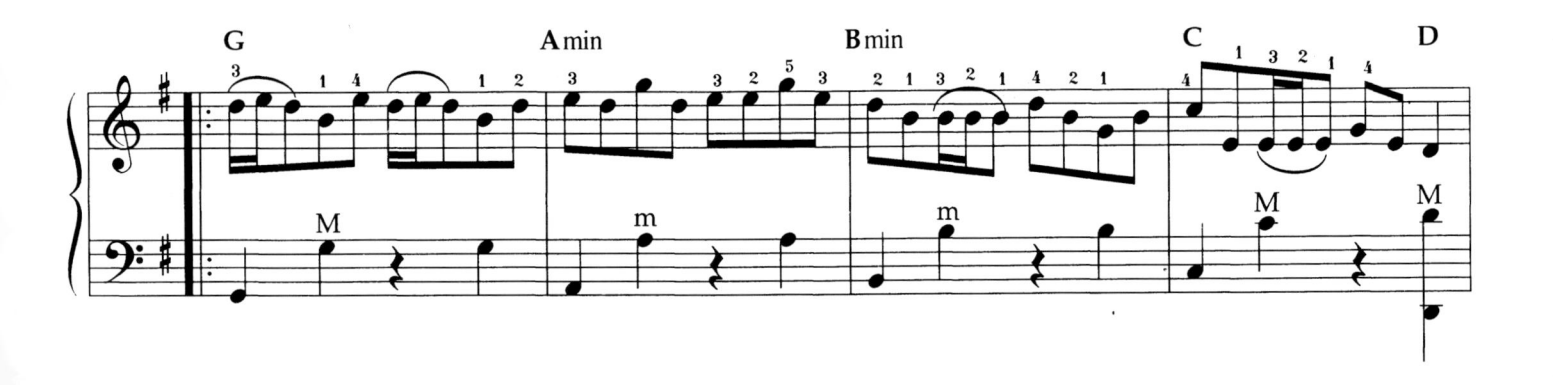

reel

James (Lad) O'Beirne

Lark on the Strand

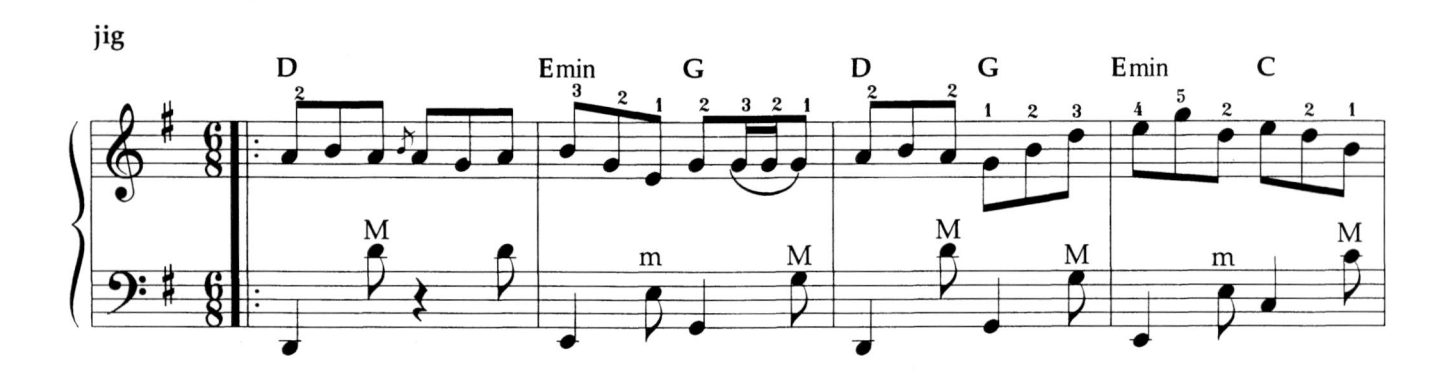

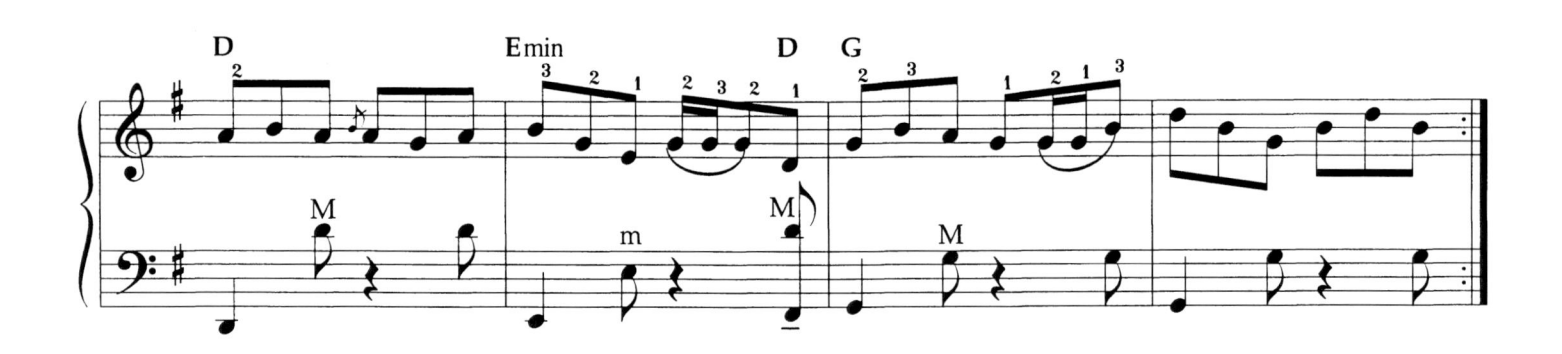

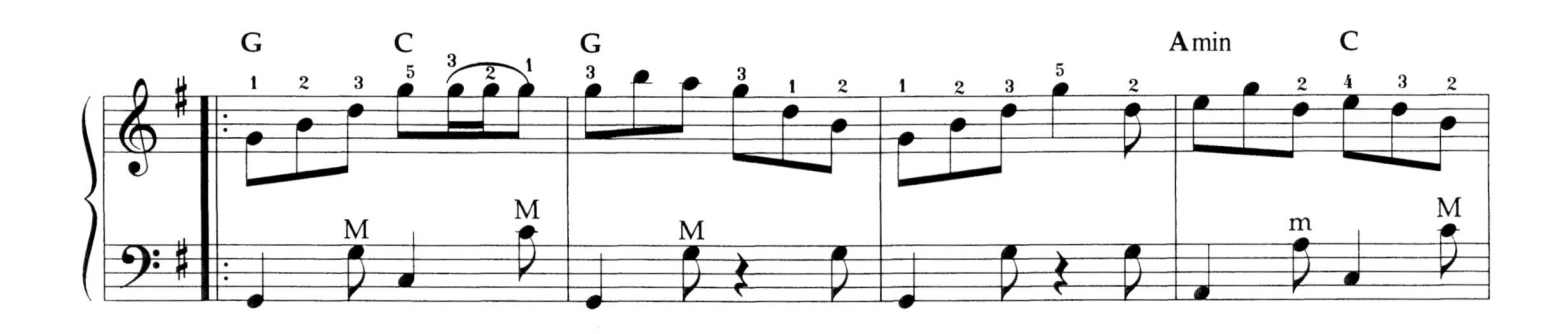

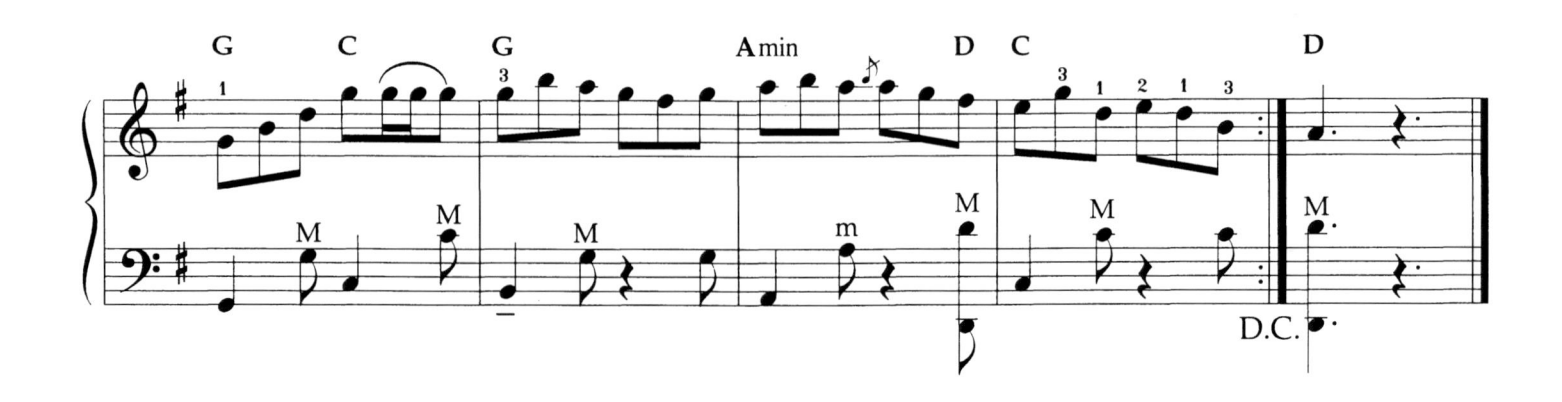

Larry Redican's Slip Jig

Larry Redican
arrangement by Jimmy Keane

slip jig

Leitrim Fancy

optional ornaments for measures 1 and 2

arr. © 1999 Mel Bay® Publications, Inc. All Rights Reserved.

The Limerick Lasses

reel, played with syncopated eighth notes

as played by Phil Cunningham

chords based on clavinet playing of Tiona Ni Dhomhnaill

Copyright © Phil Cunningham. All Rights Reserved. Used by Permission.

The Lonesome Jig
(Rolling Waves, McGuire's March)

as played by John Williams

Note - John plays both keyboard accordion and Anglo concertina on this recording.

arr. © Green Linnet Music/Doolins Music (ASCAP). All Rights Reserved. Used by Permission.

Maggie in the Woods

Maid Behind the Bar

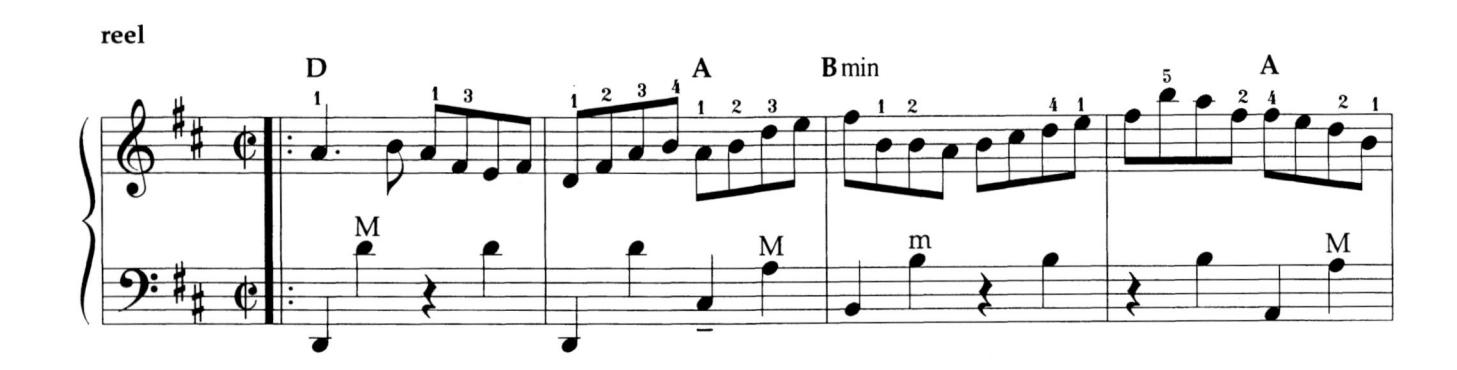

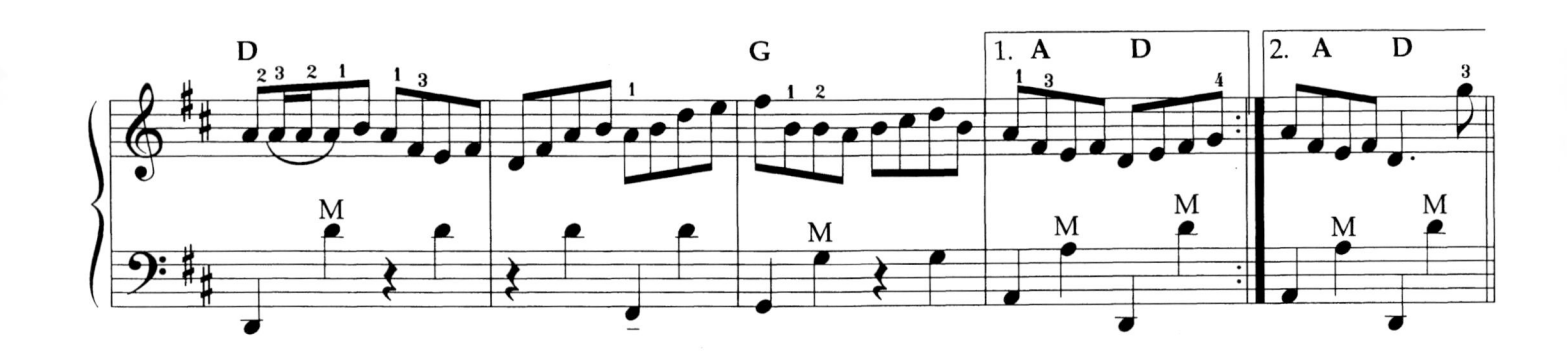

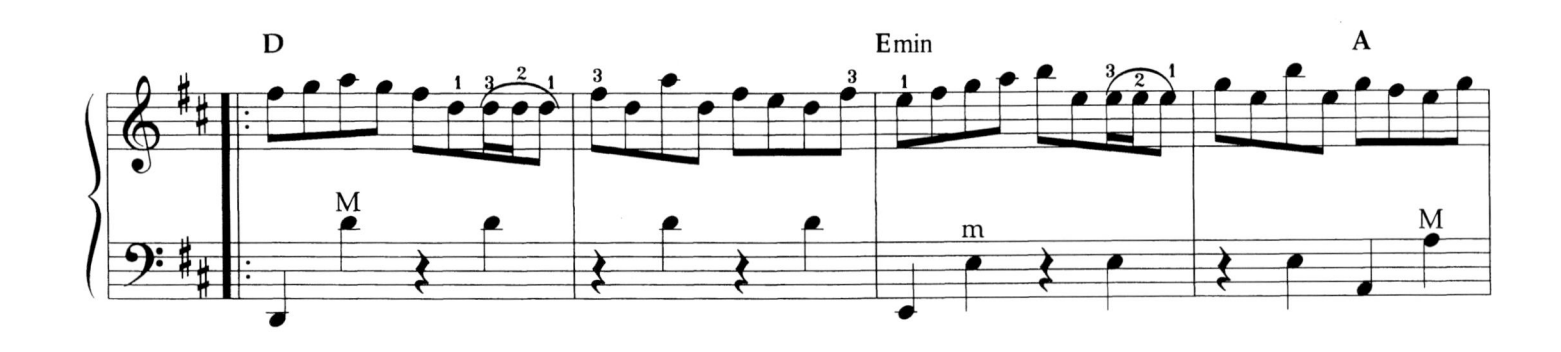

Maid of Ardagh

Mary McMahon's

Master Crowley's

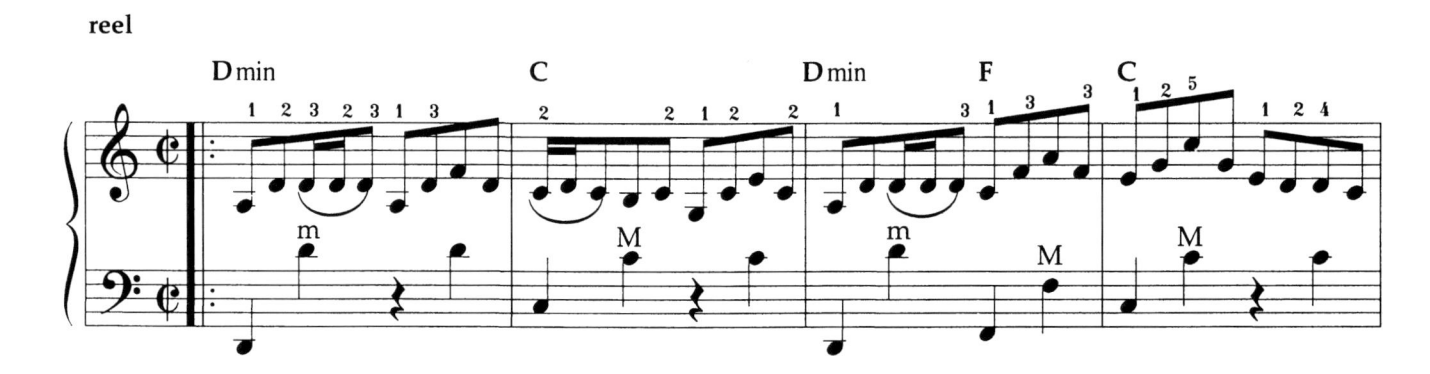

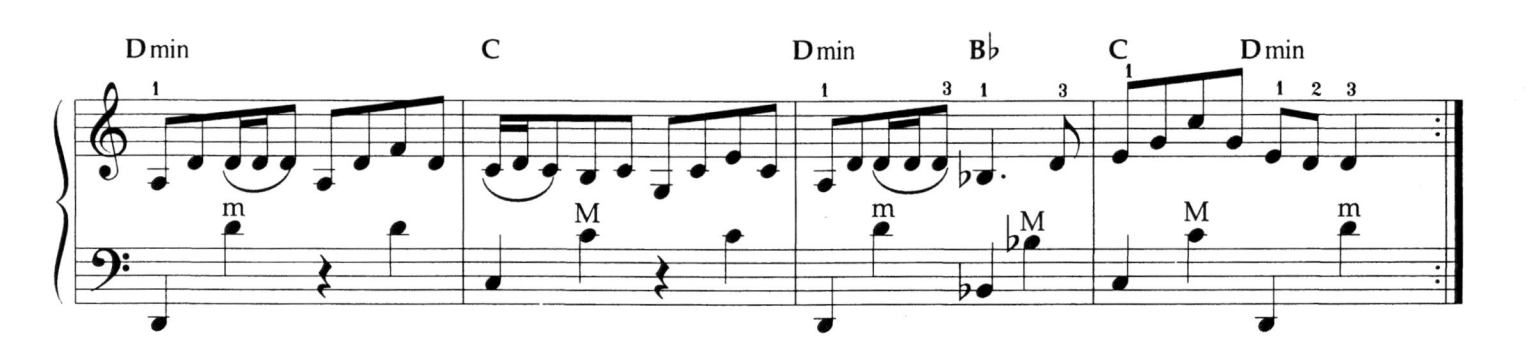

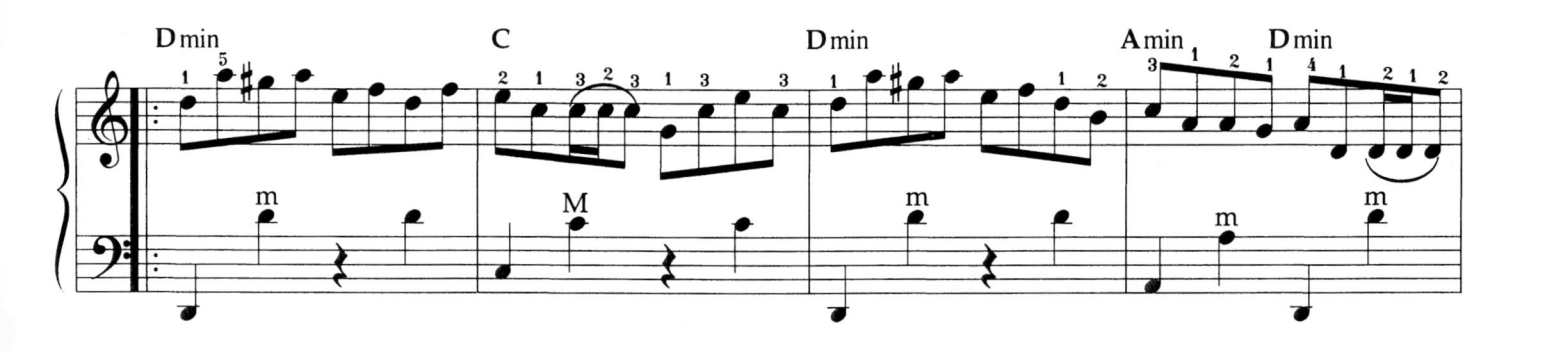

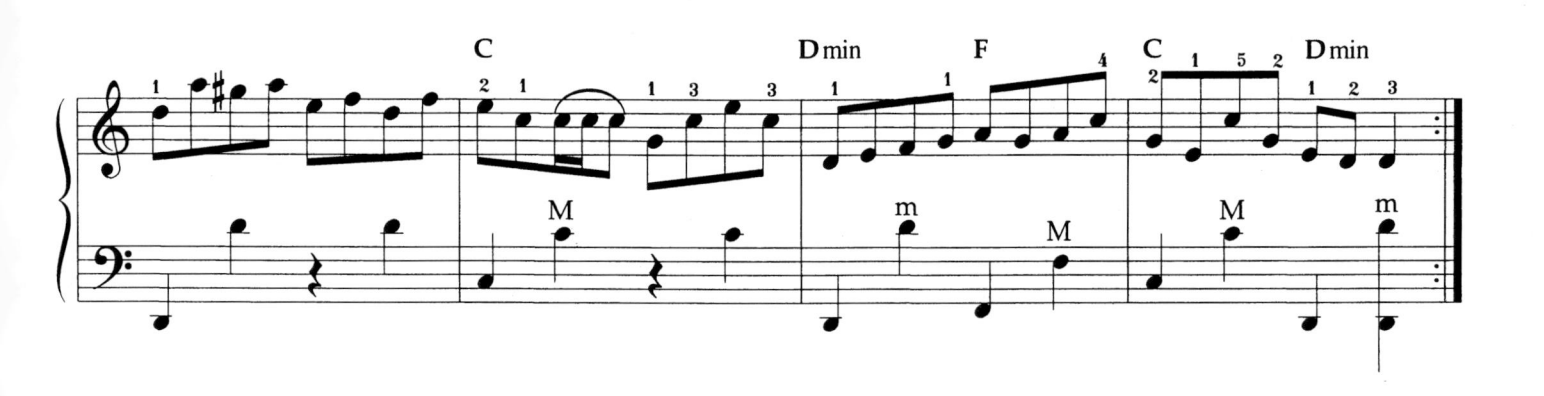

Matt the Thrasher

reel   as played by Alan Kelly

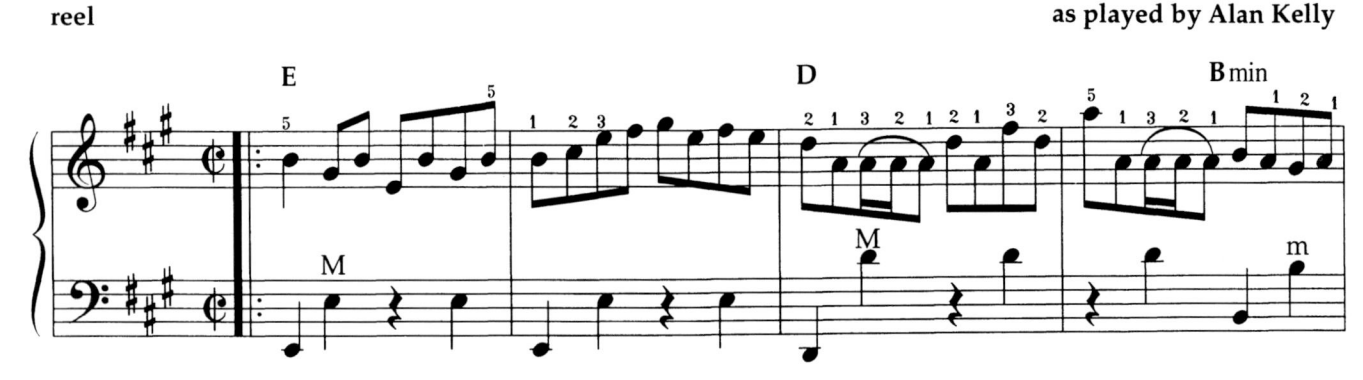

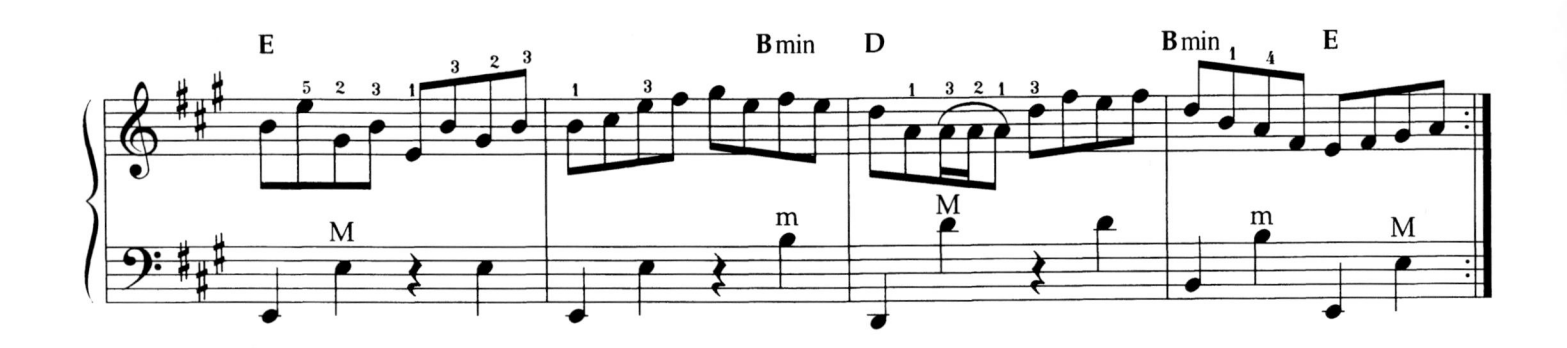

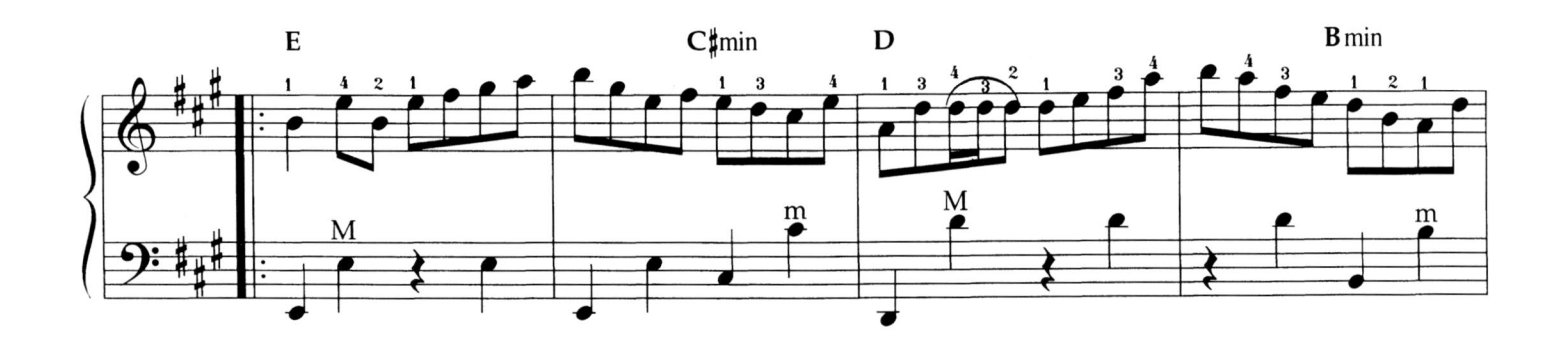

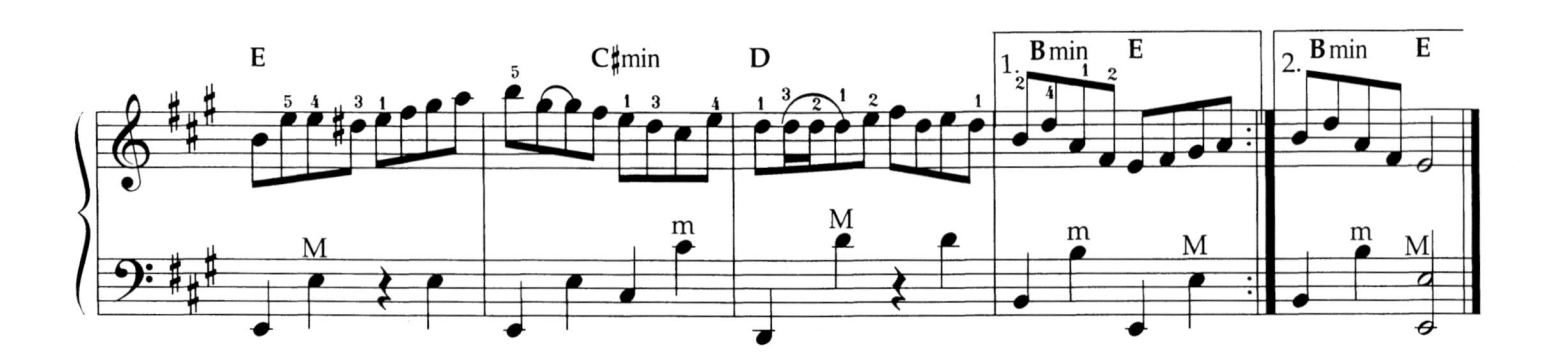

Chords based on guitar playing of Donogh Hennessey.

arr. © Acorn Music, Ltd (Ireland). All Rights Reserved. Used by Permission.

Maudabawn Chapel

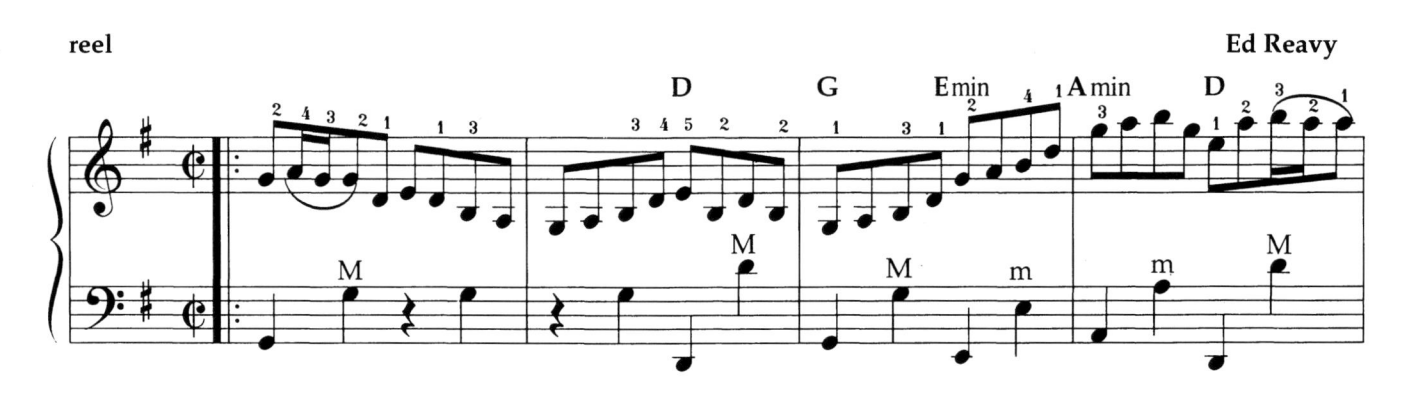

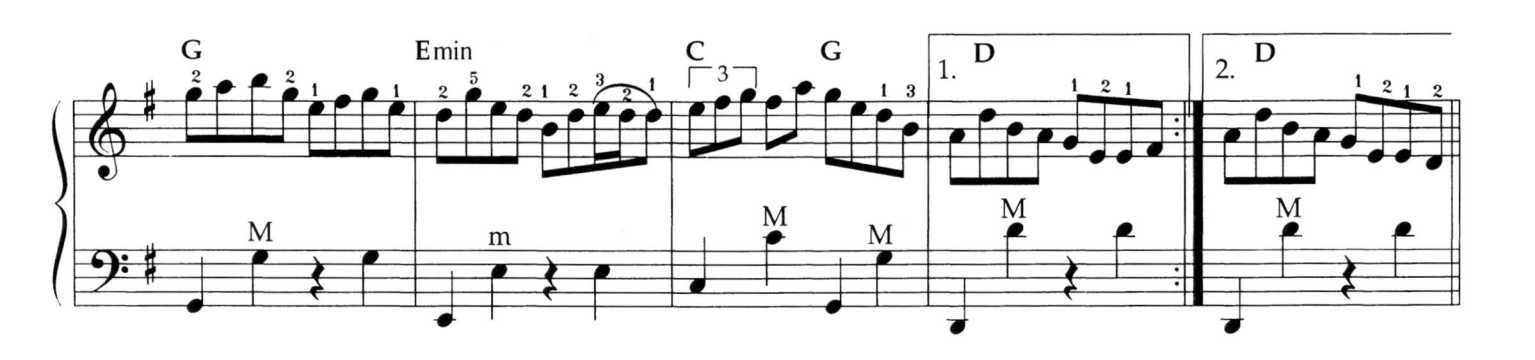

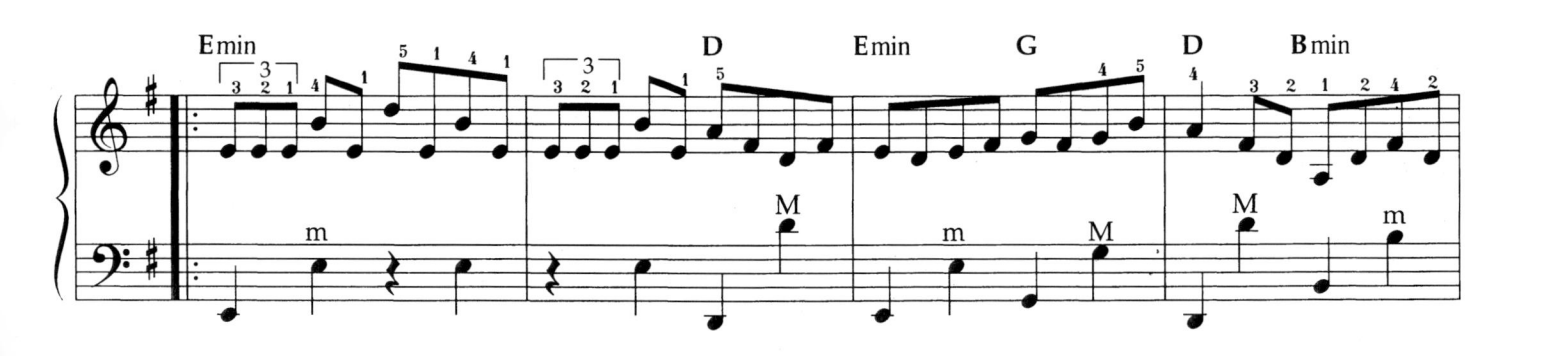

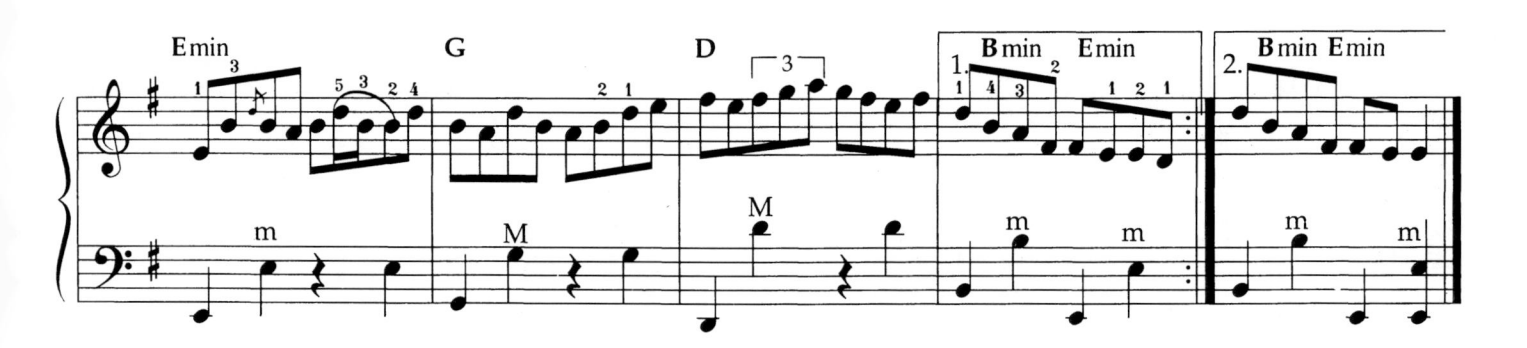

reel

Ed Reavy

© Joseph M. Reavy. All Rights Reserved. Used by Permission.

McDermitt's

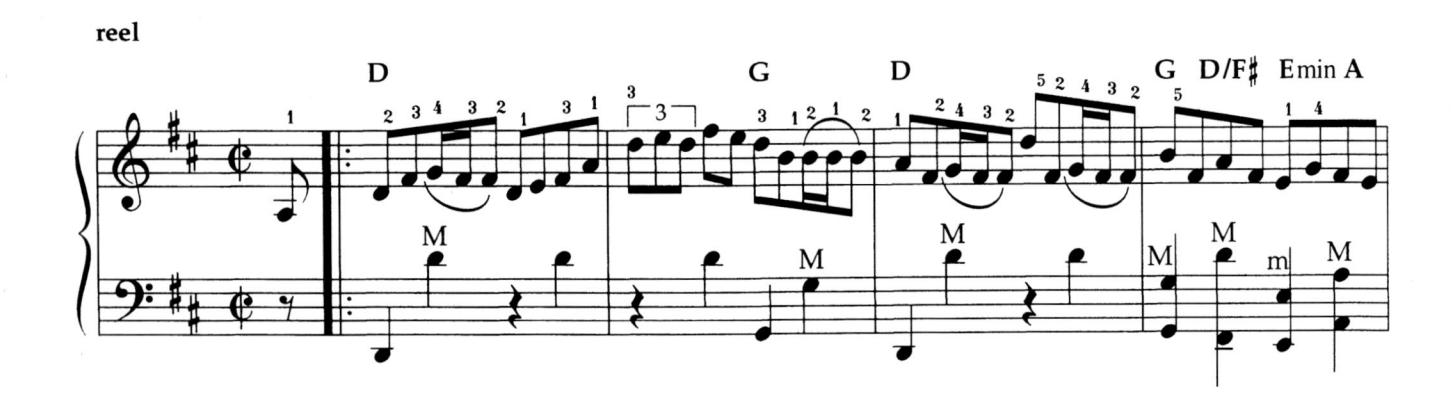

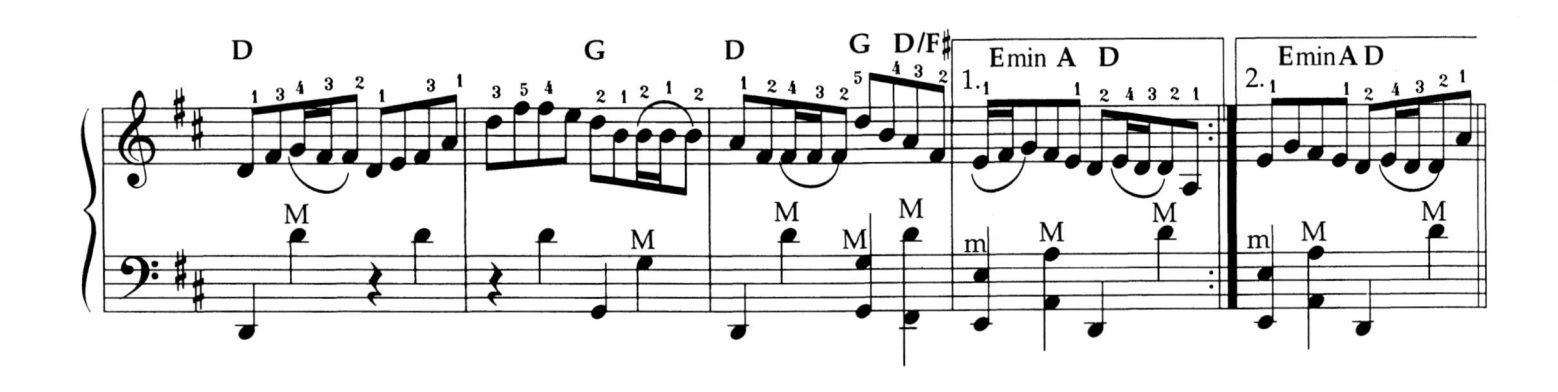

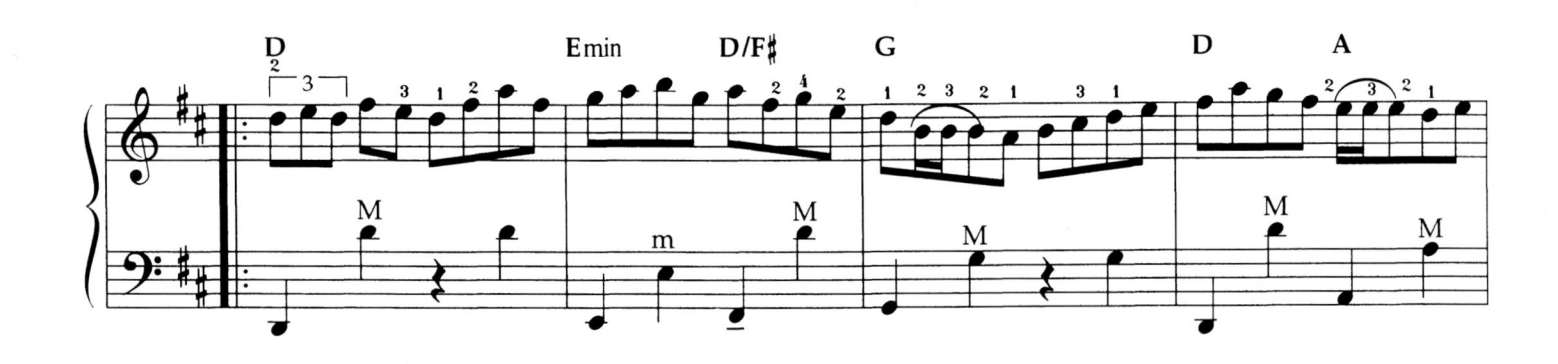

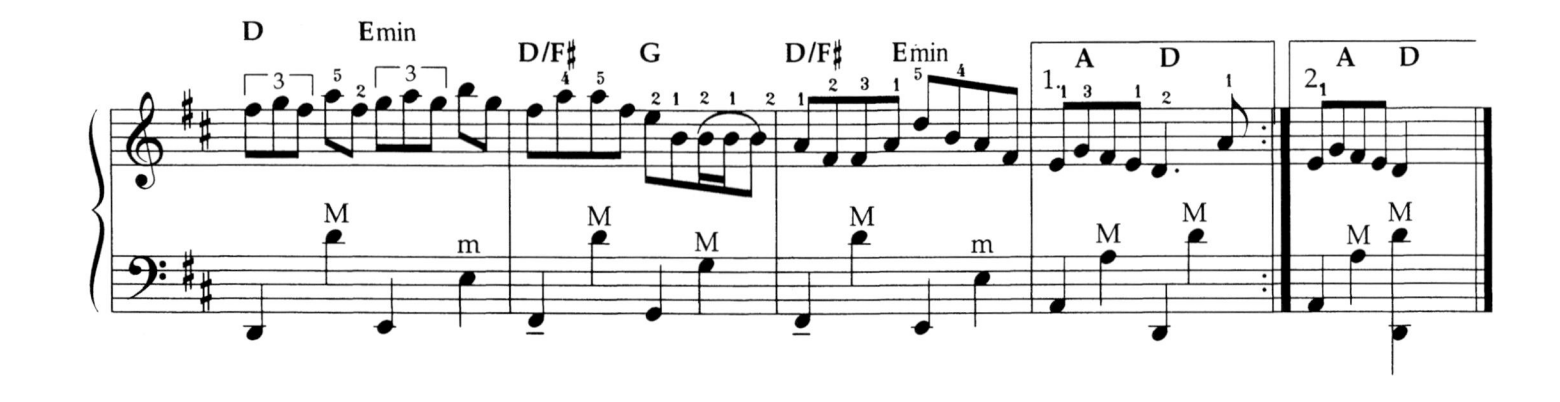

McMahon's
(The Banshee)

reel

James McMahon

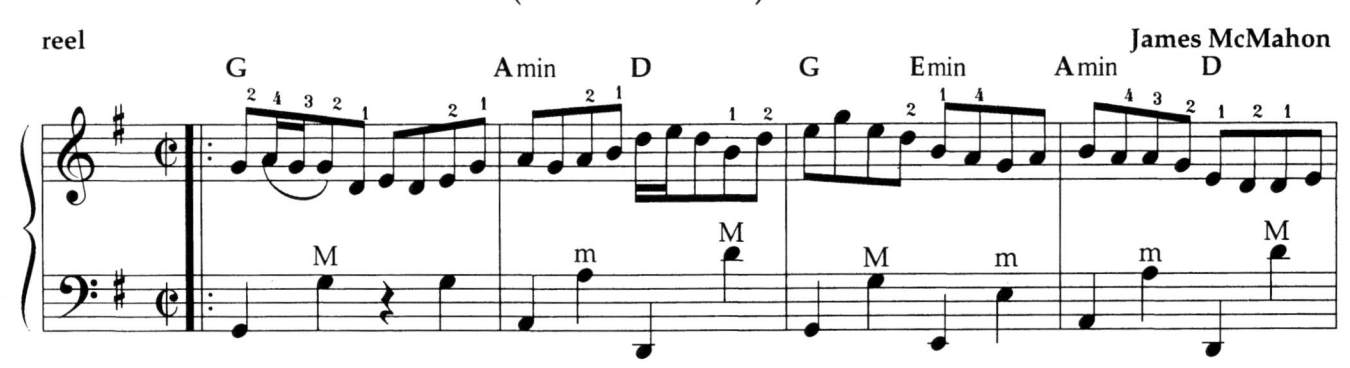

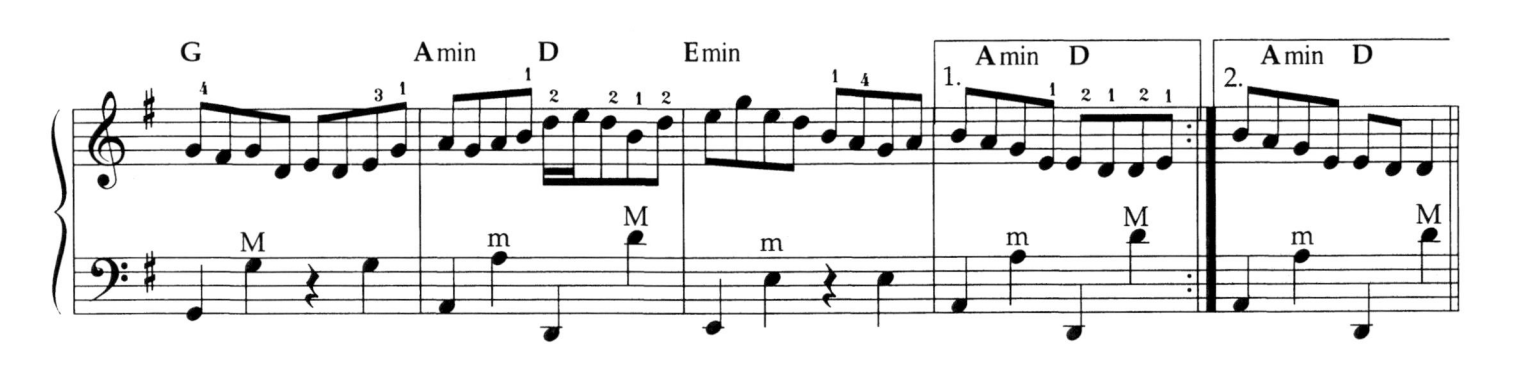

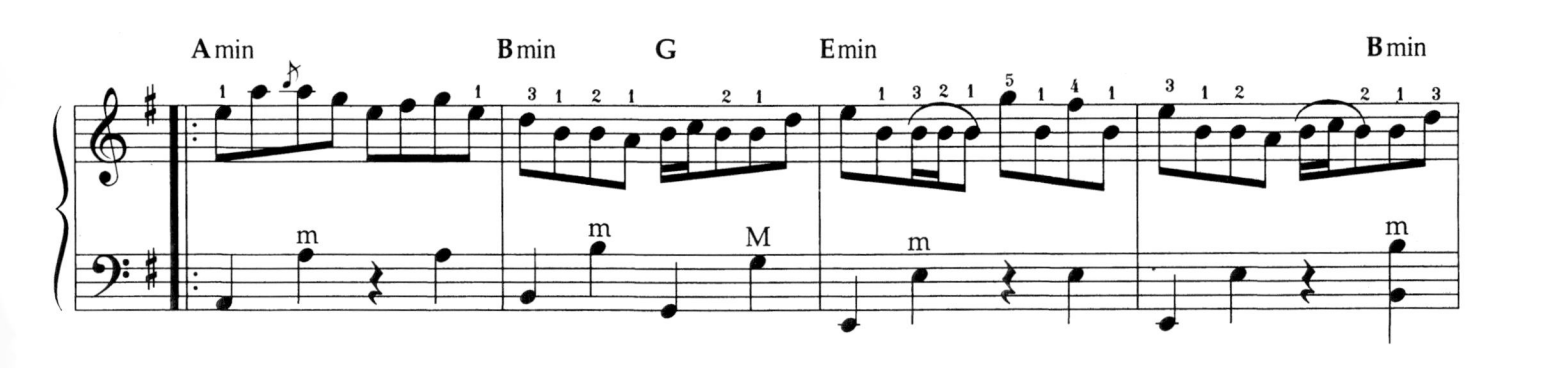

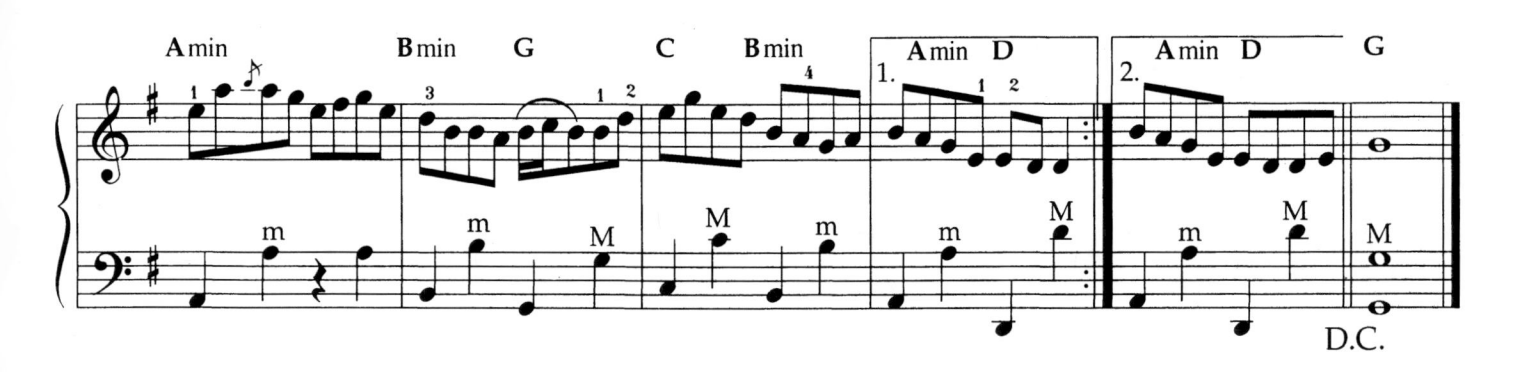

Merrily Kiss the Quaker

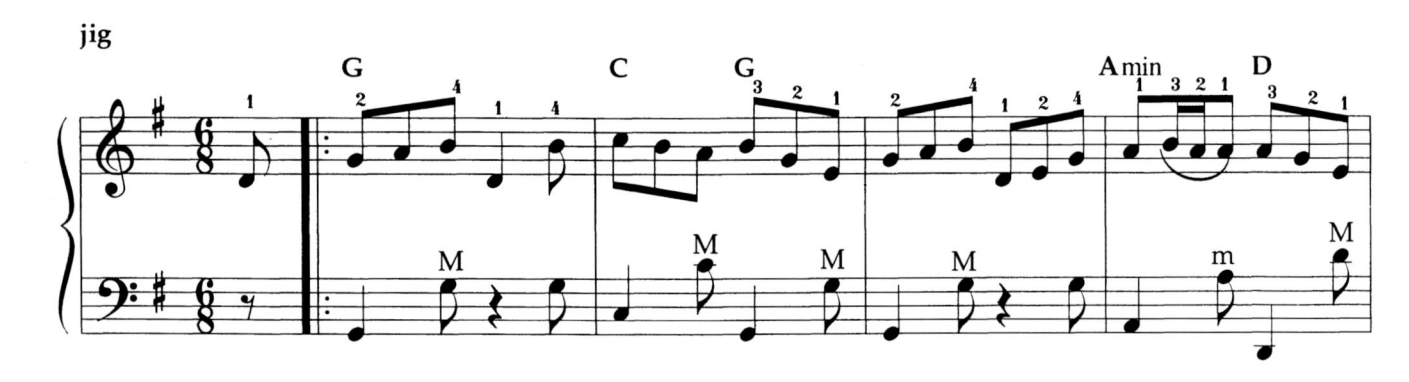

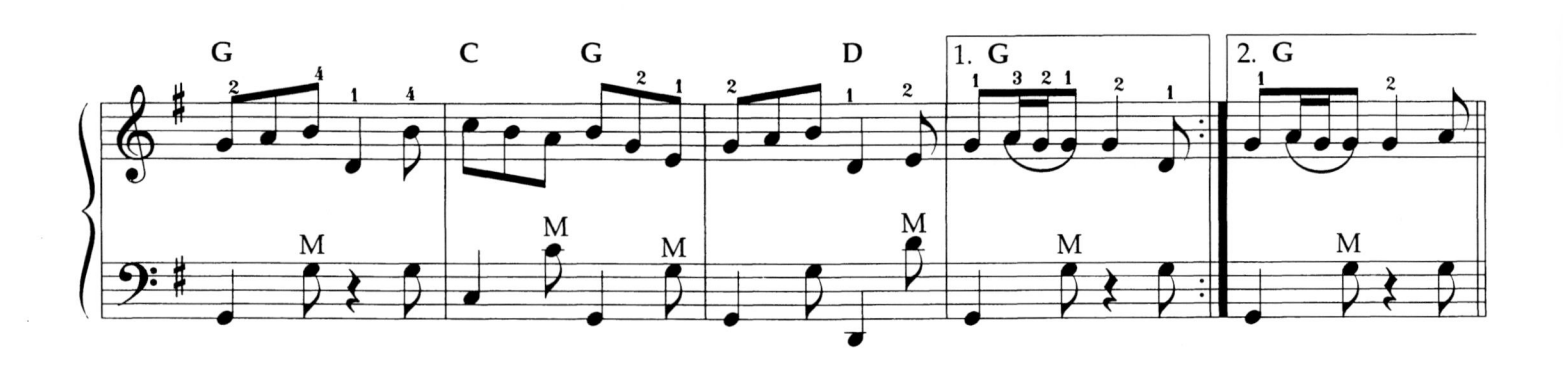

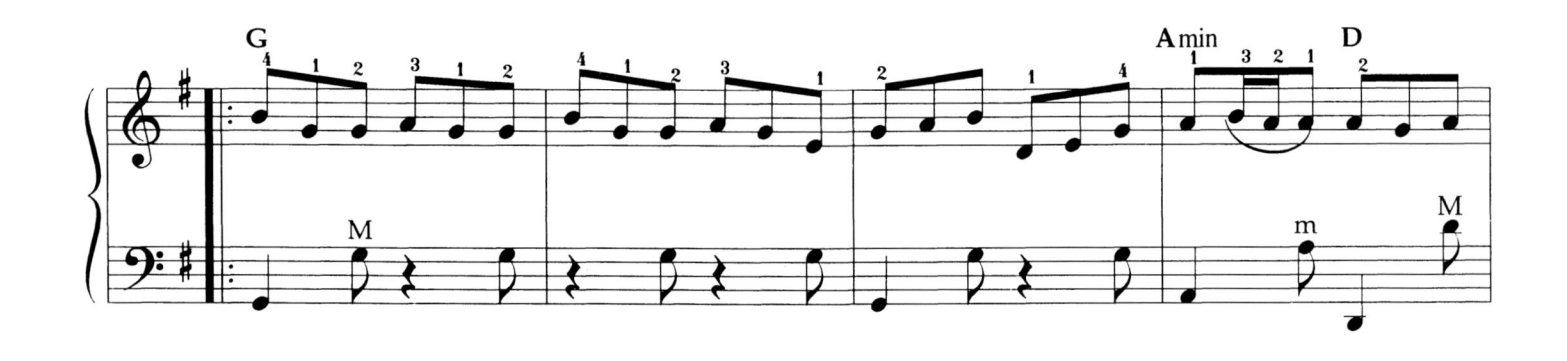

optional 2nd part

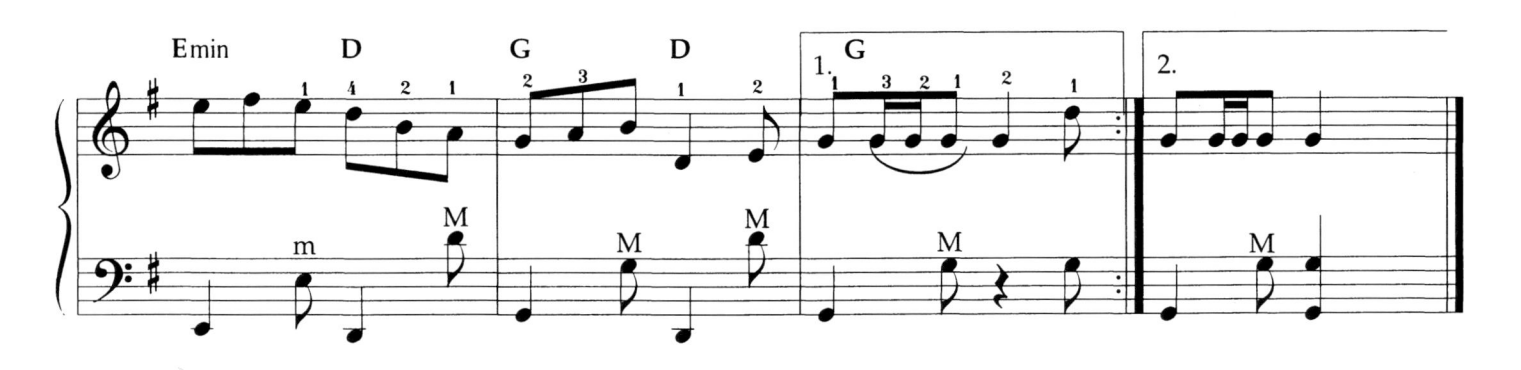

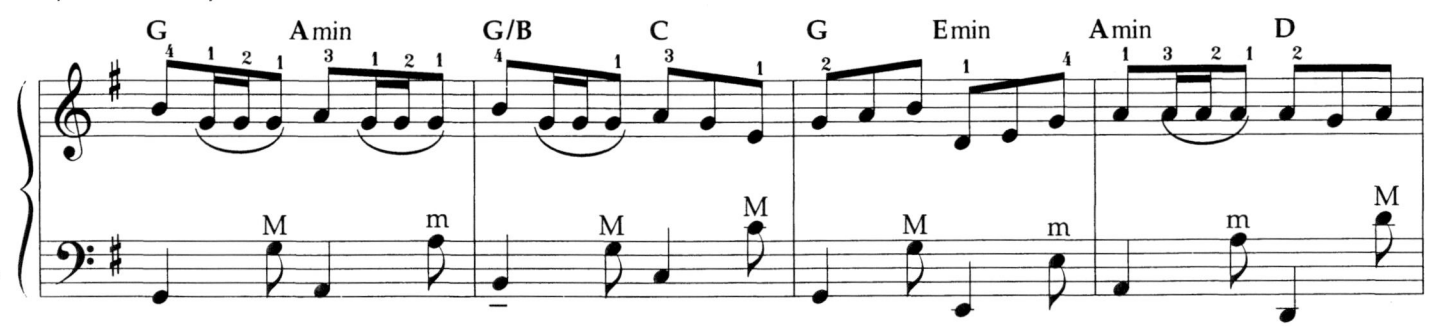

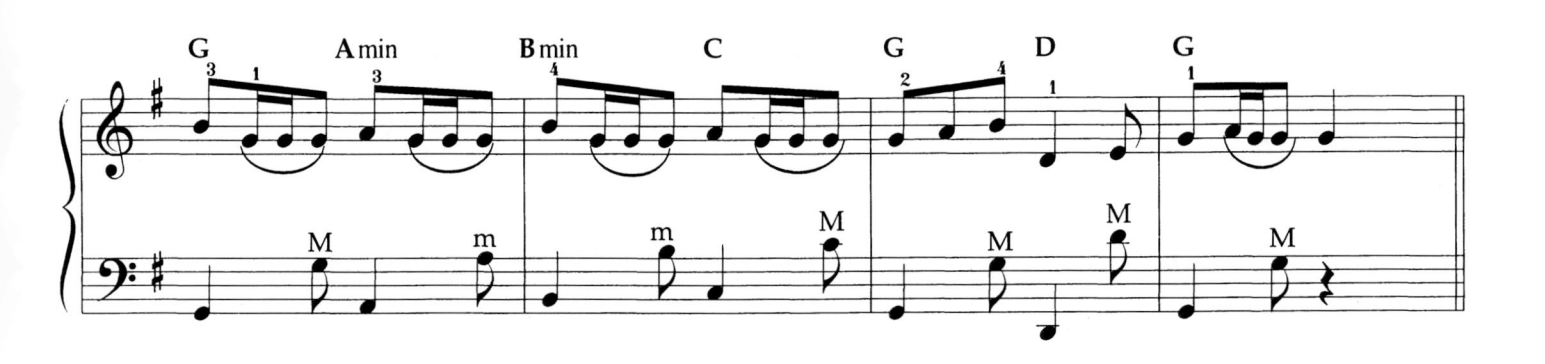

A Merry Christmas

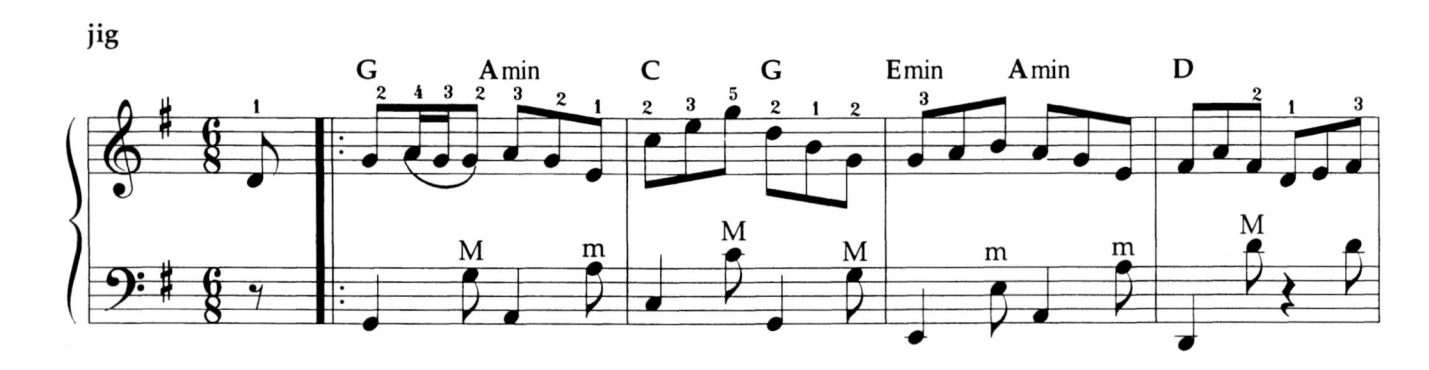

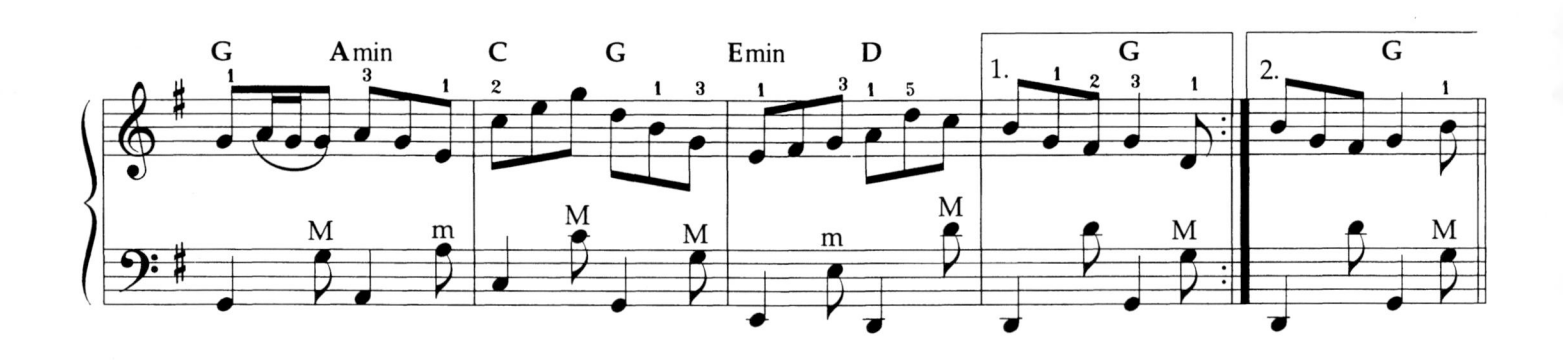

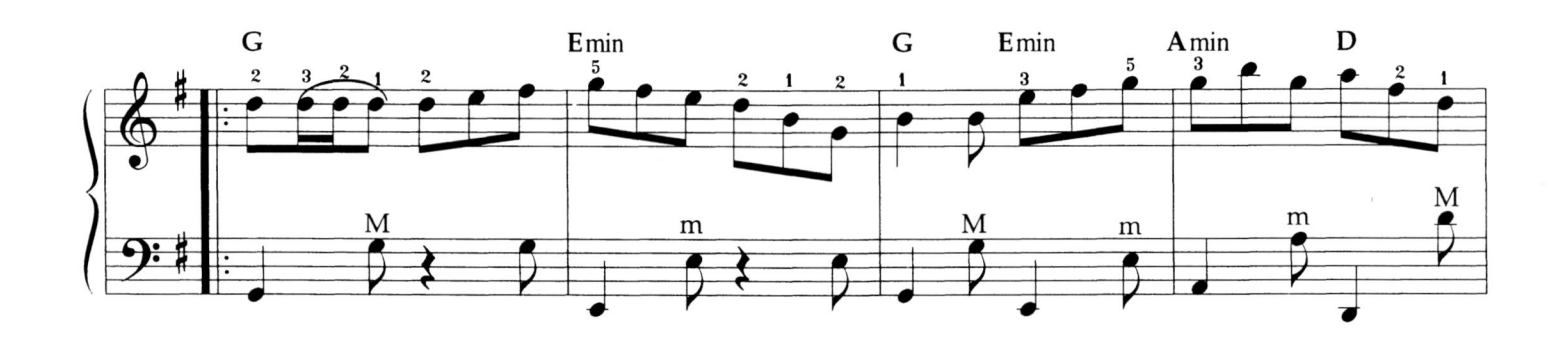

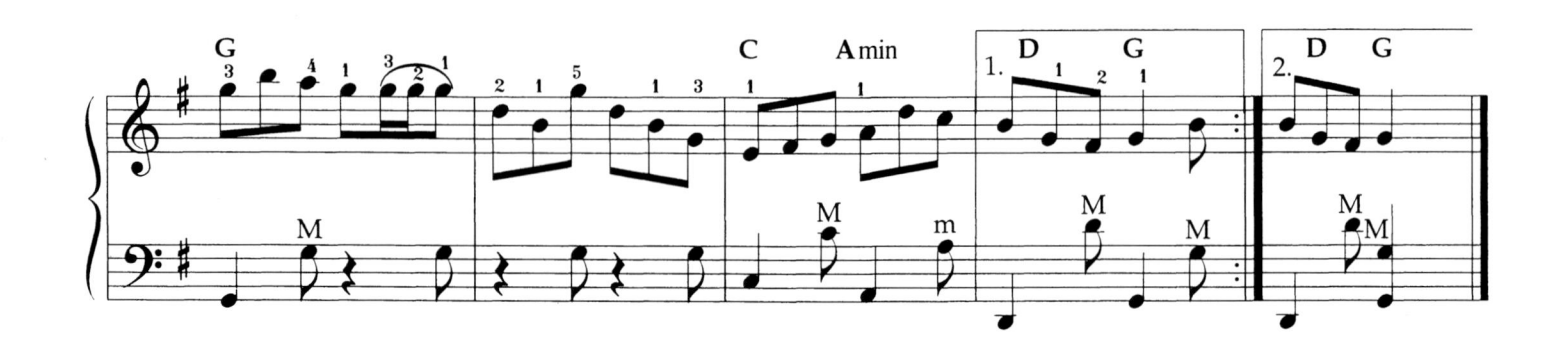

The Millpond

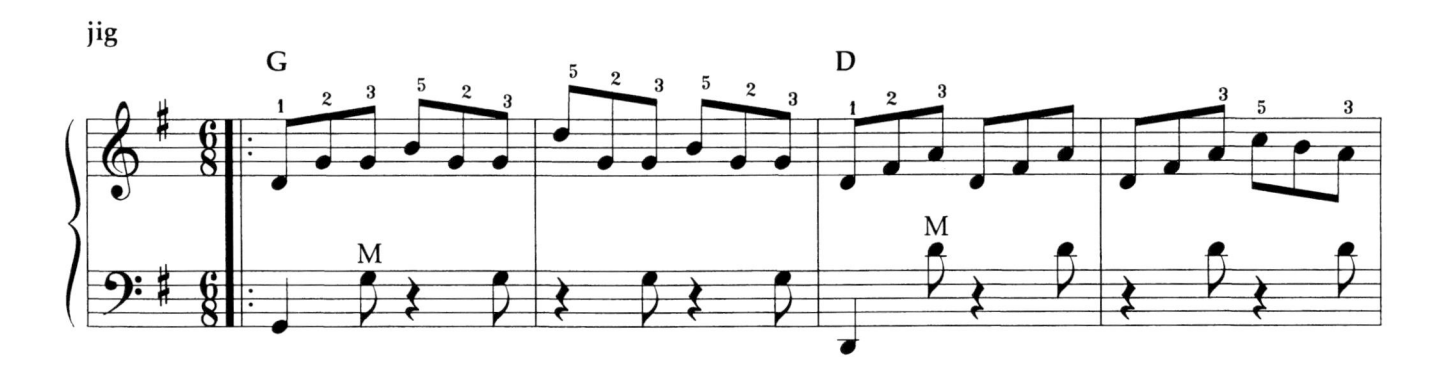

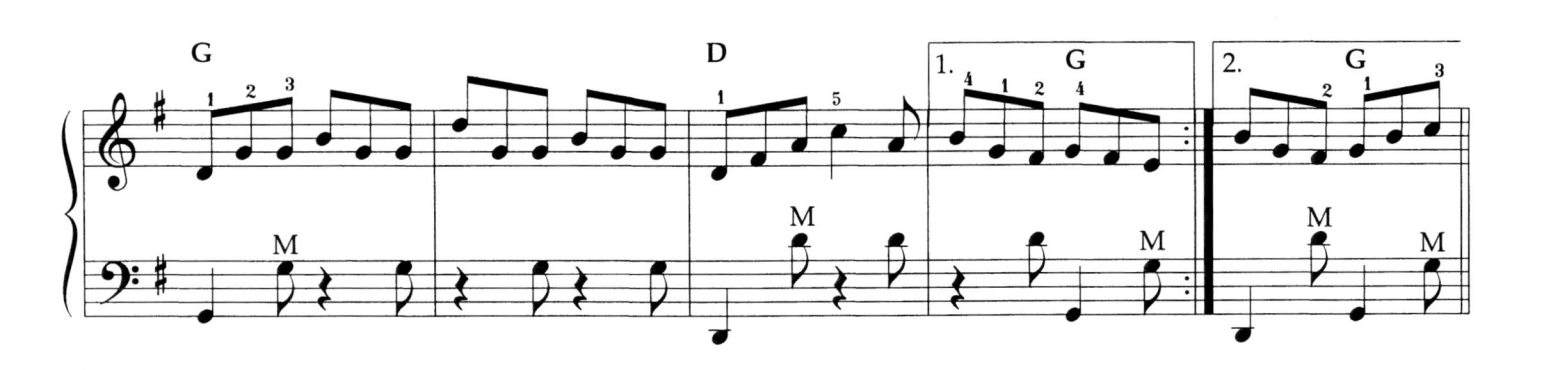

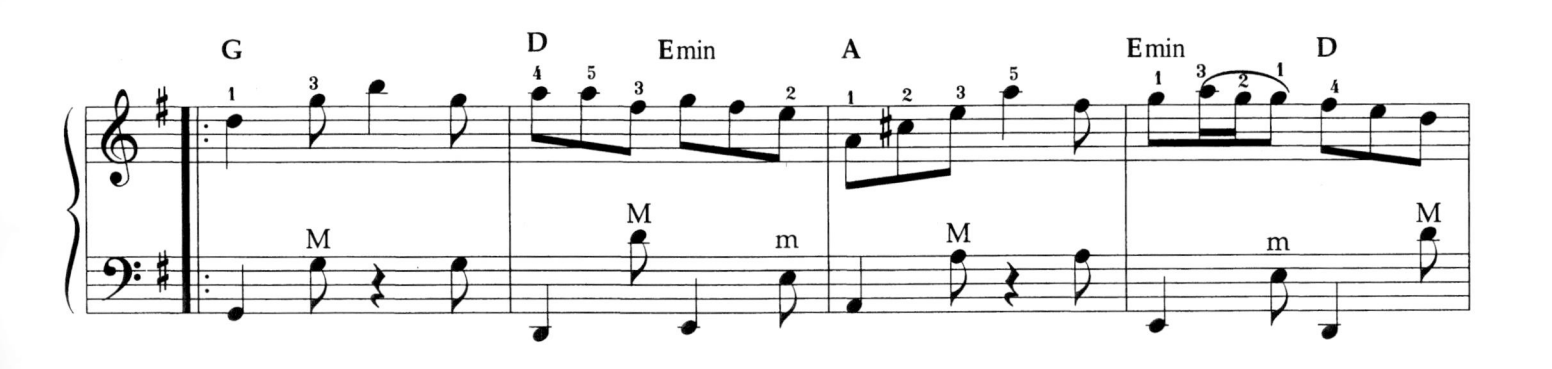

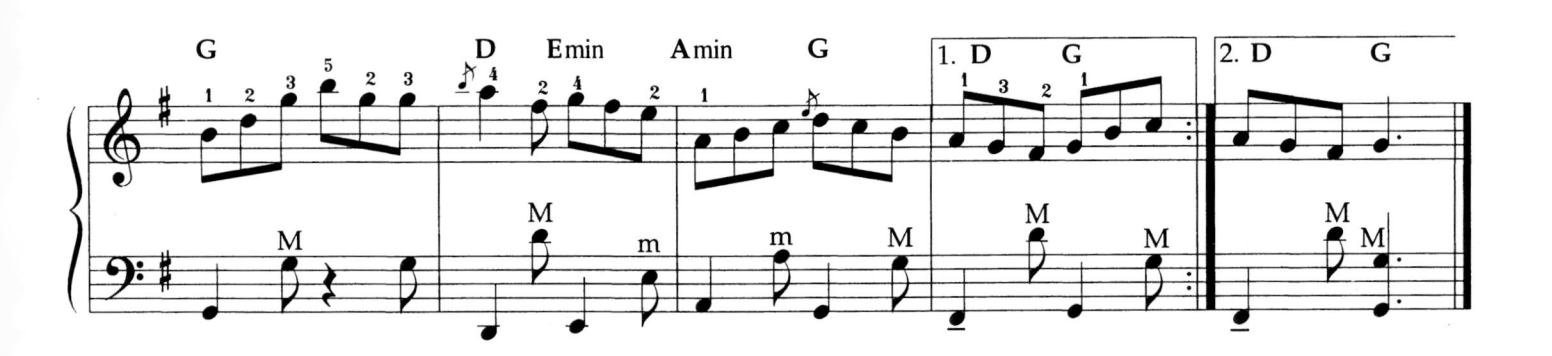

Miss Monaghan's

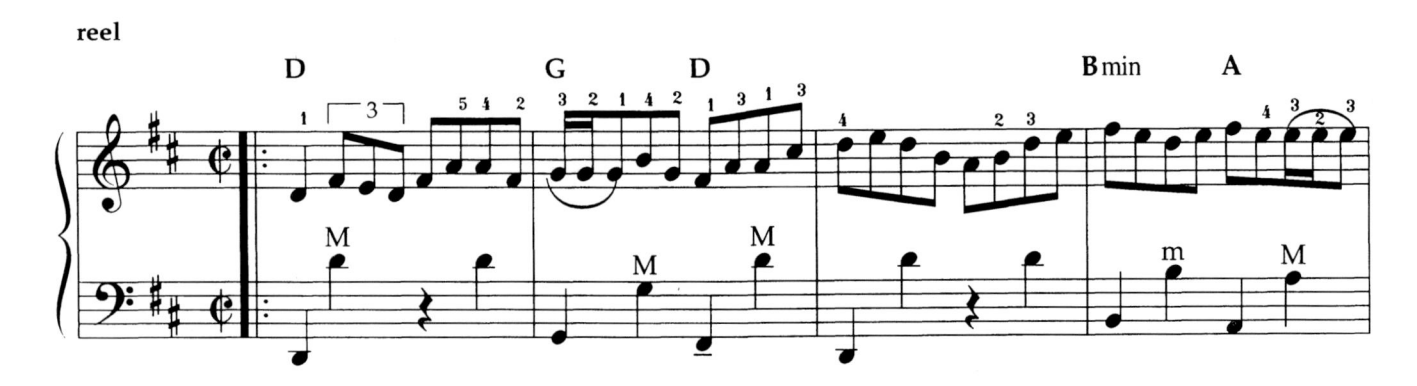

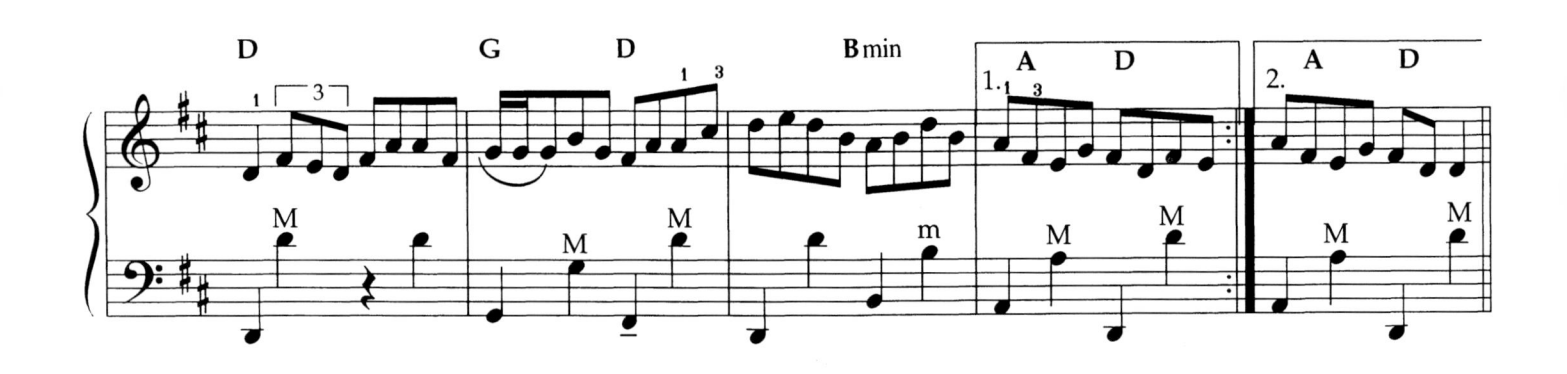

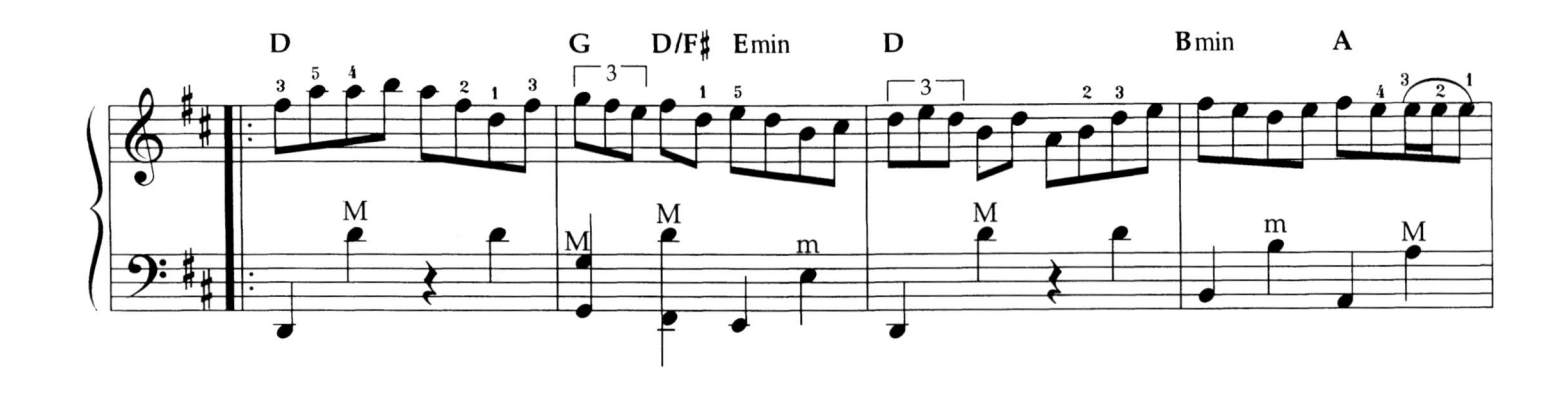

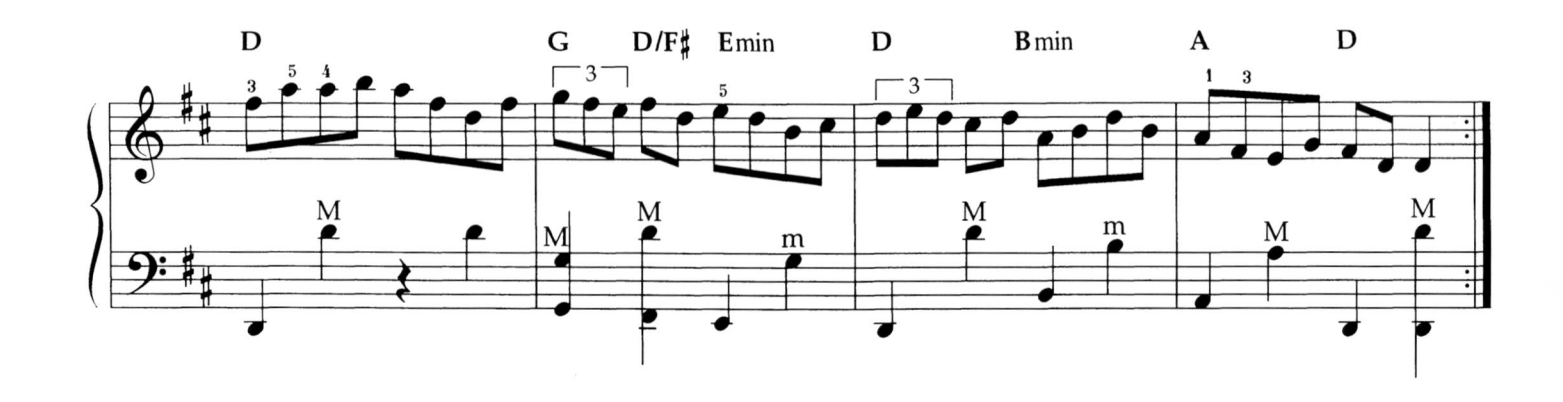

The Mullingar Races

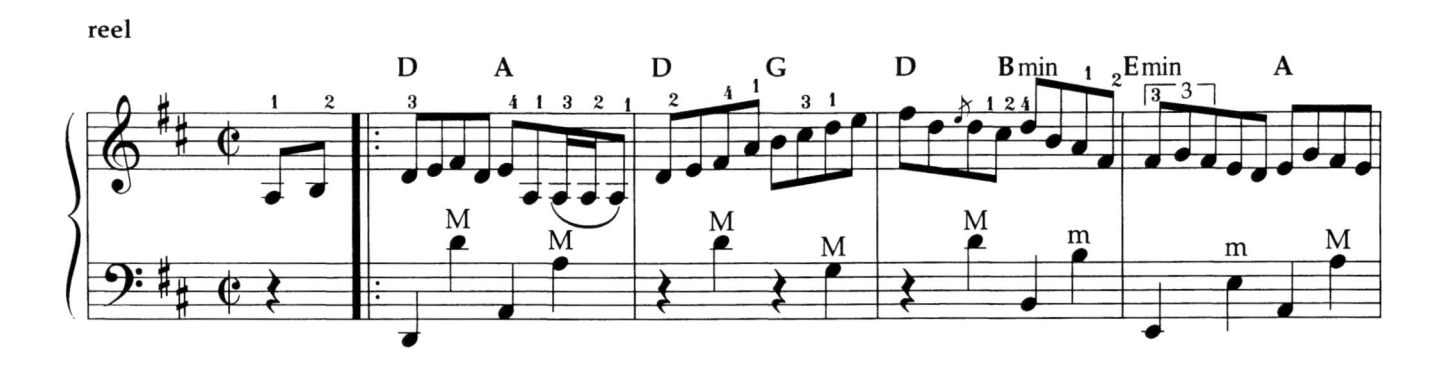

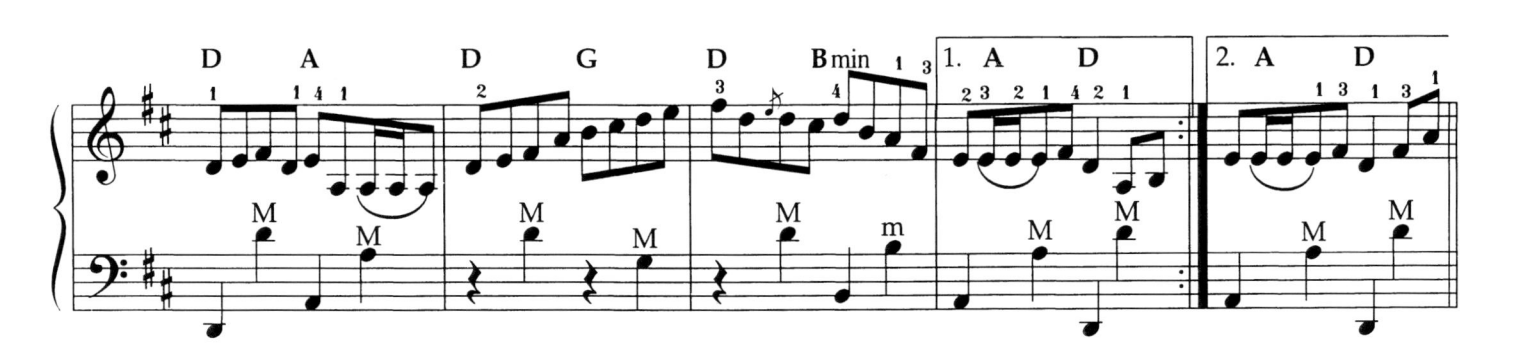

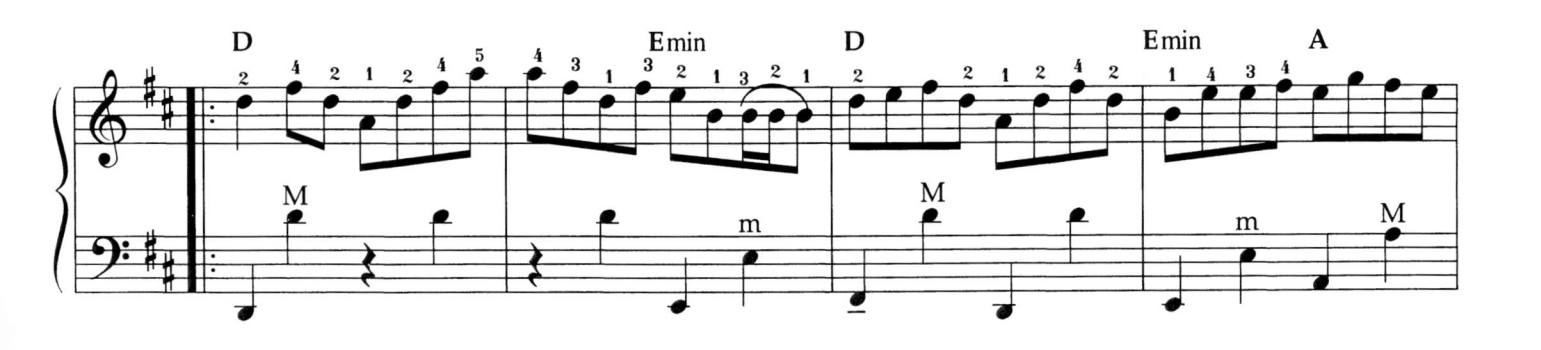

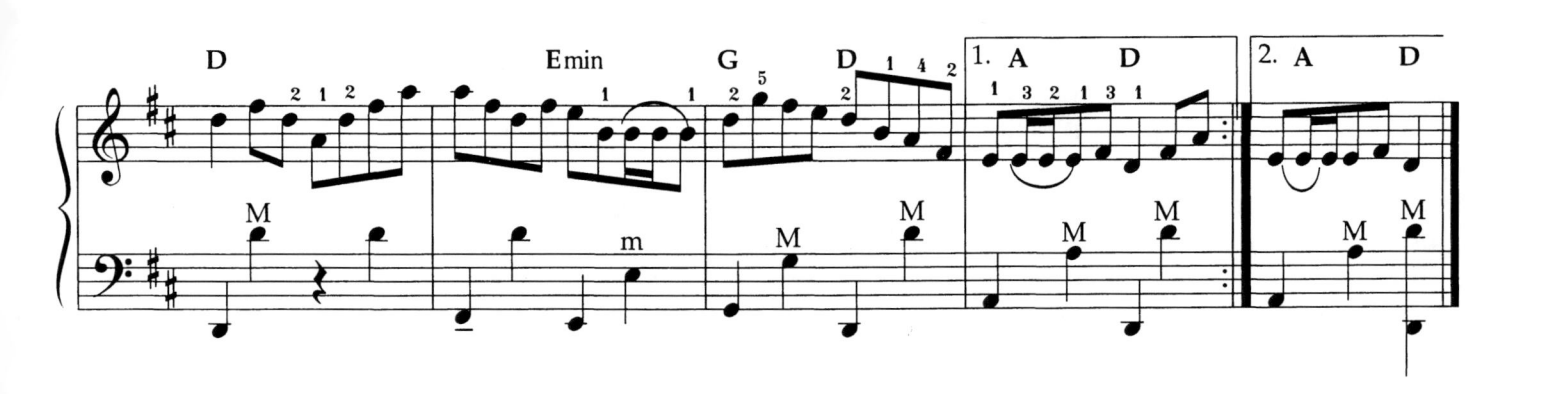

Murphy's

hornpipe, played with syncopated eighth notes

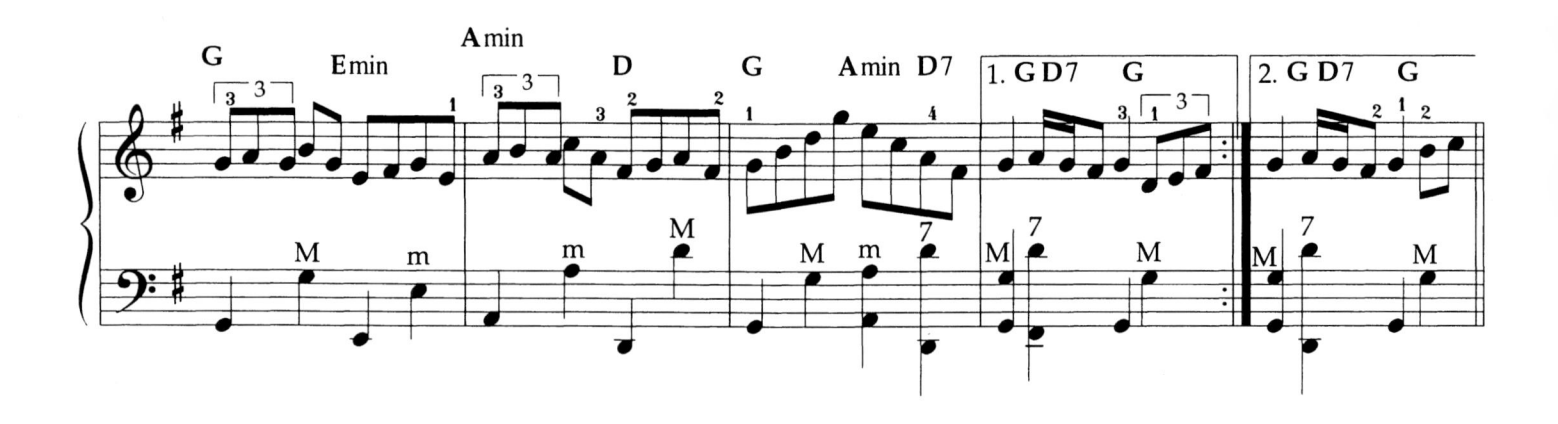

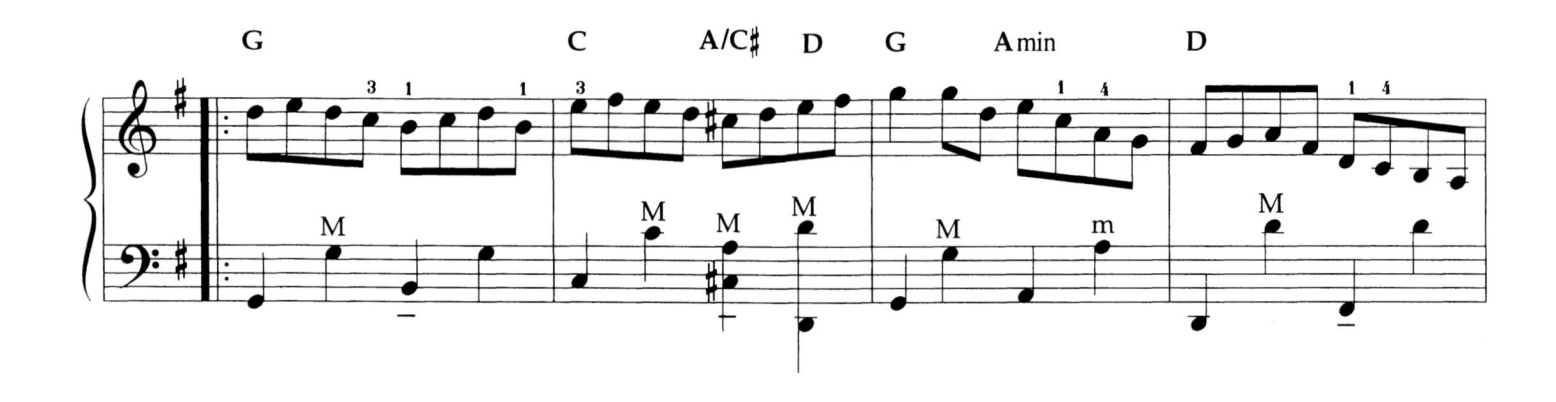

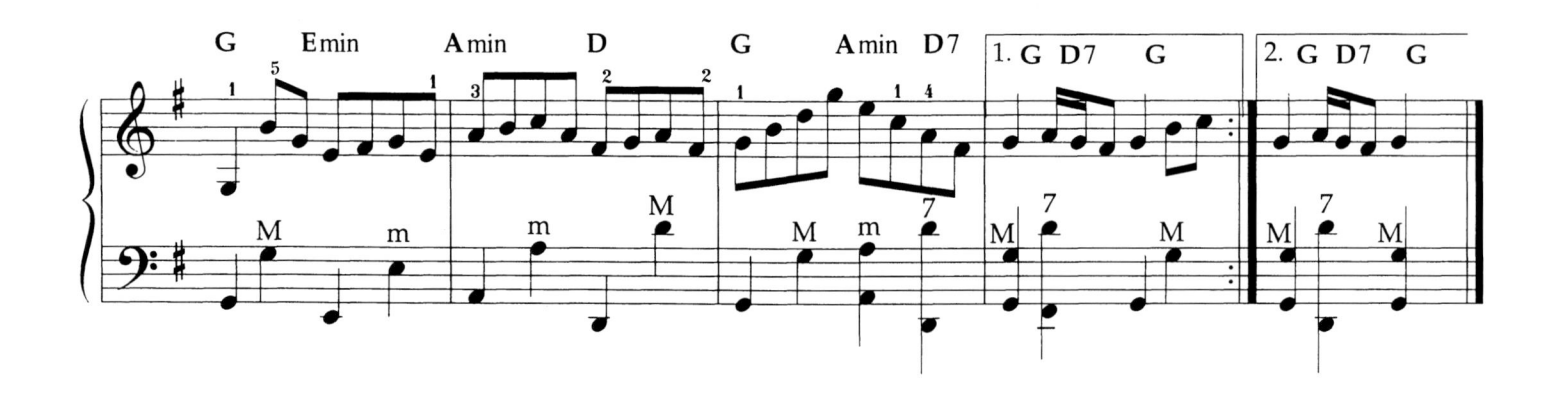

The Musical Priest

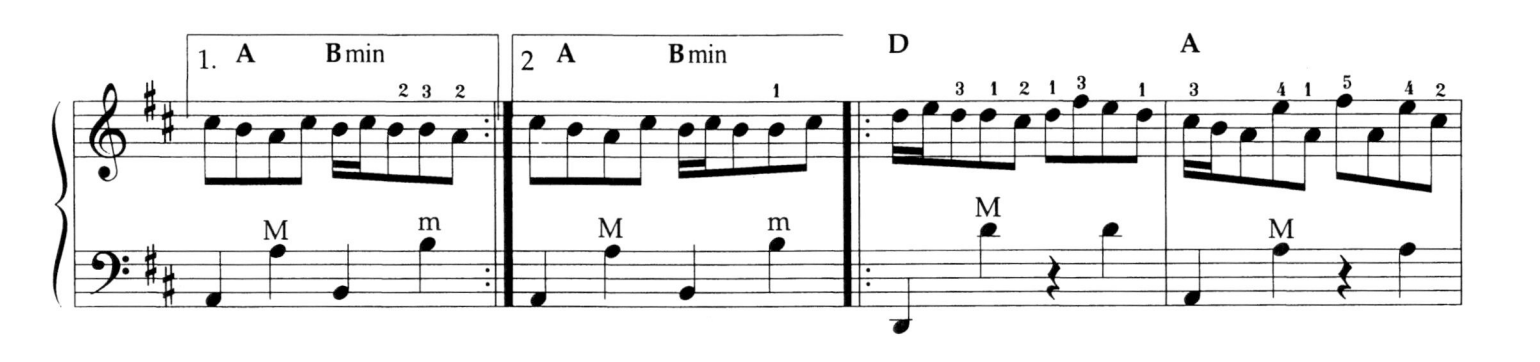

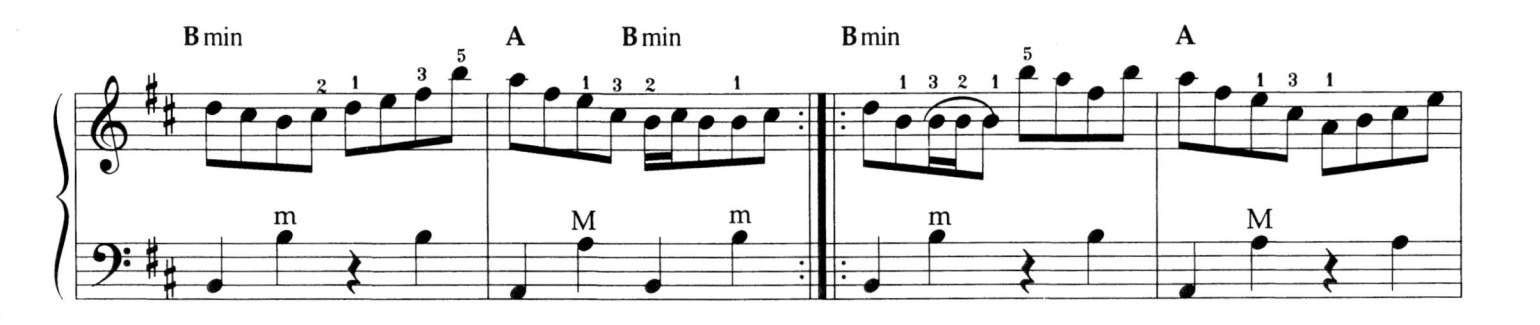

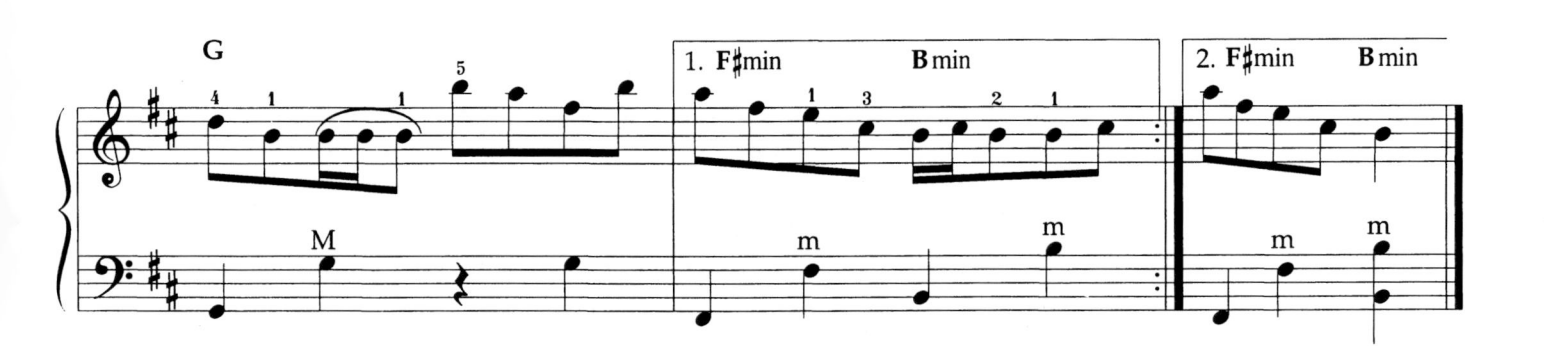

Nine Points of Roguery

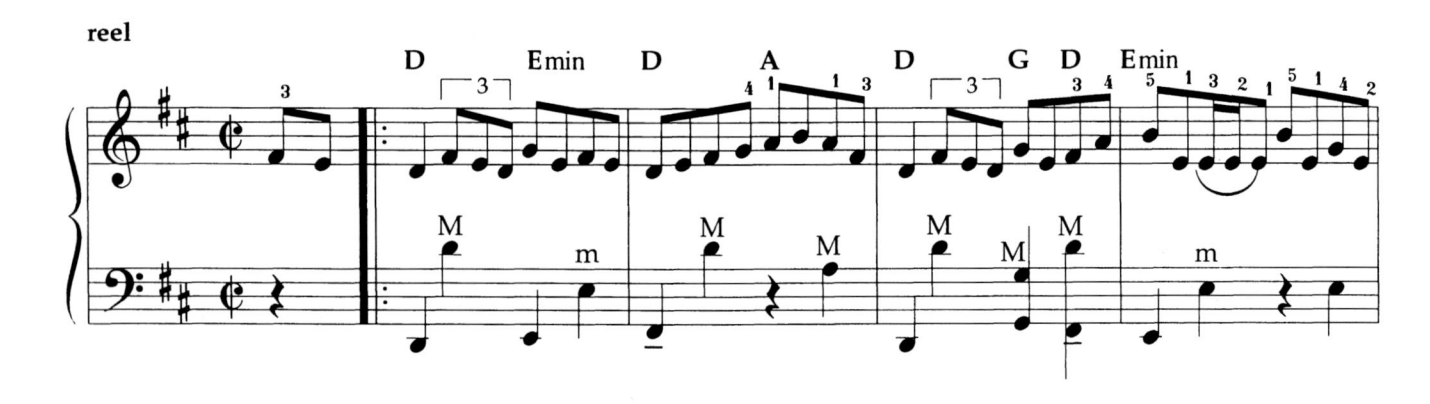

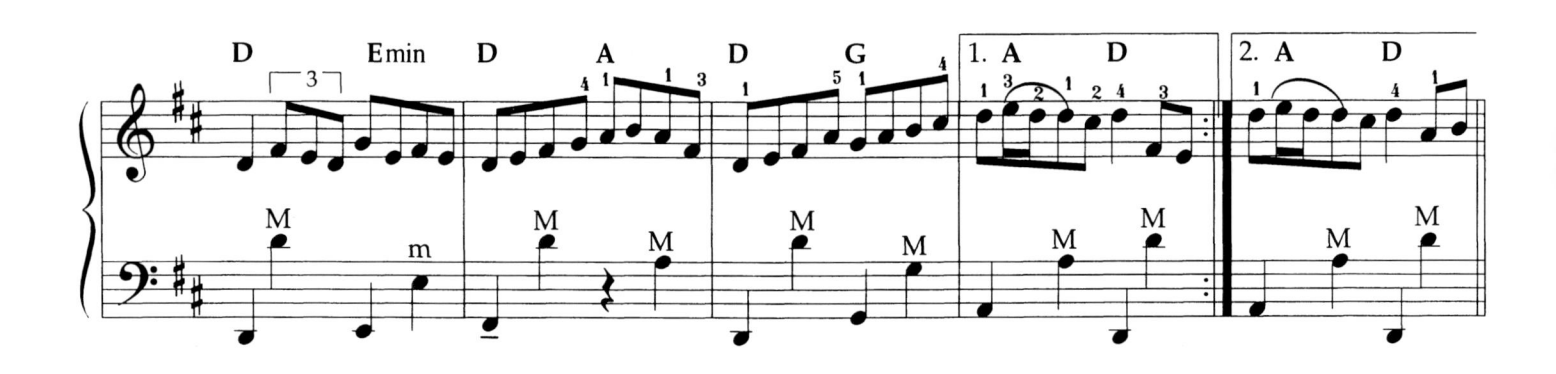

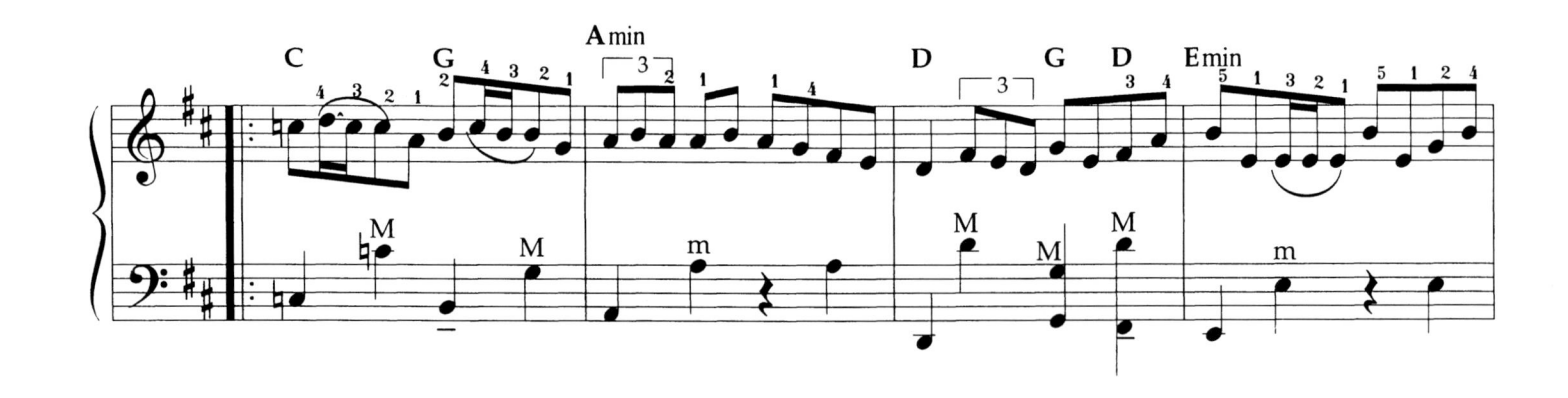

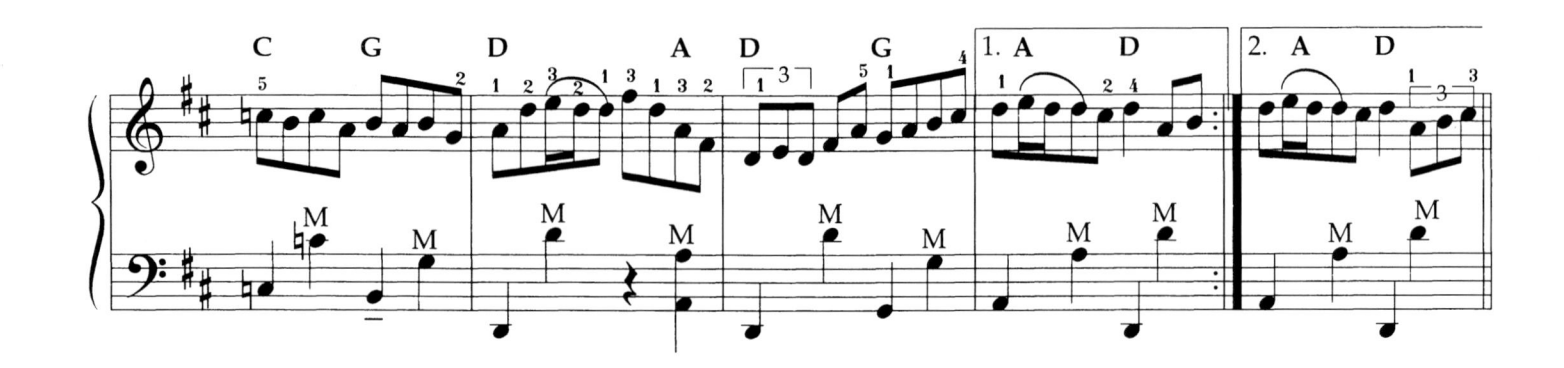

D Emin D A D G D Emin
D Emin D A D A D
D A D C G Amin
D G D Emin C G
D A D G A D A D

O'Keefe's Slide

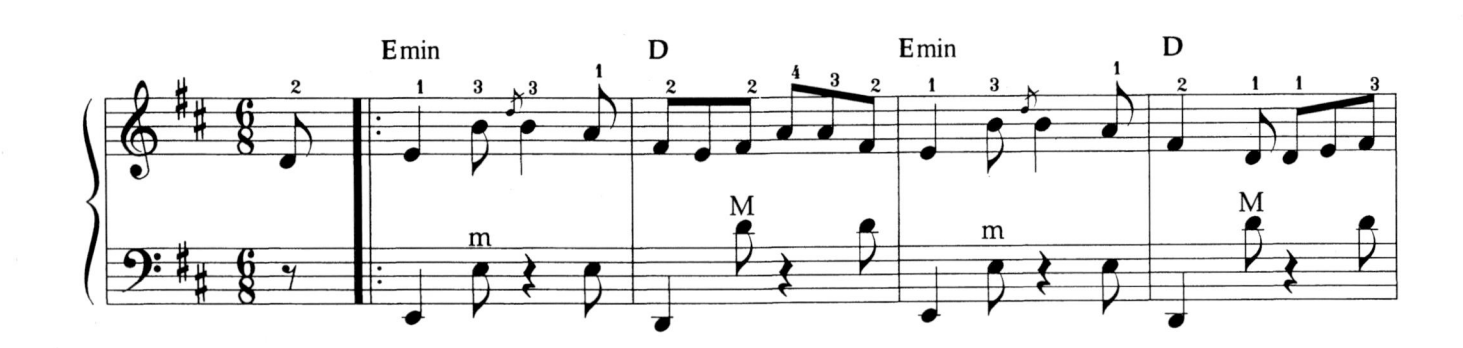

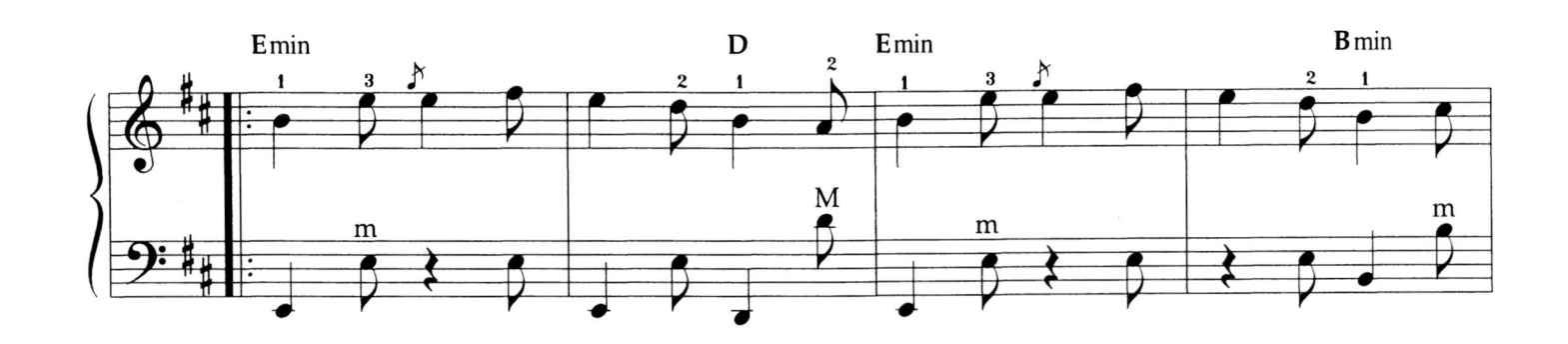

The Old Copper Plate

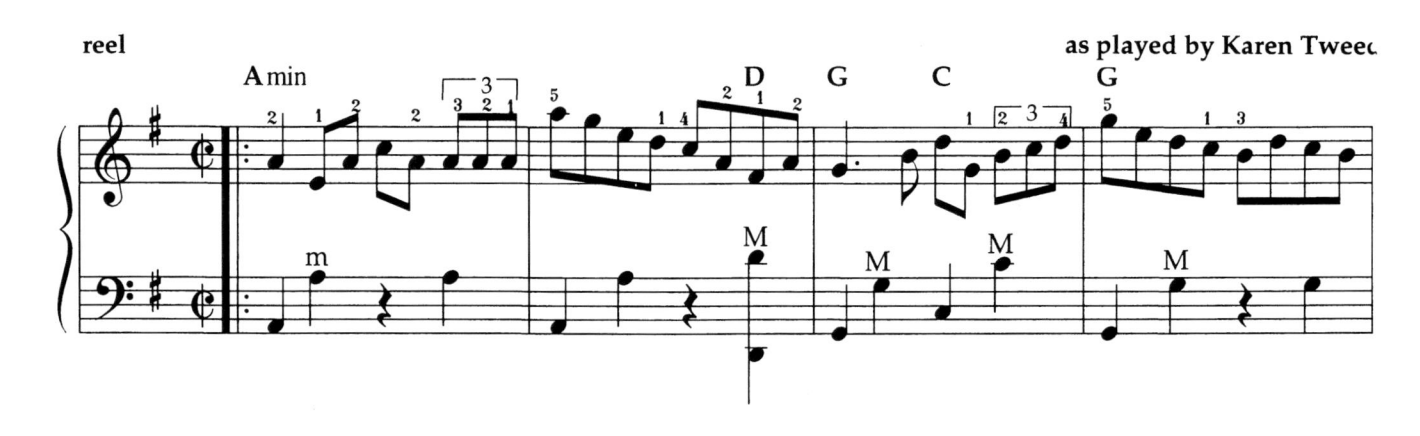

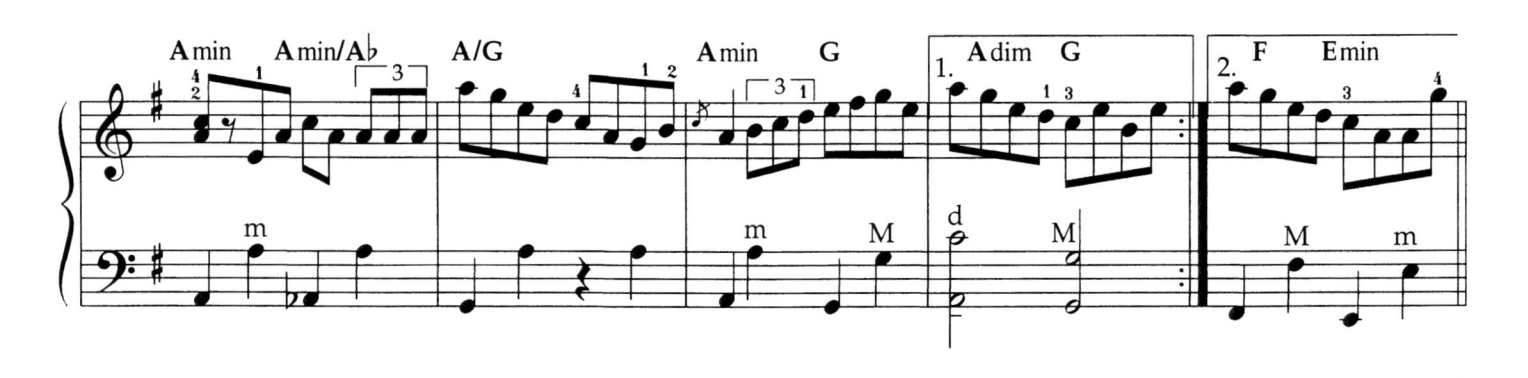

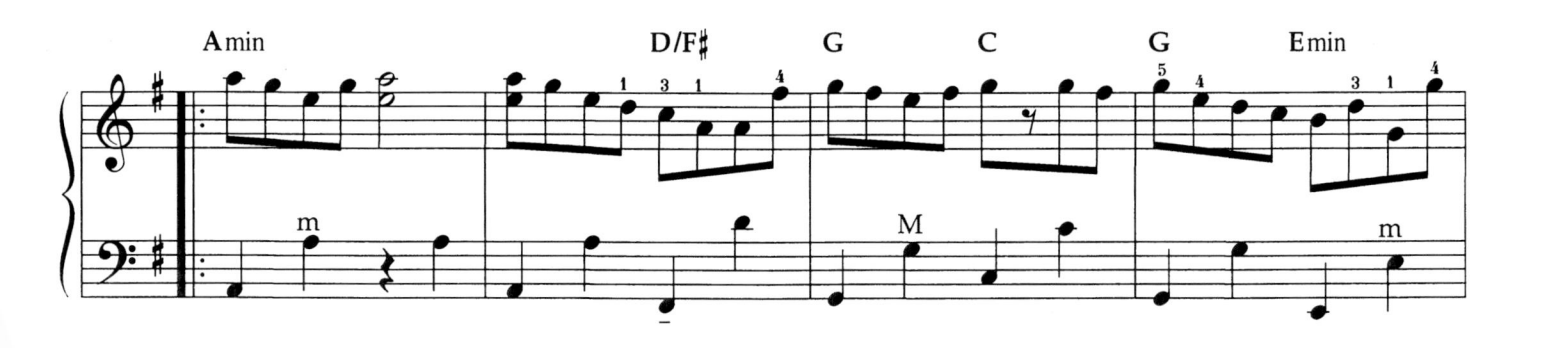

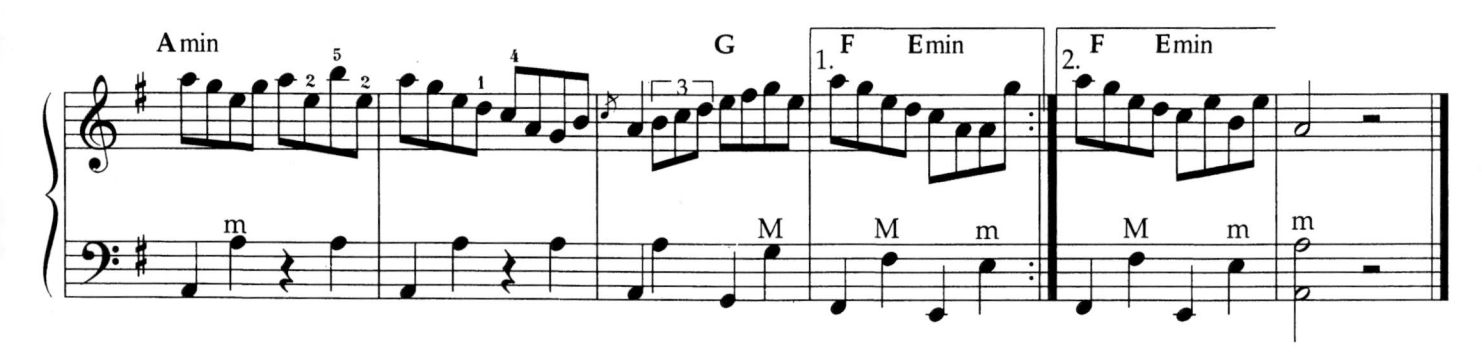

reel
as played by Karen Tweed

Chords based on piano playing of Seamus O'Sullivan

arr. © Dave Mallison Publications. All Rights Reserved. Used by Permission.

Out on the Ocean

Paddy Clancy's

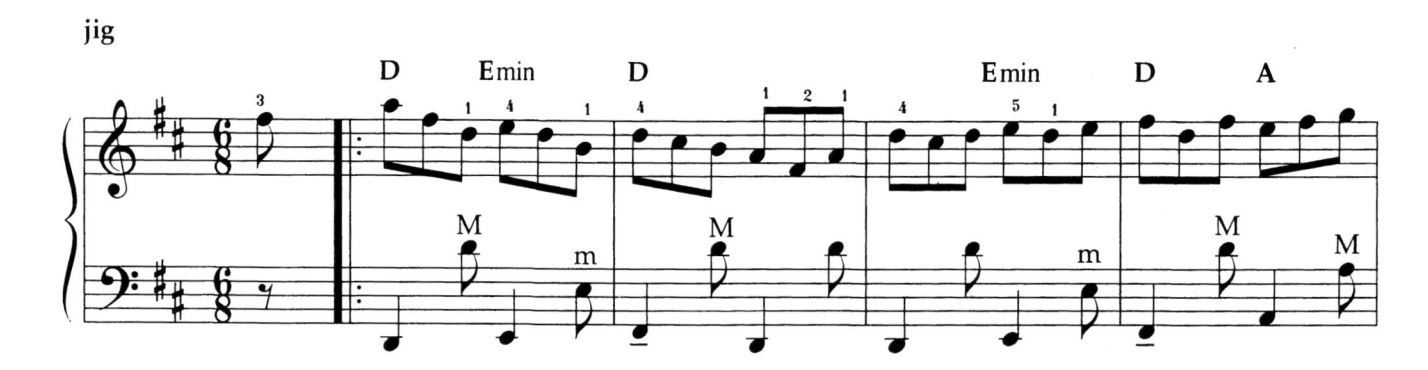

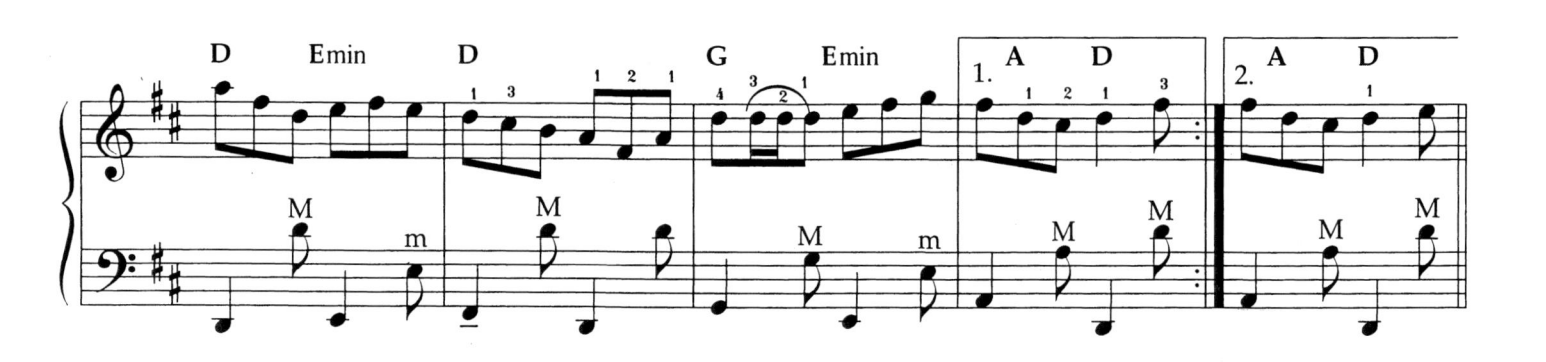

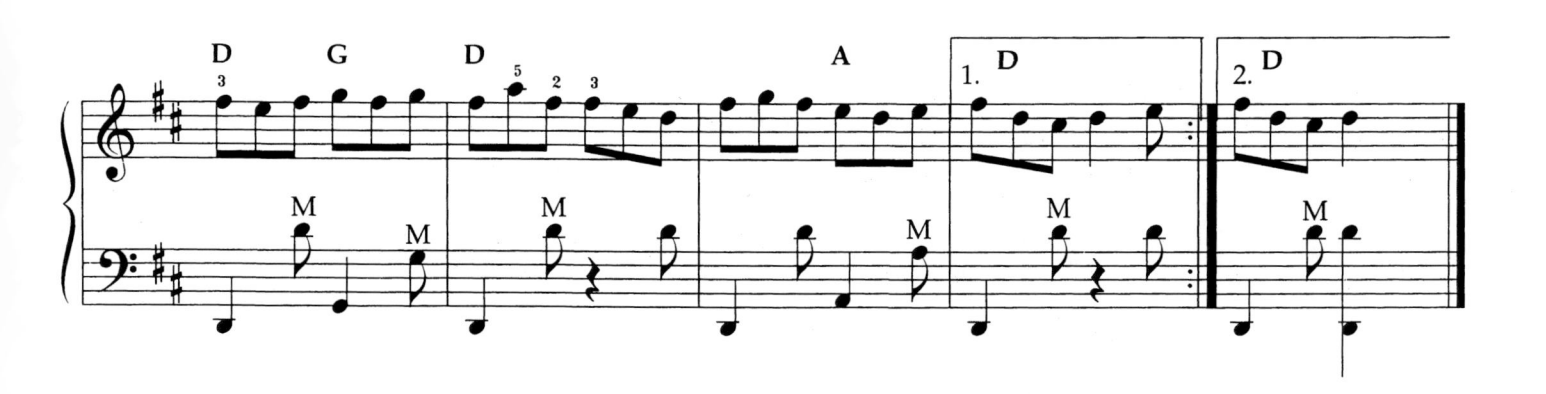

Paddy Fahy's Reel

Paddy Fahy

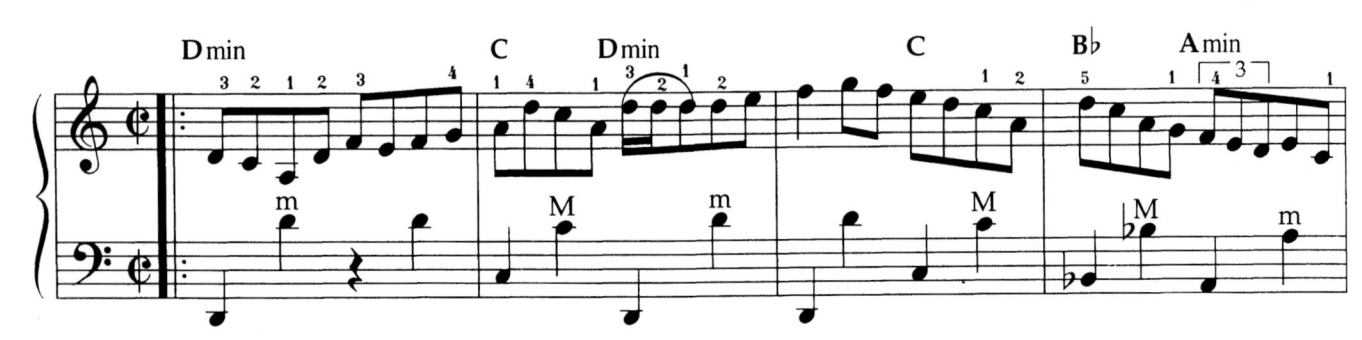

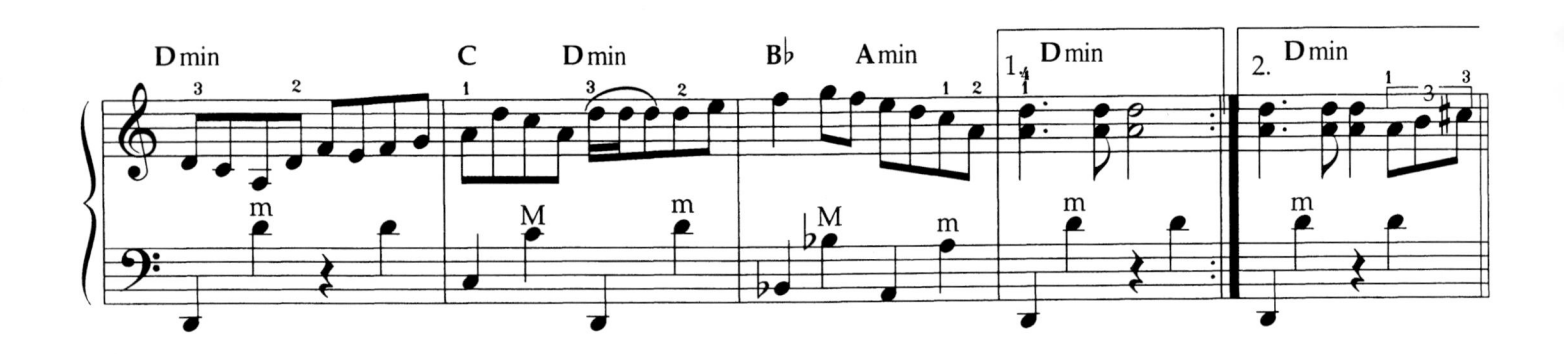

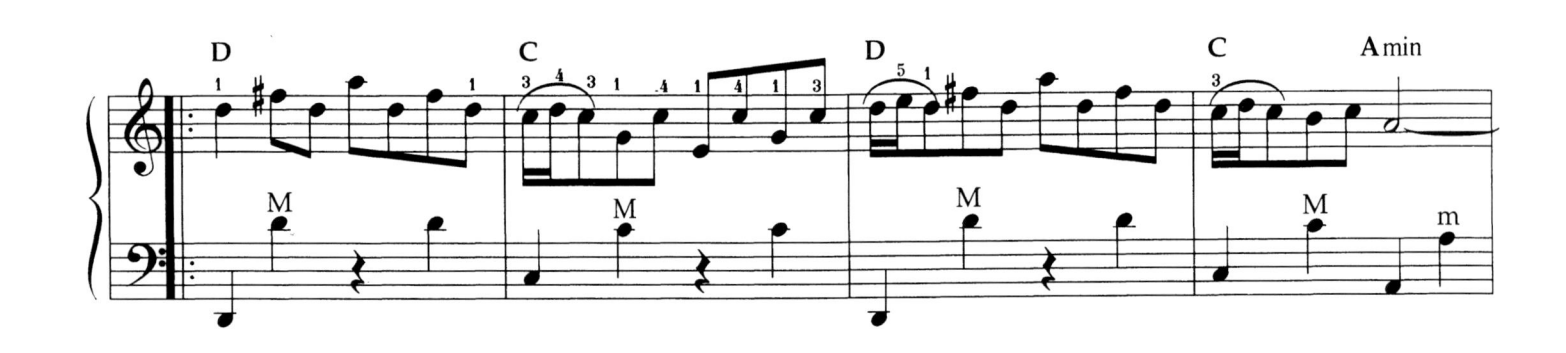

Pigeon on the Gate

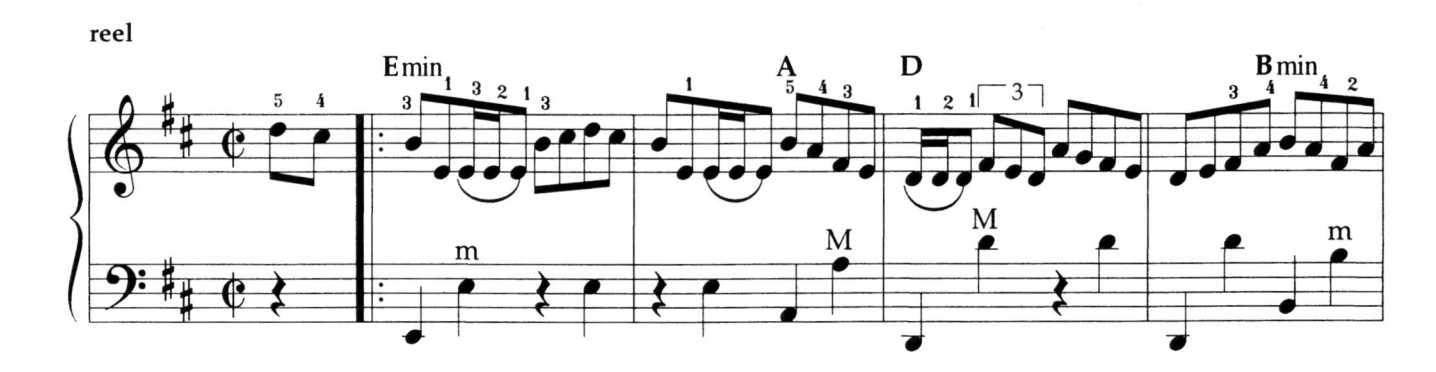

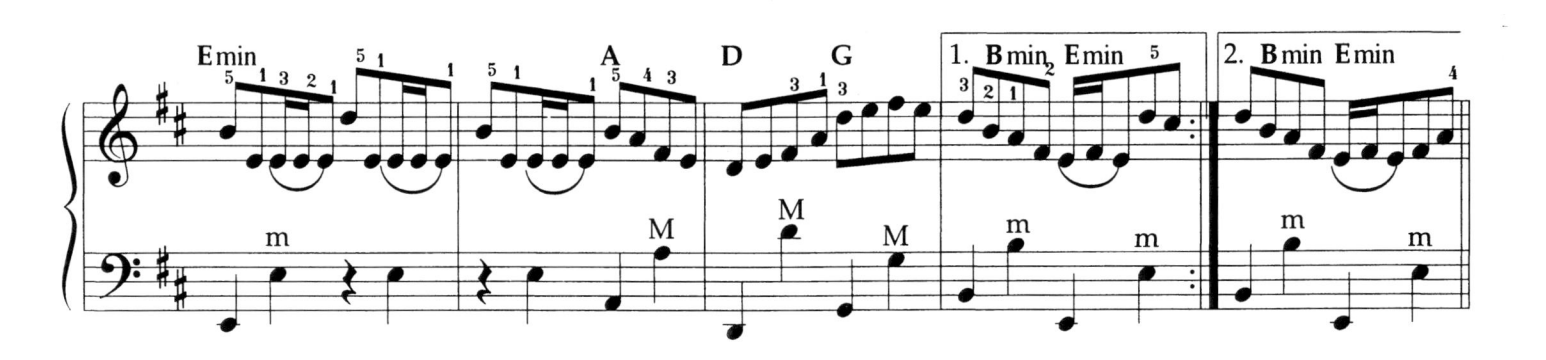

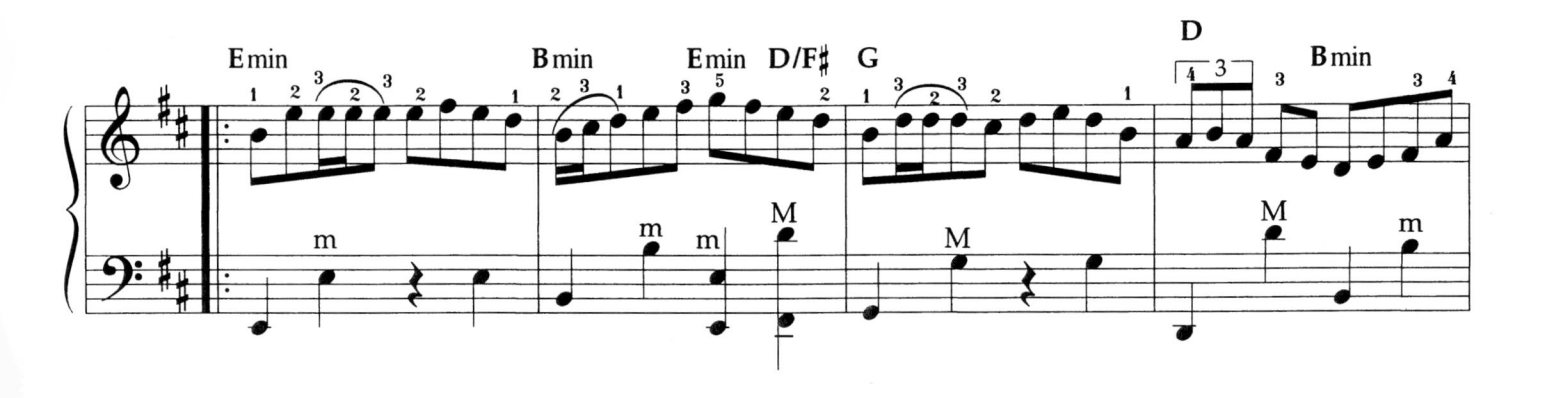

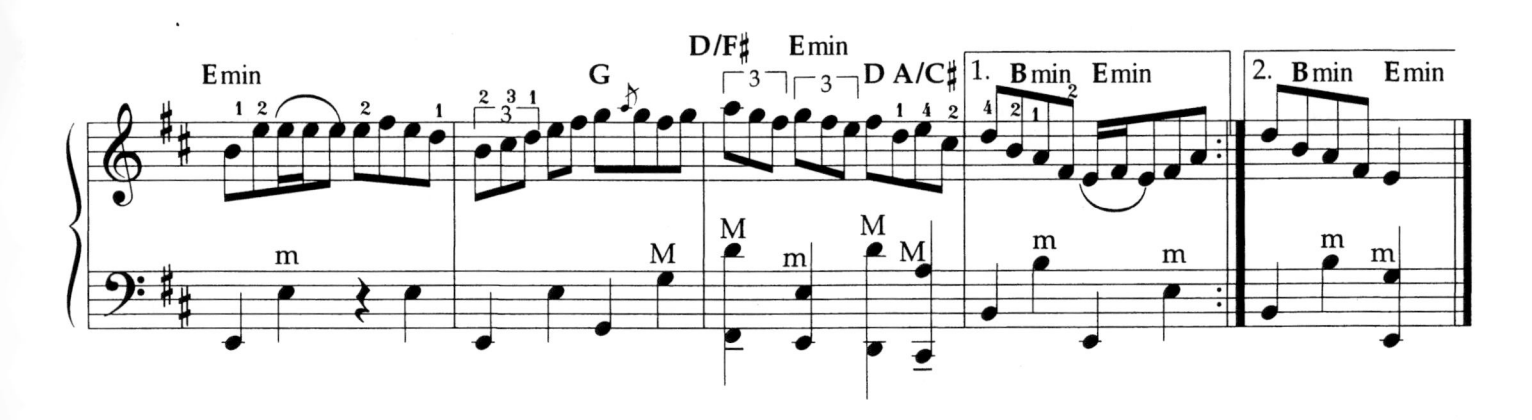

Pipe on the Hob

Pretty Girls of Mayo

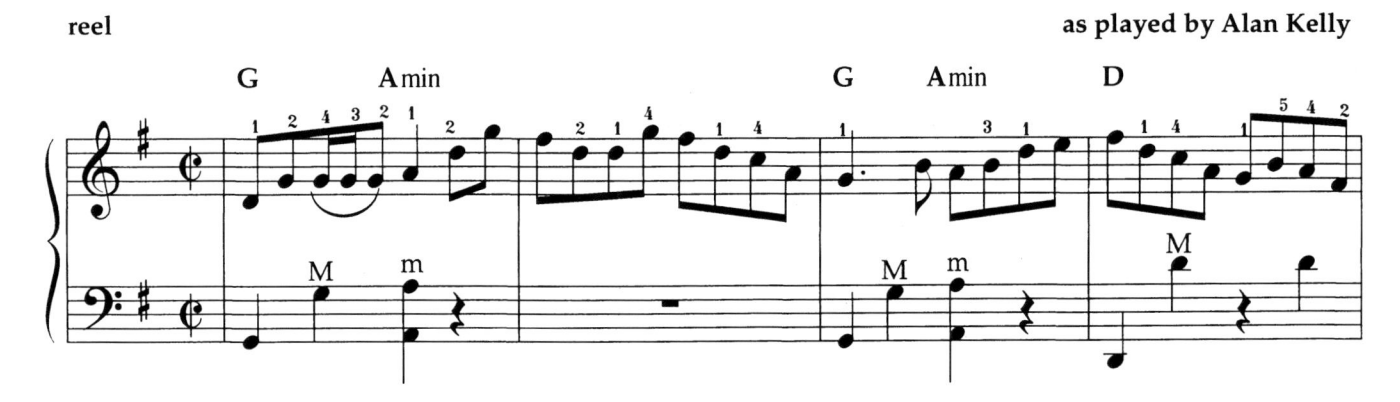

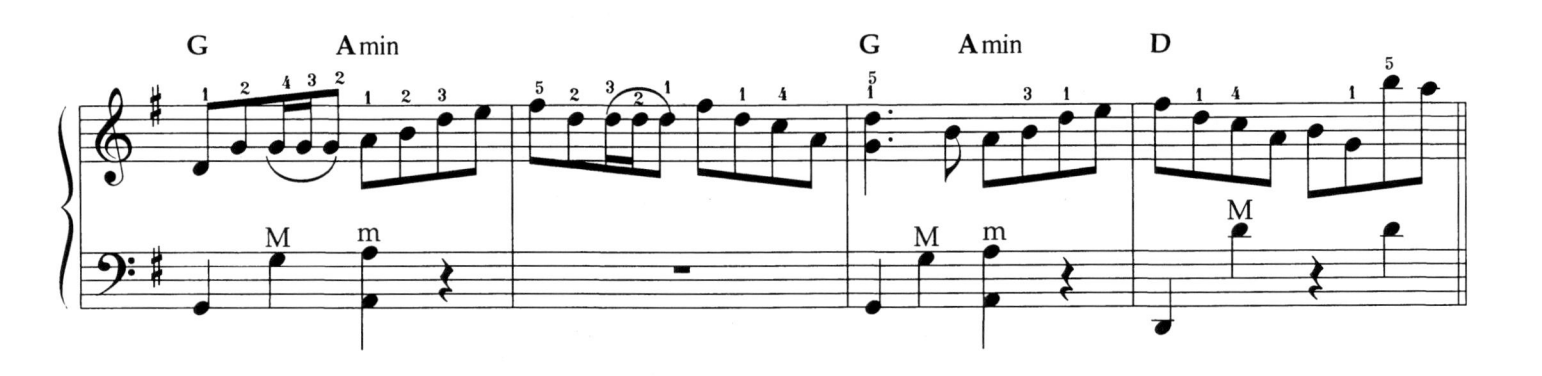

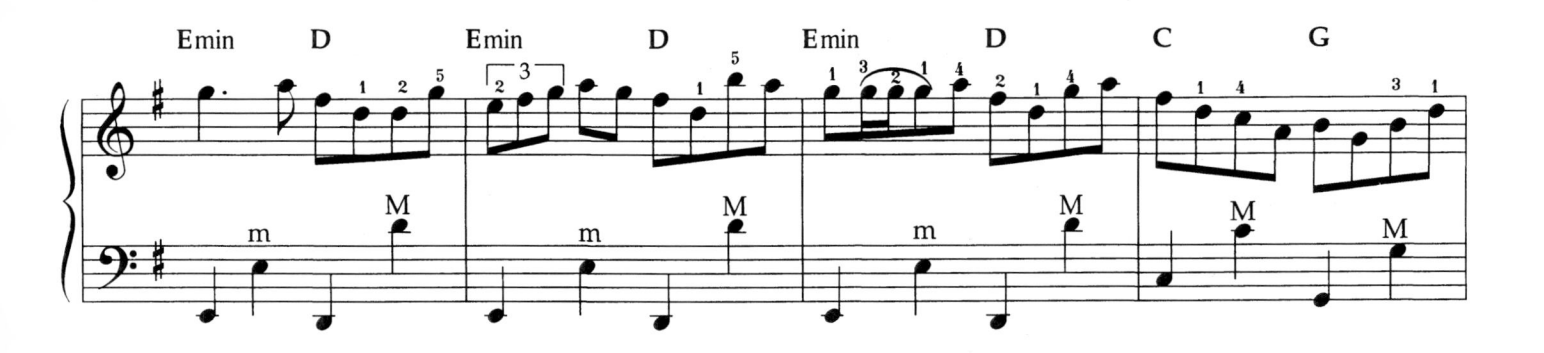

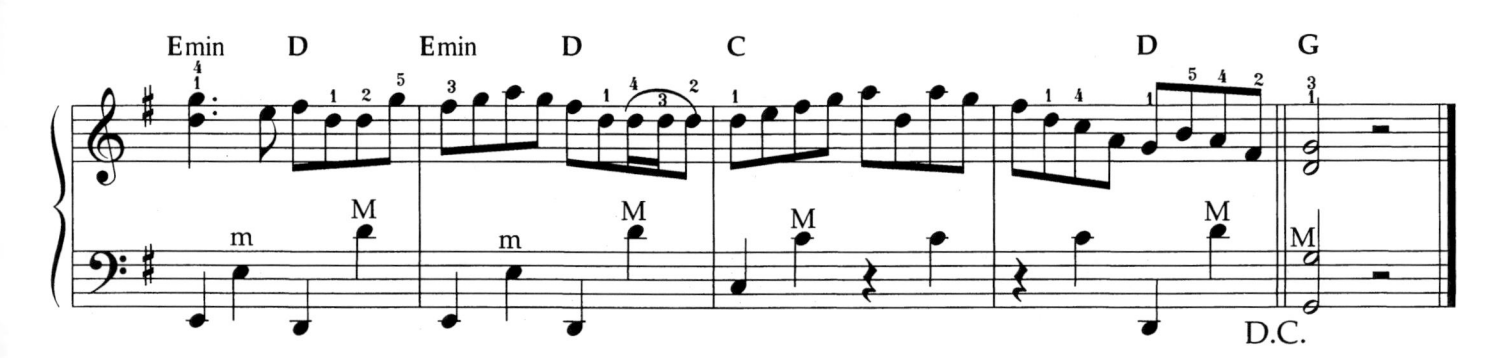

reel
as played by Alan Kelly

Chords based on guitar playing of Donogh Hennessey.

arr. © Acorn Music, Ltd (Ireland). All Rights Reserved. Used by Permission.

The Rakes of Kildare

Reel

as played by Noel Hill
and Tony MacMahon

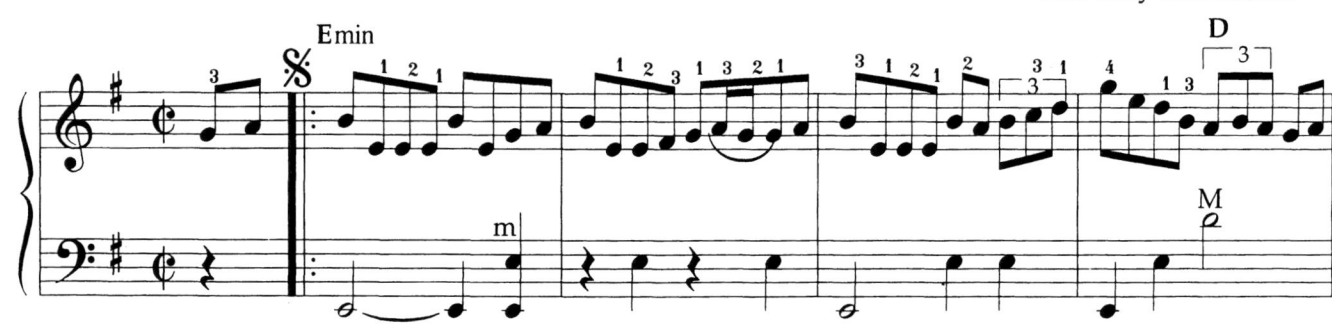

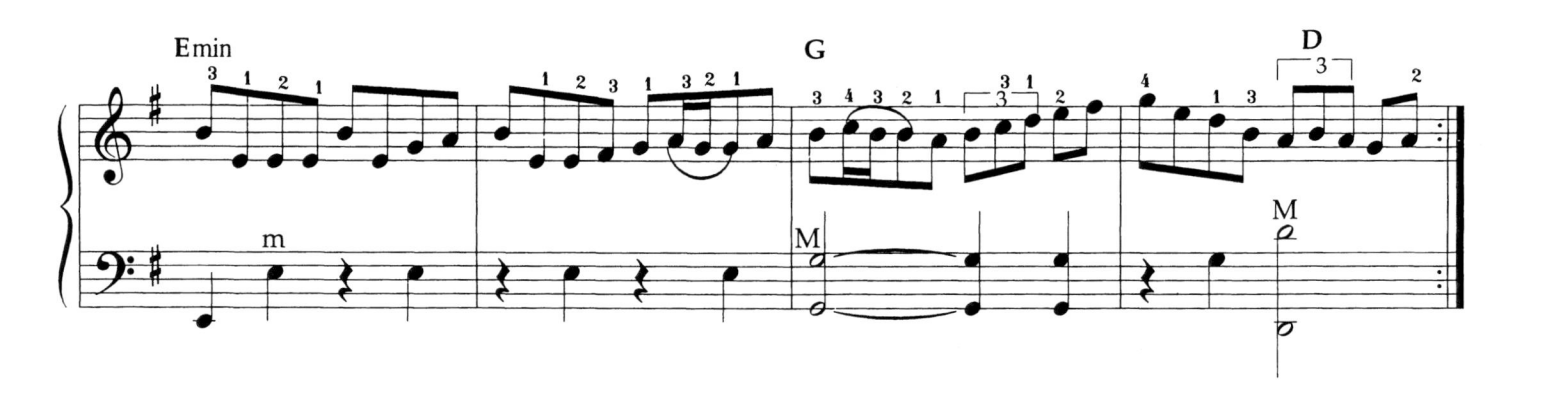

arr. © Hill, MacMahon. All Rights Reserved. Used by Permission.

Road to Lisdoonvarna

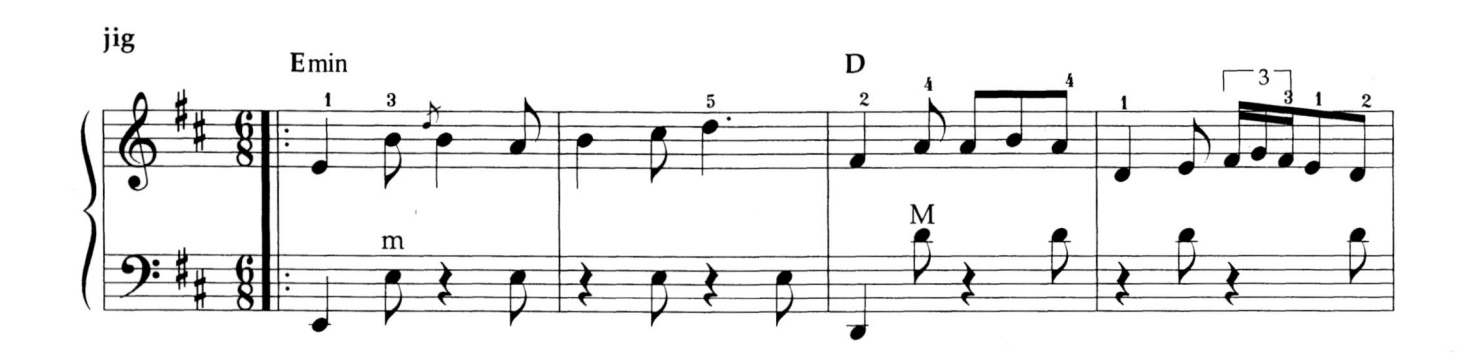

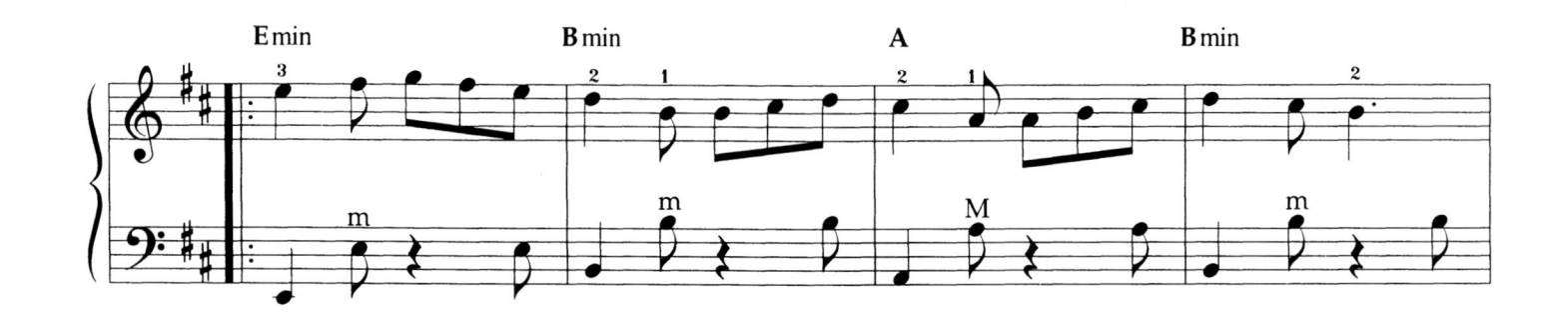

Sally Gardens

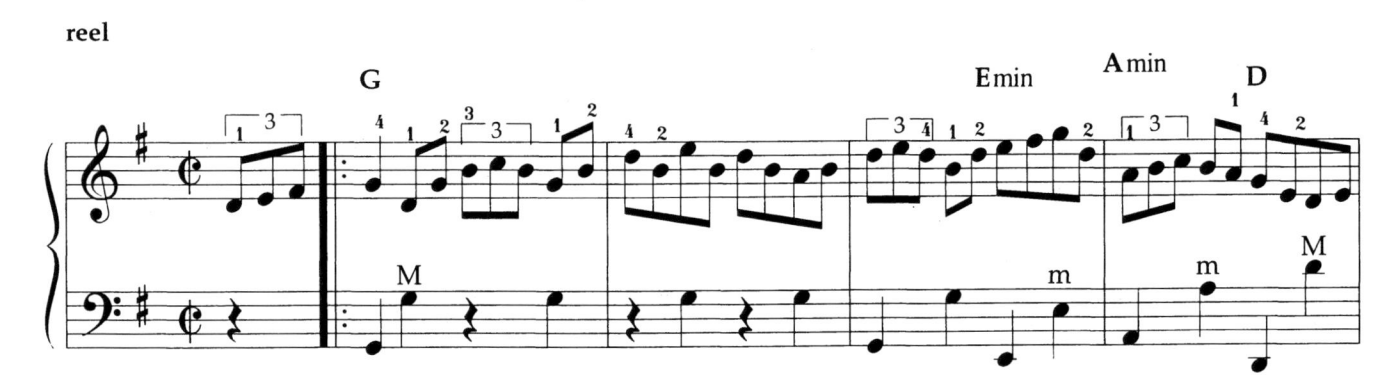

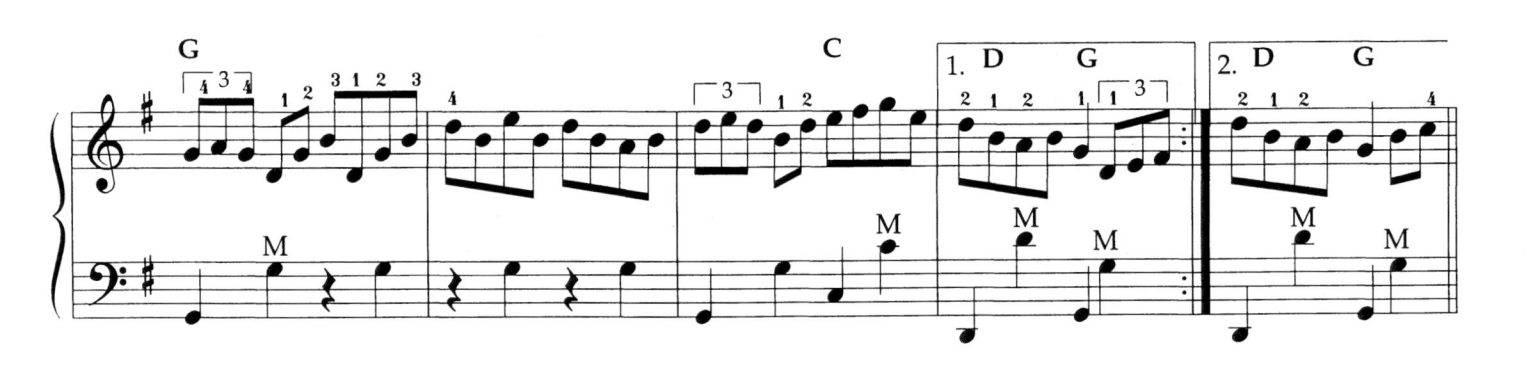

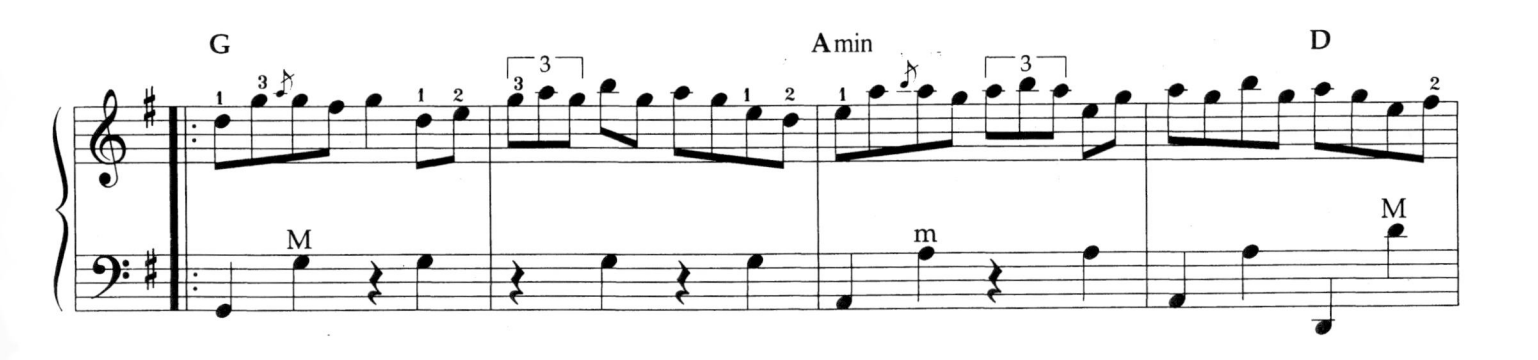

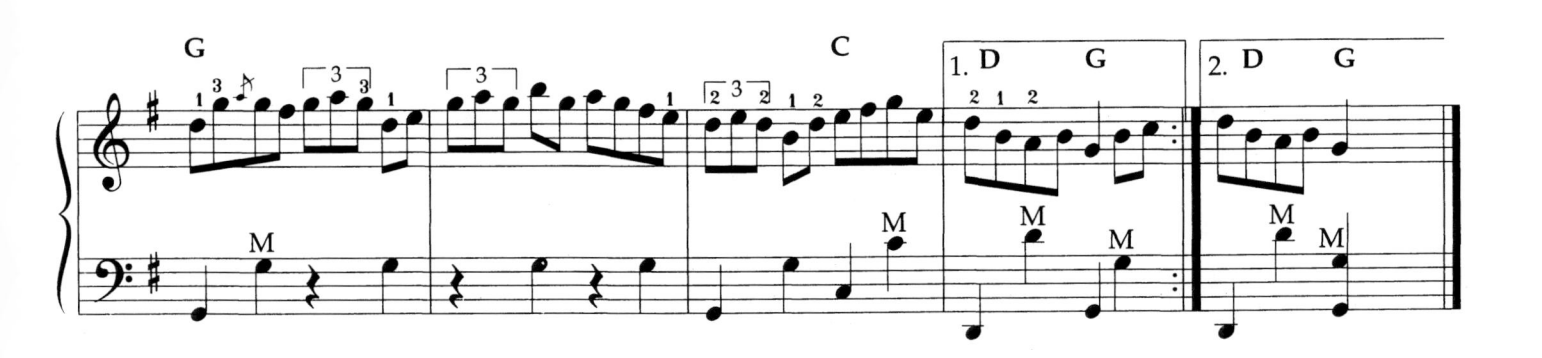

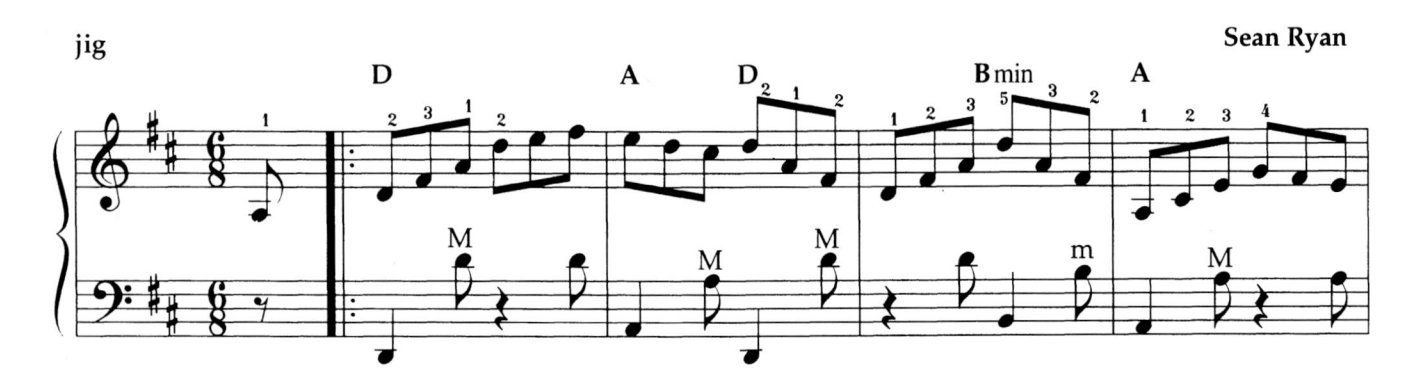

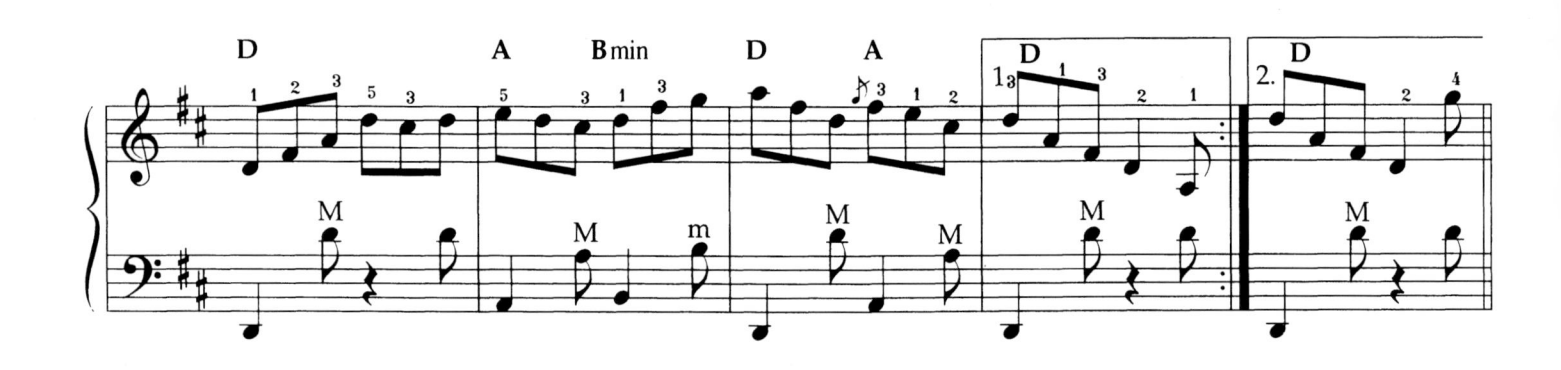

Sean Ryan's

jig

Sean Ryan

Sean Ryan's Jig

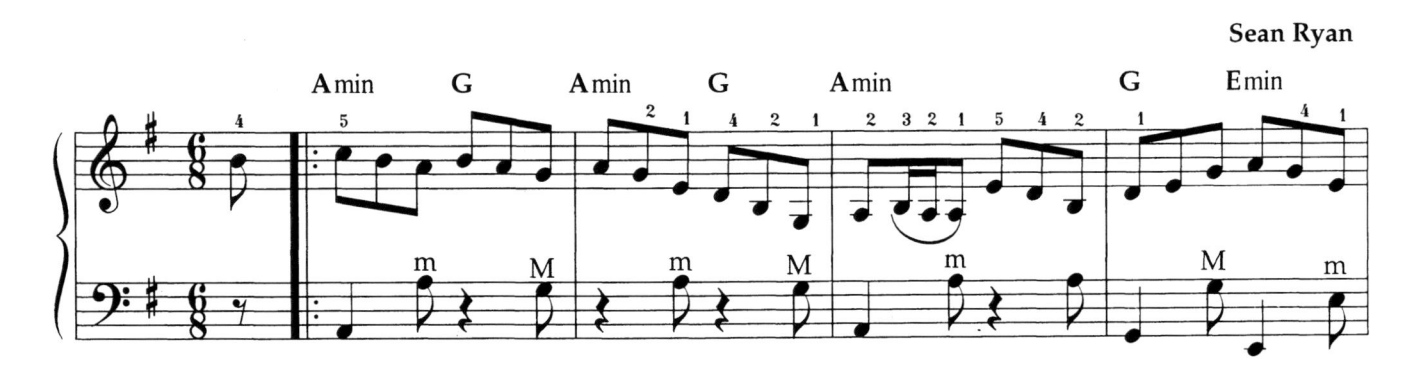

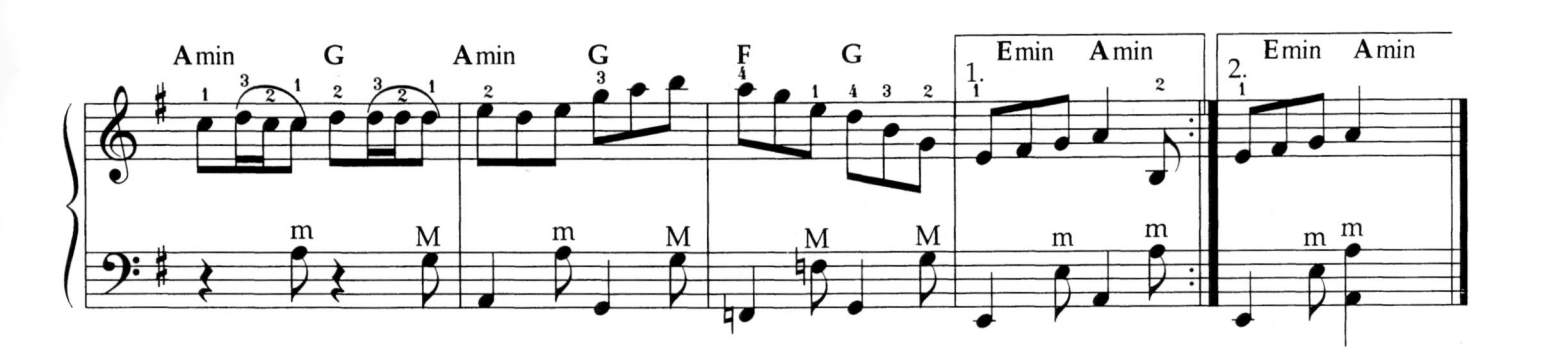

Sean Ryan

Ships are Sailing

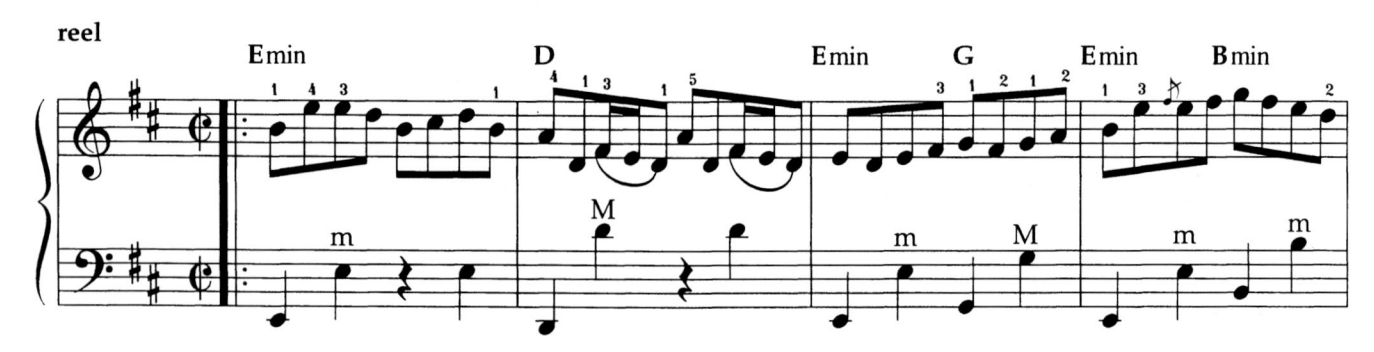

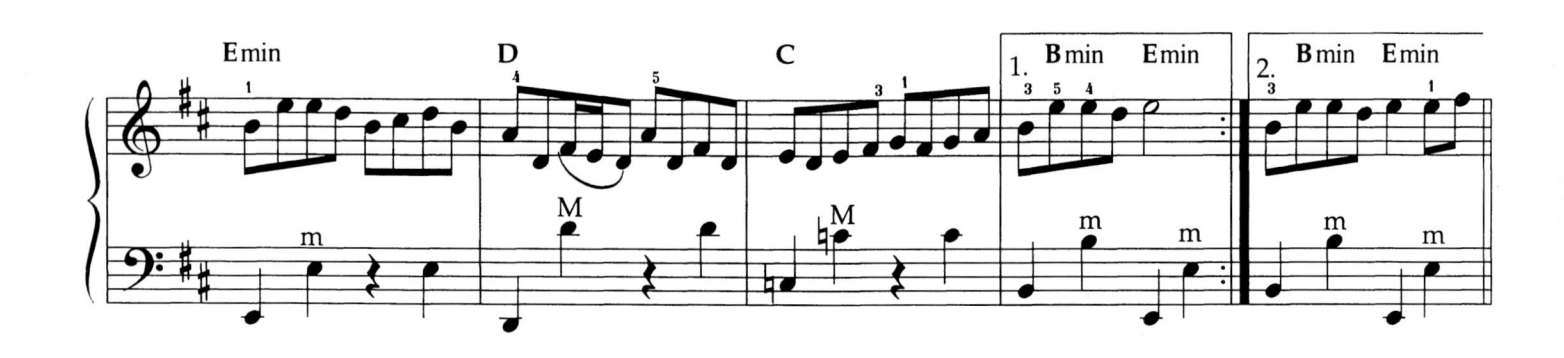

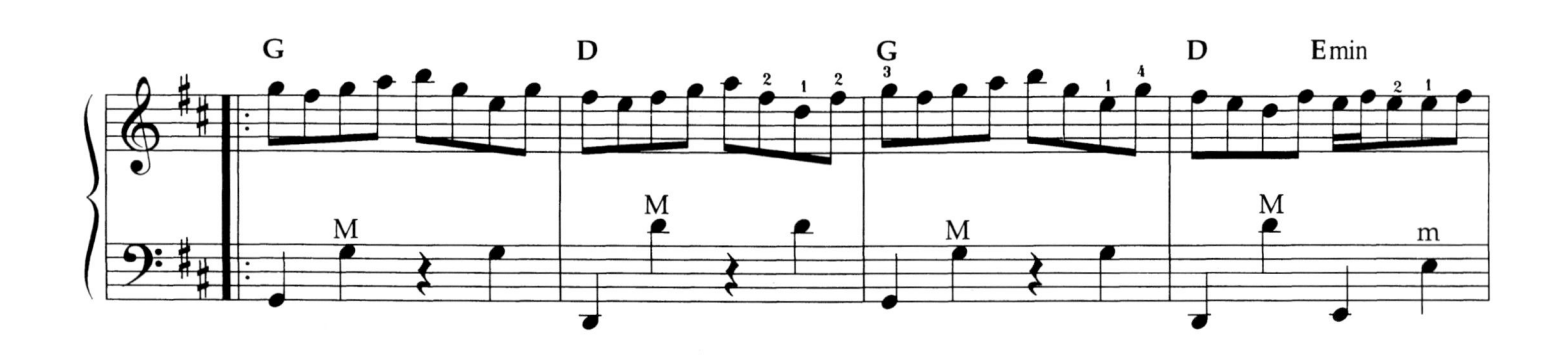

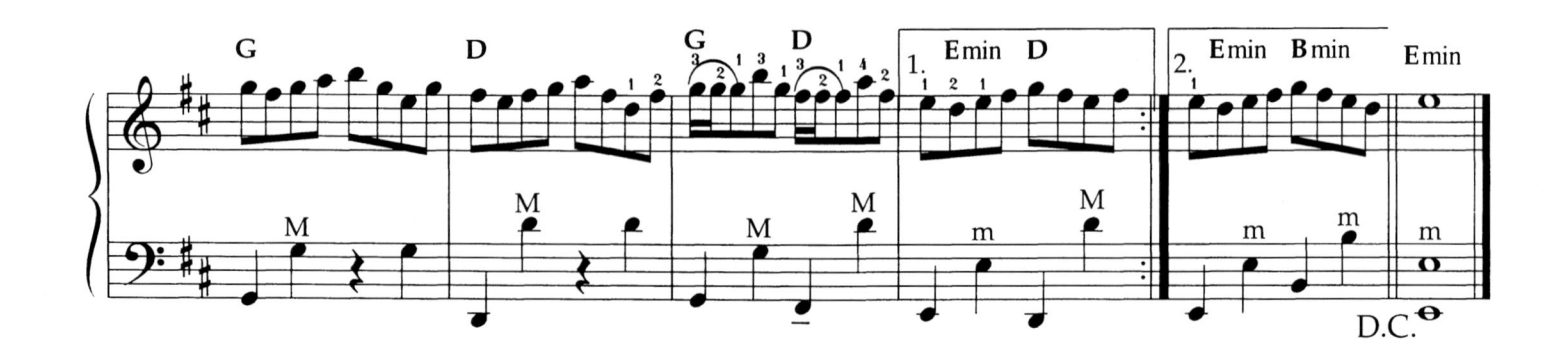

Silver Spear

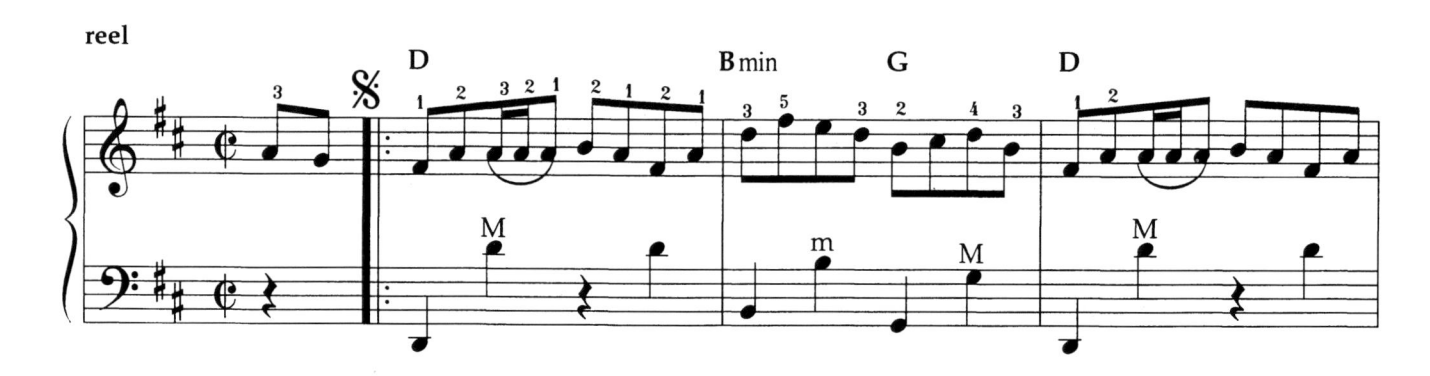

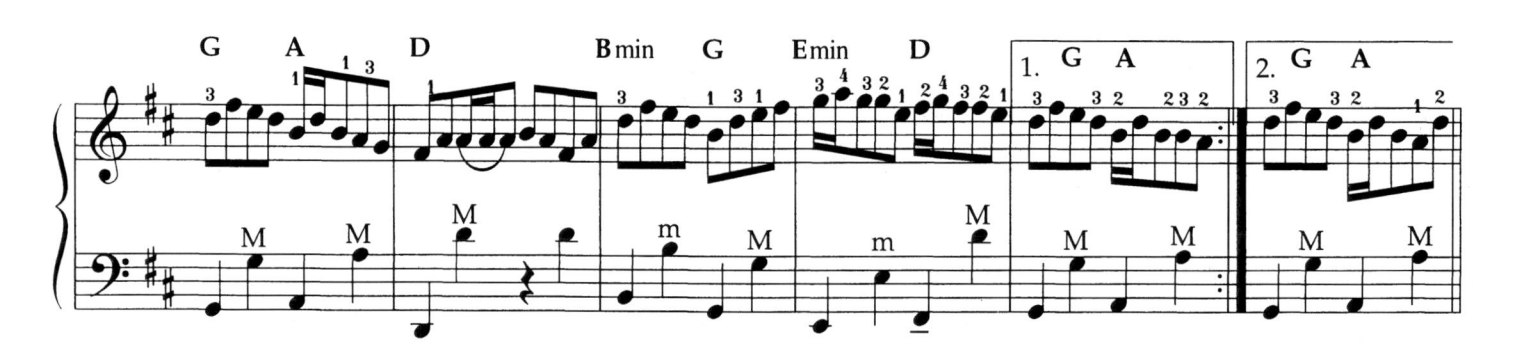

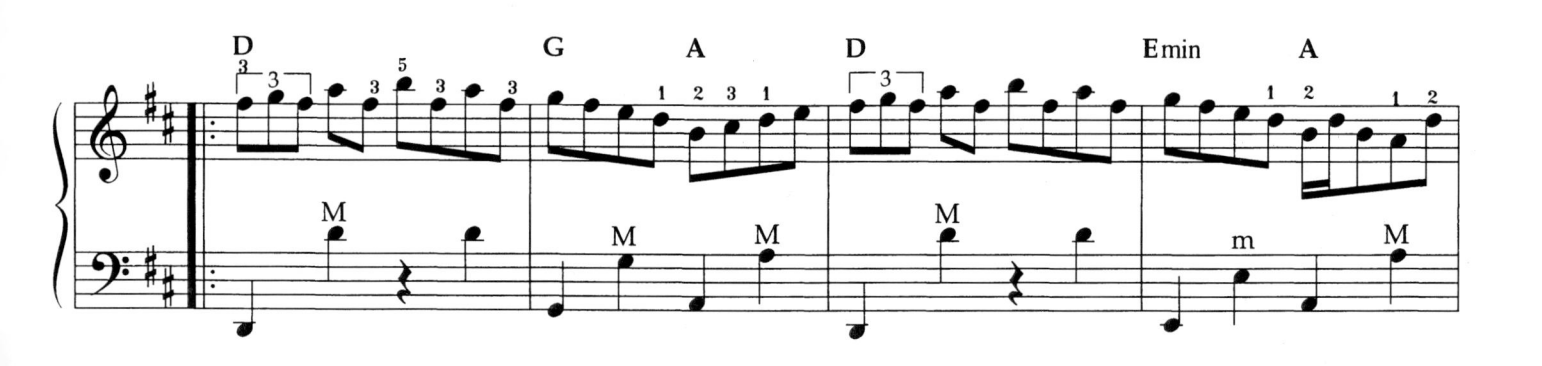

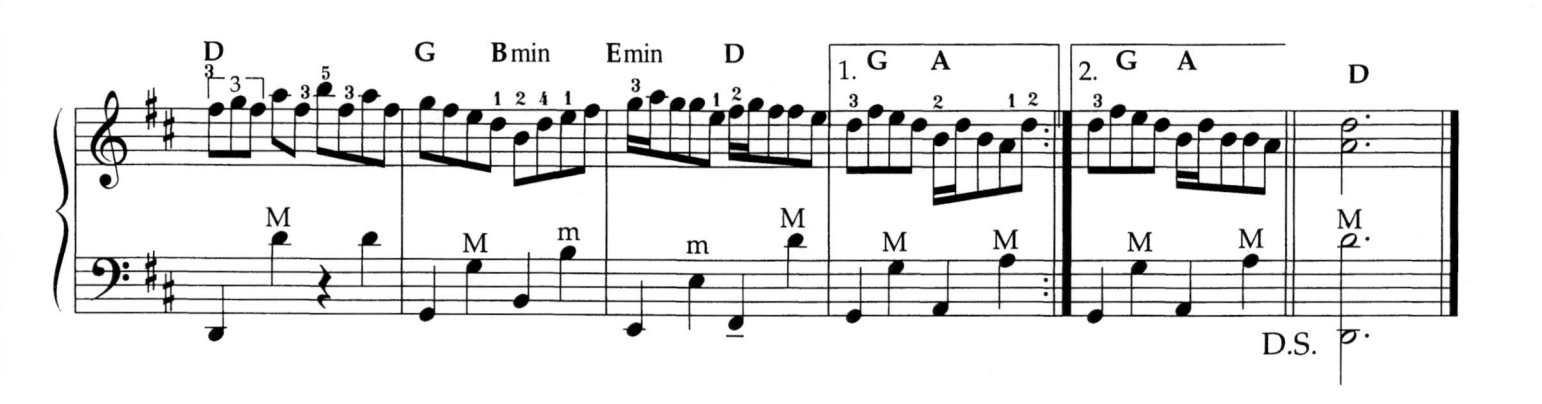

The Skylark

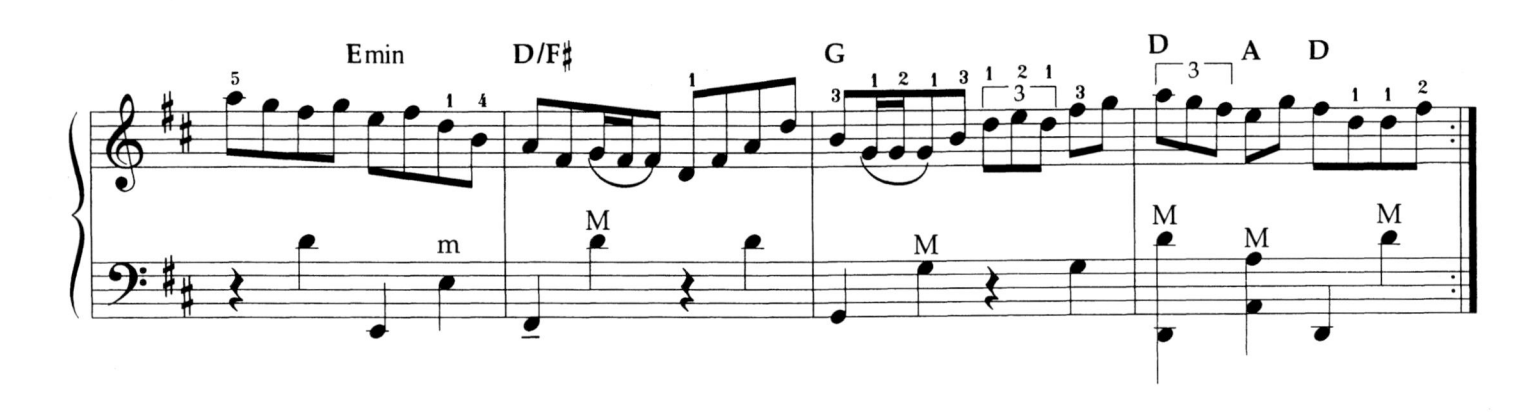

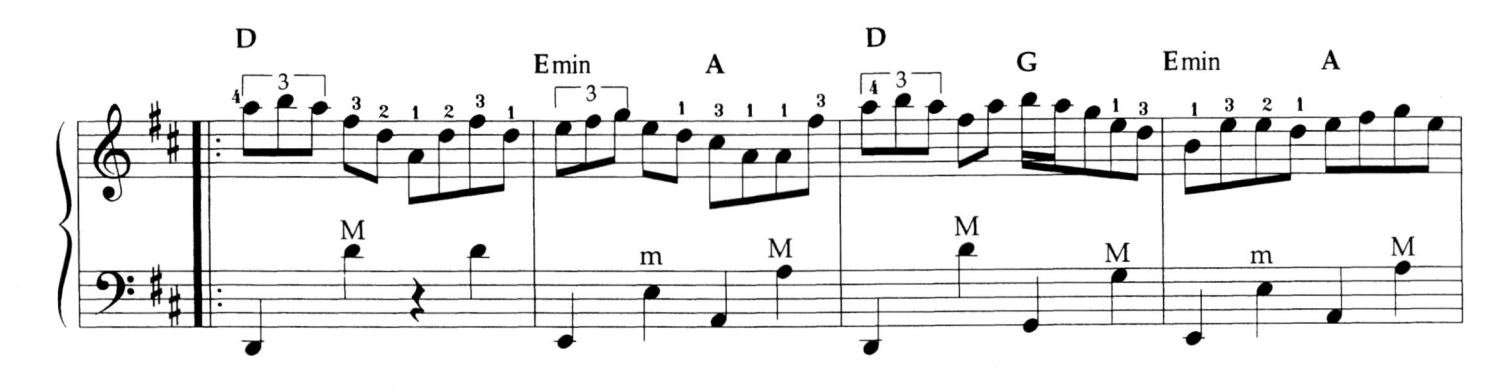

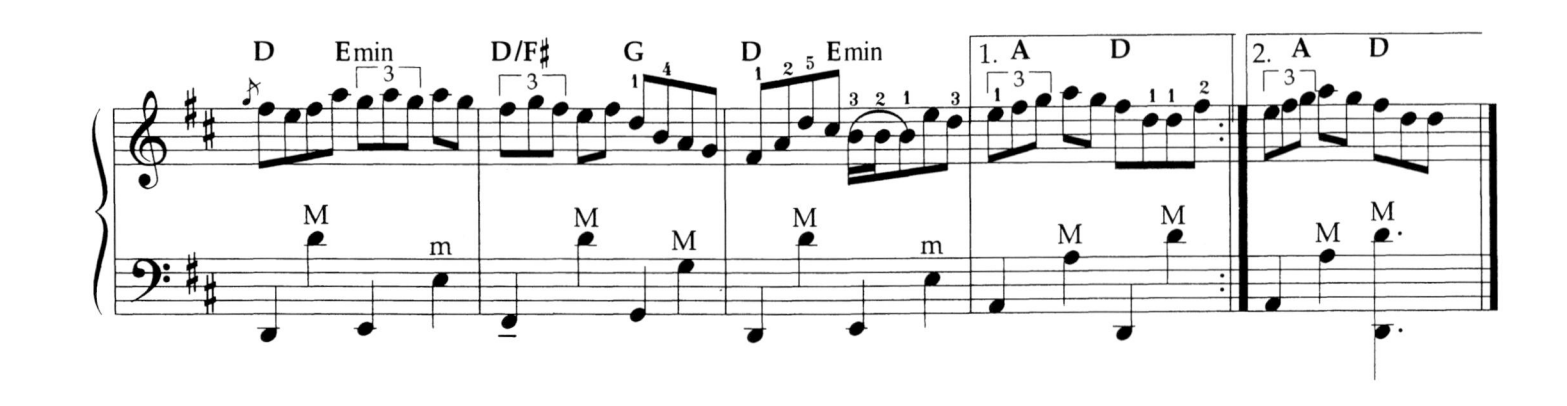

Slieve Russel

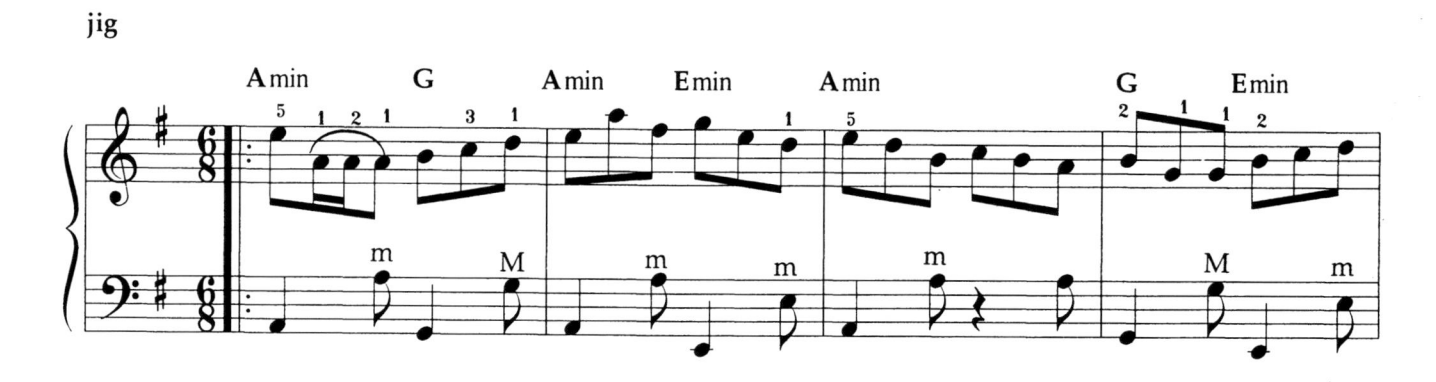

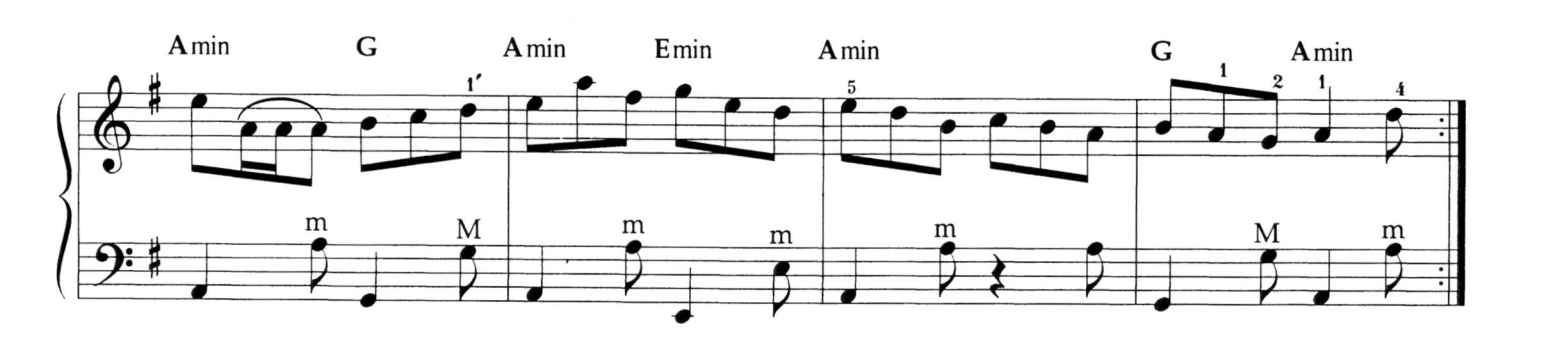

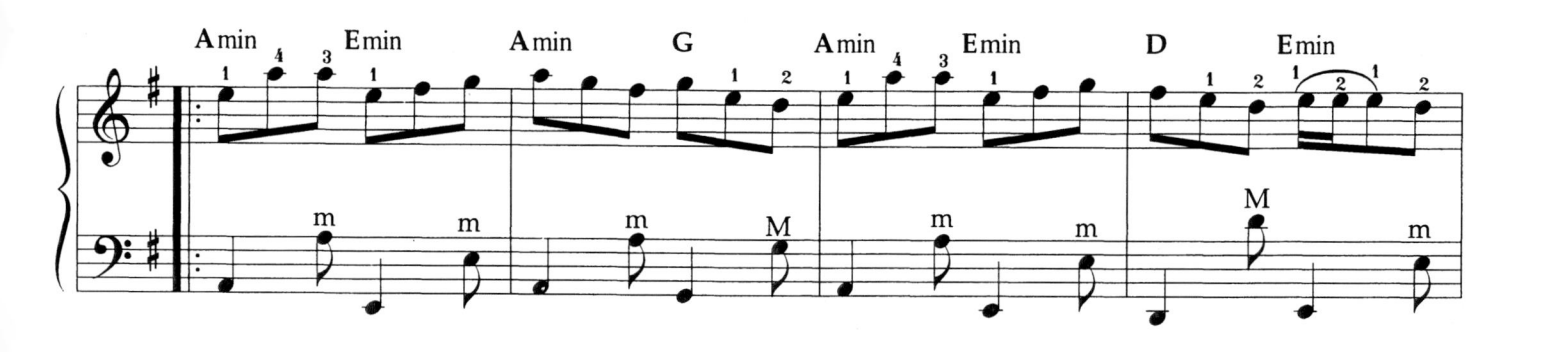

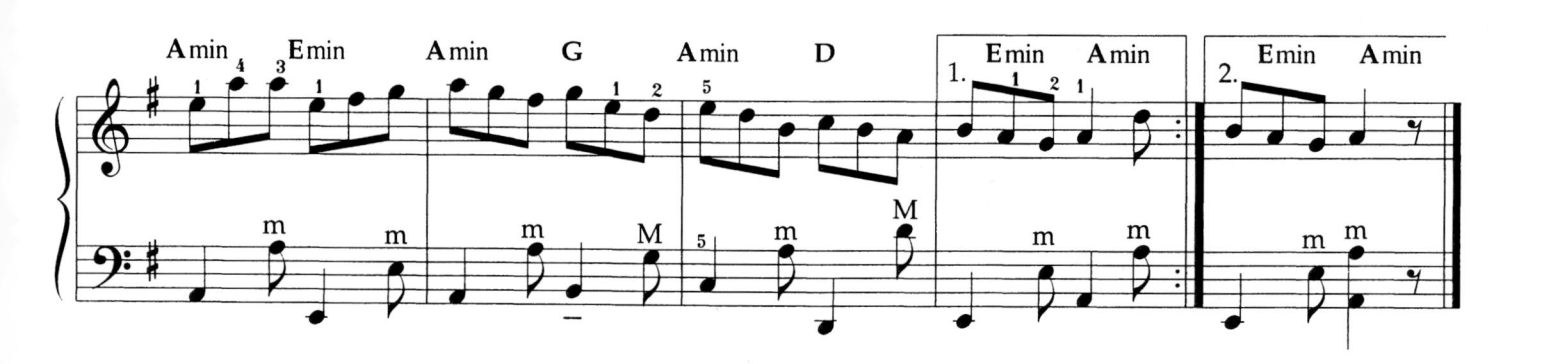

jig

arr. © 1999 Mel Bay® Publications, Inc. All Rights Reserved.

Snug in a Blanket

*This page has been
left blank to avoid
awkward page turns*

The Spike Island Lassies

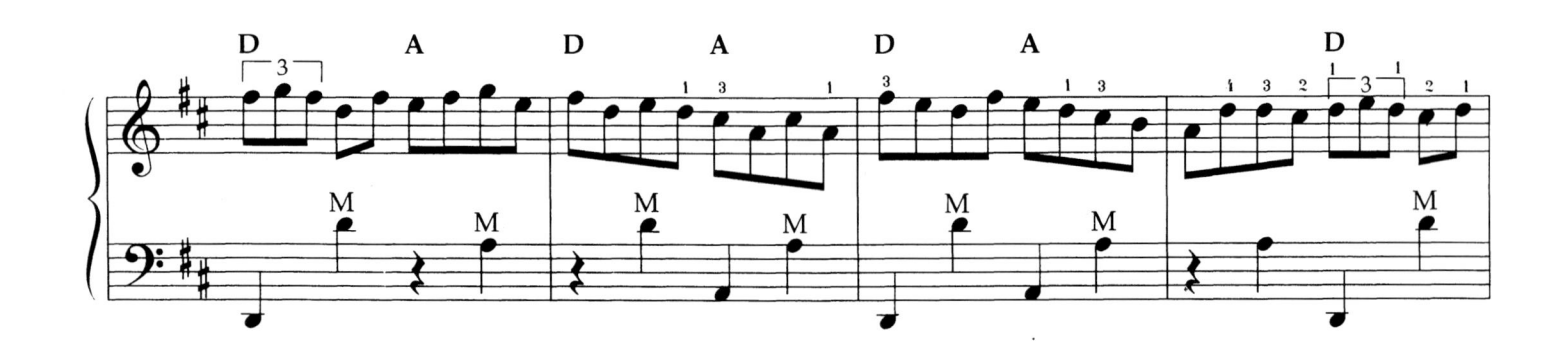

103

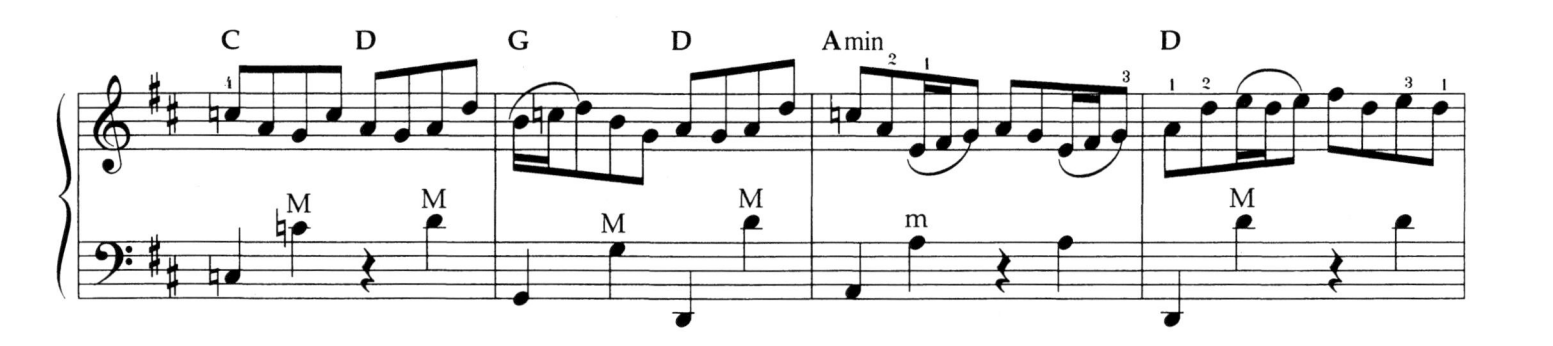

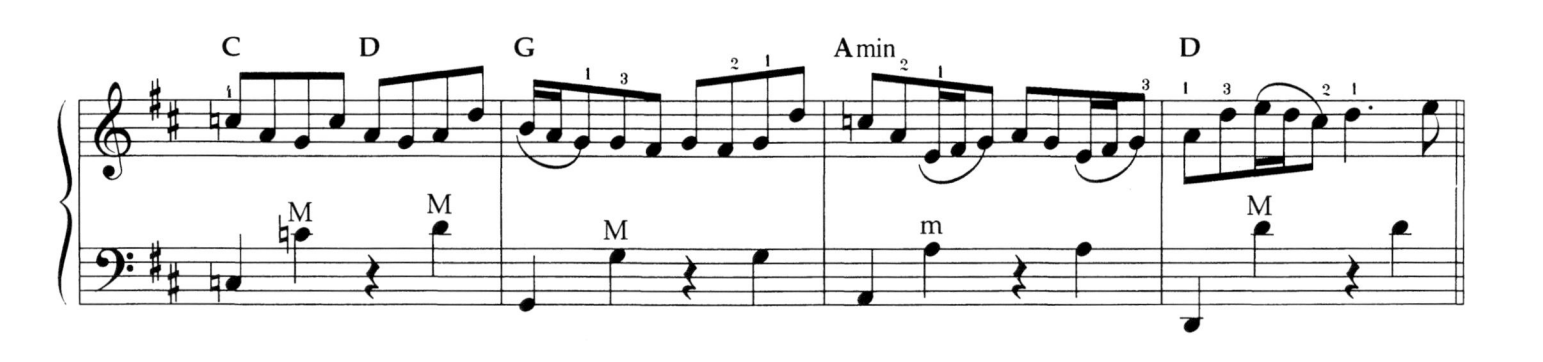

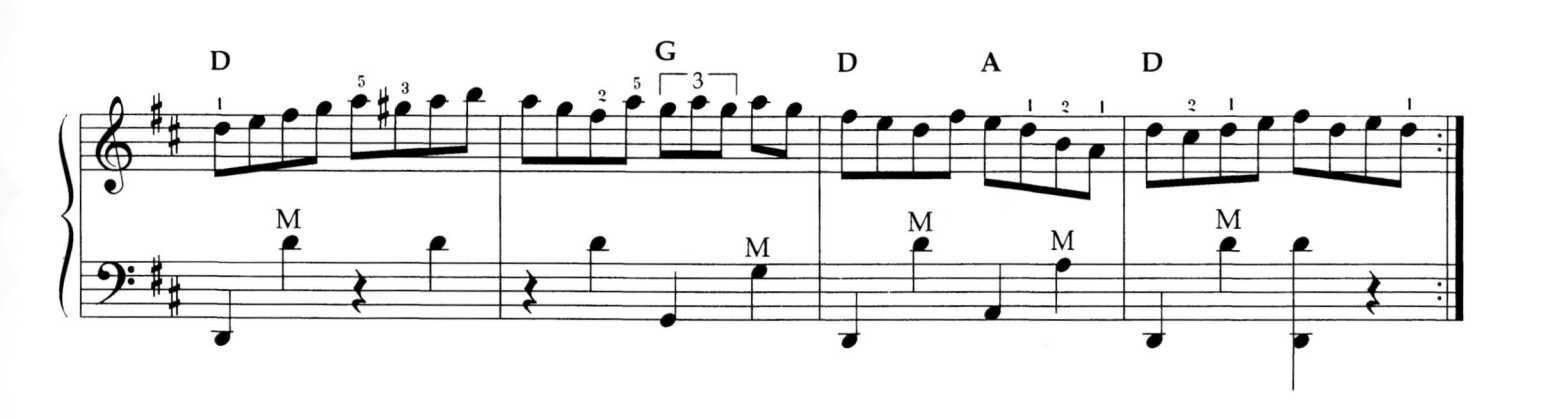

Sportin' Pat

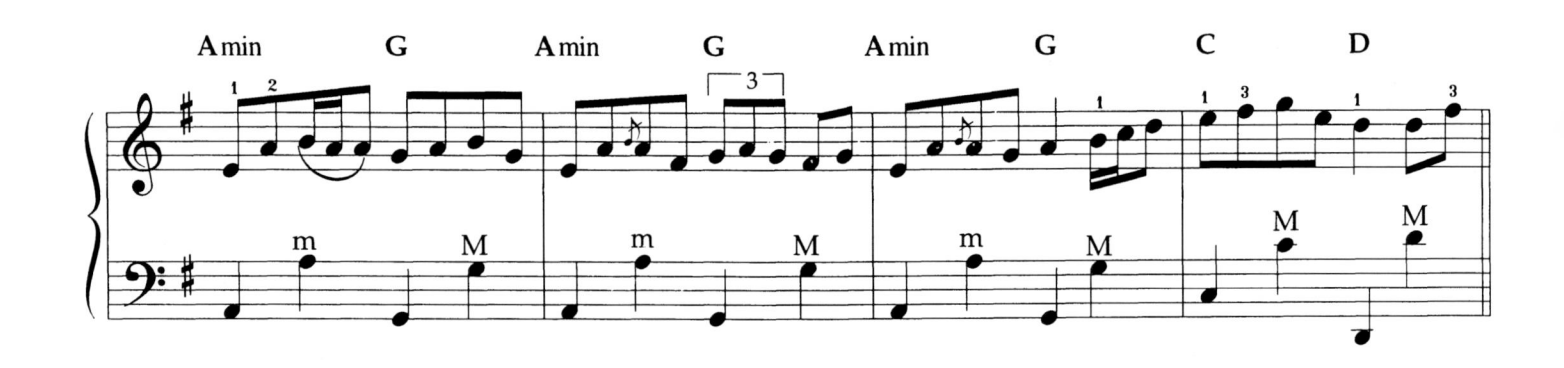

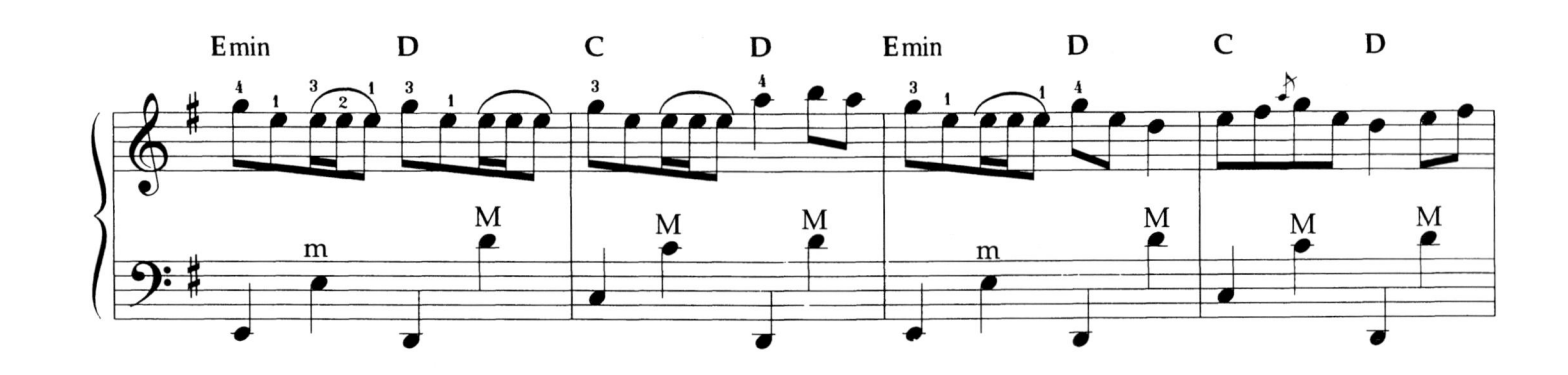

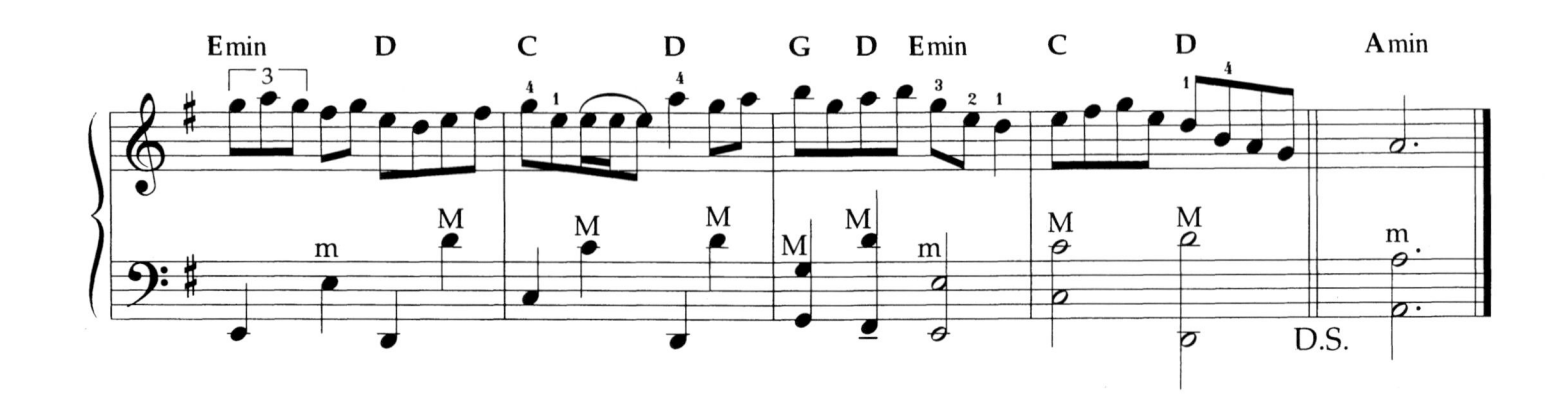

This page has been left blank to avoid awkward page turns

Star of Munster

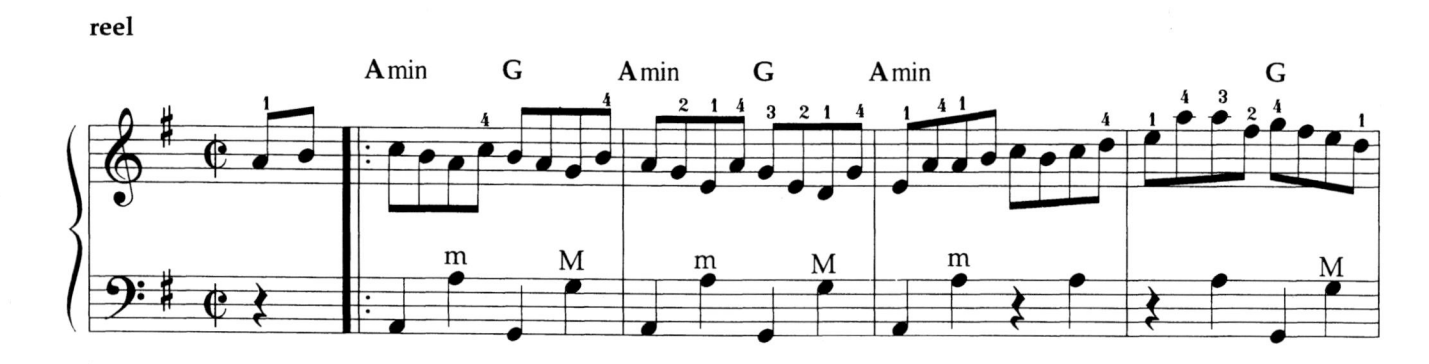

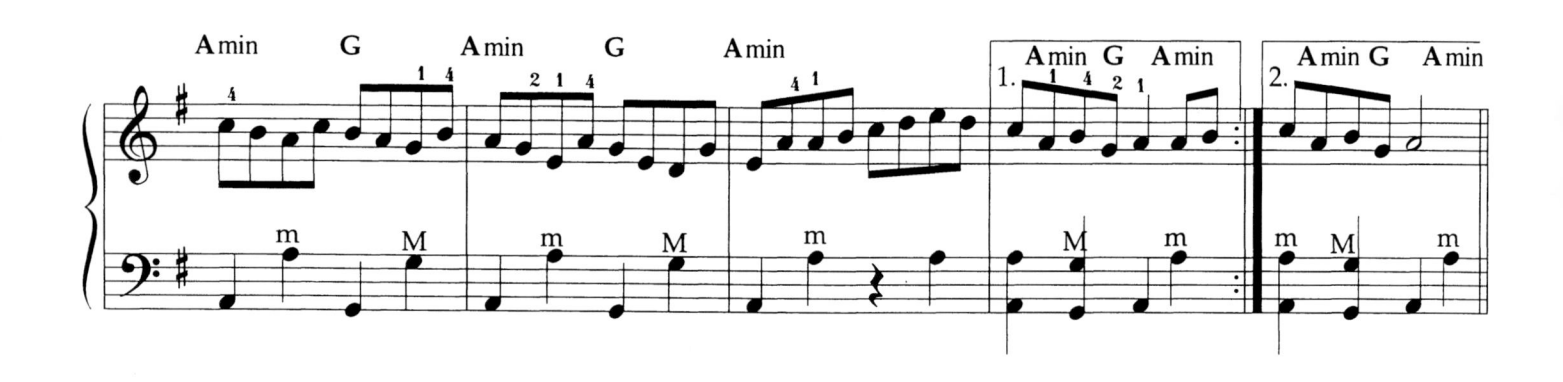

reel

variation

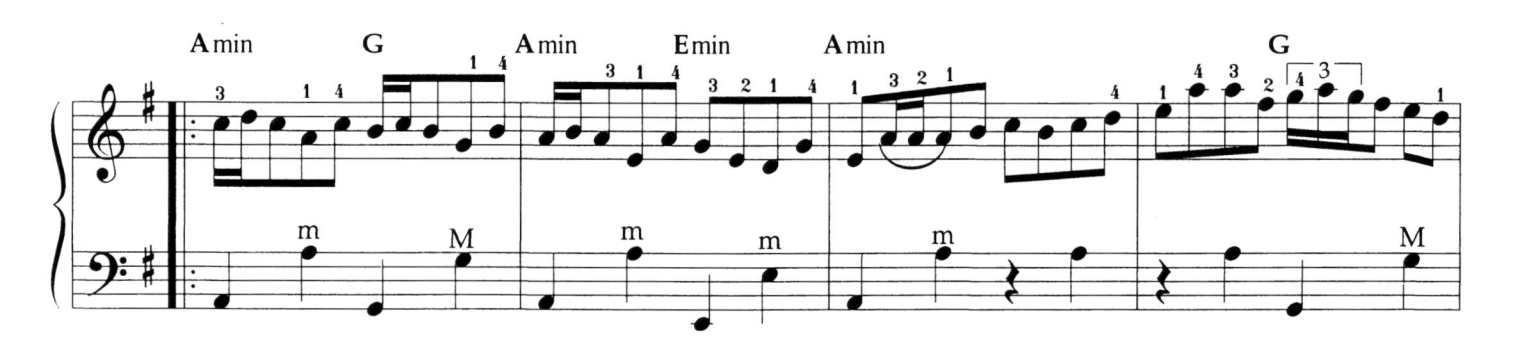

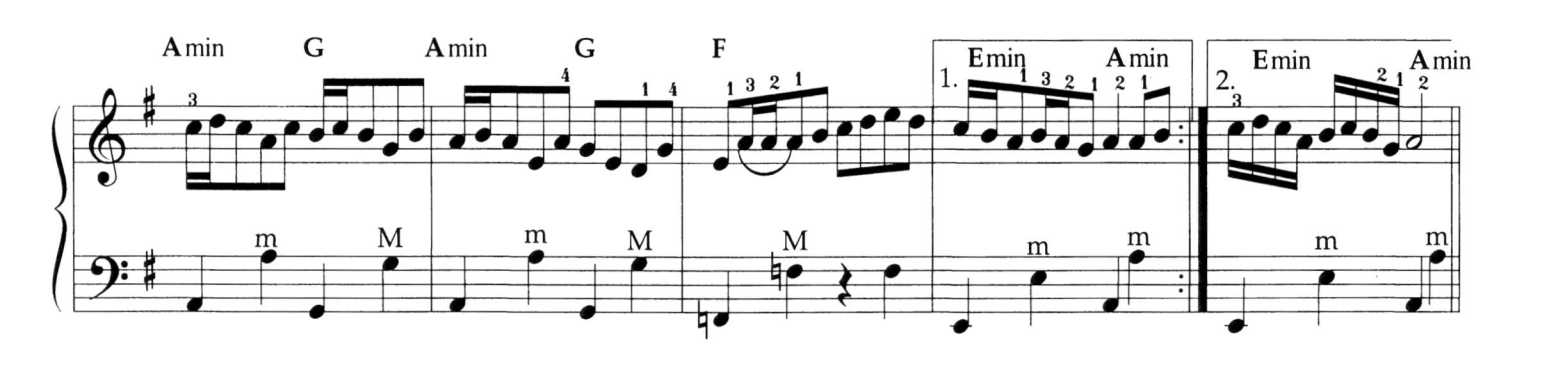

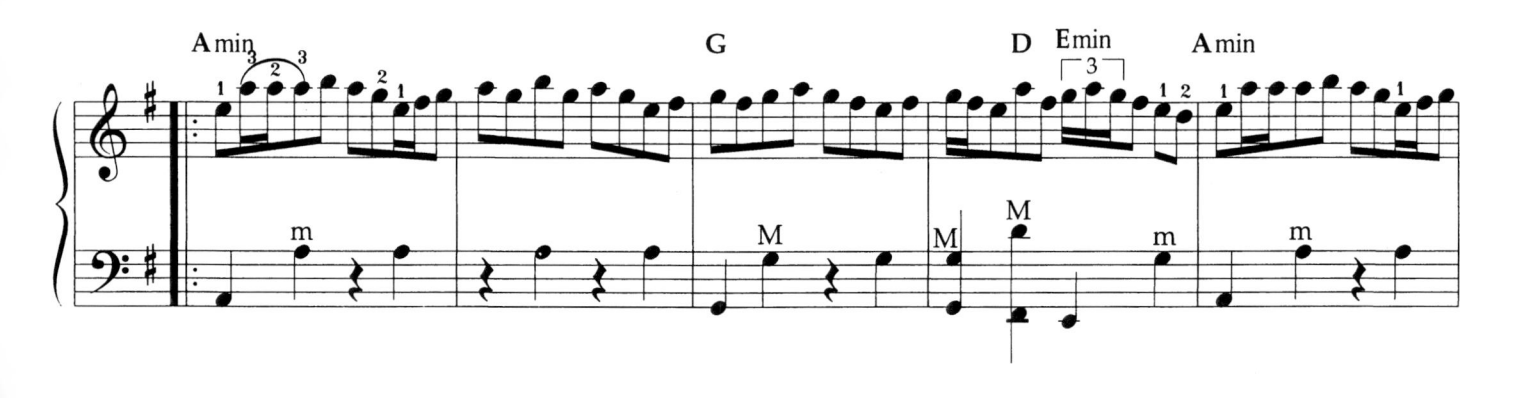

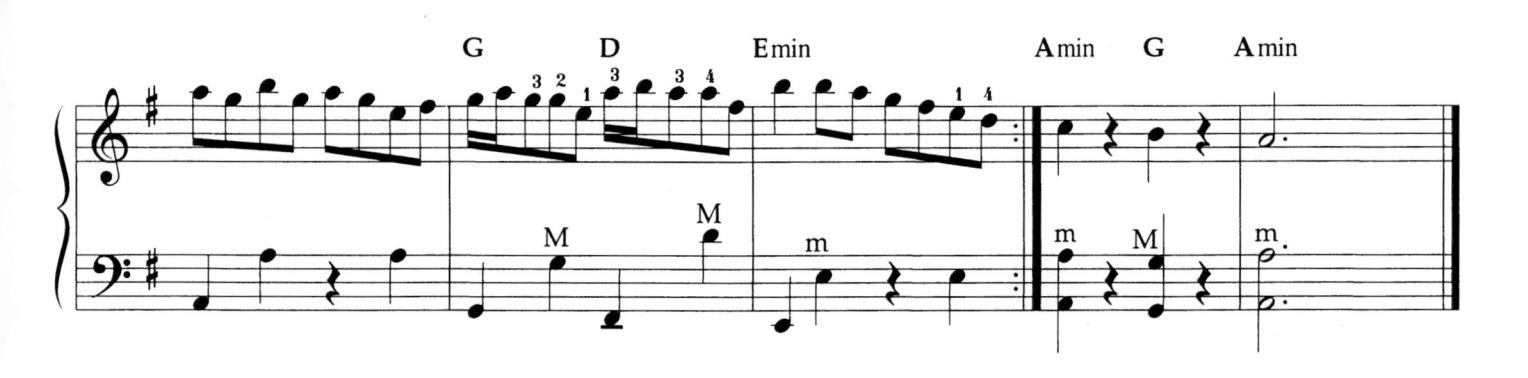

The Steeplechase

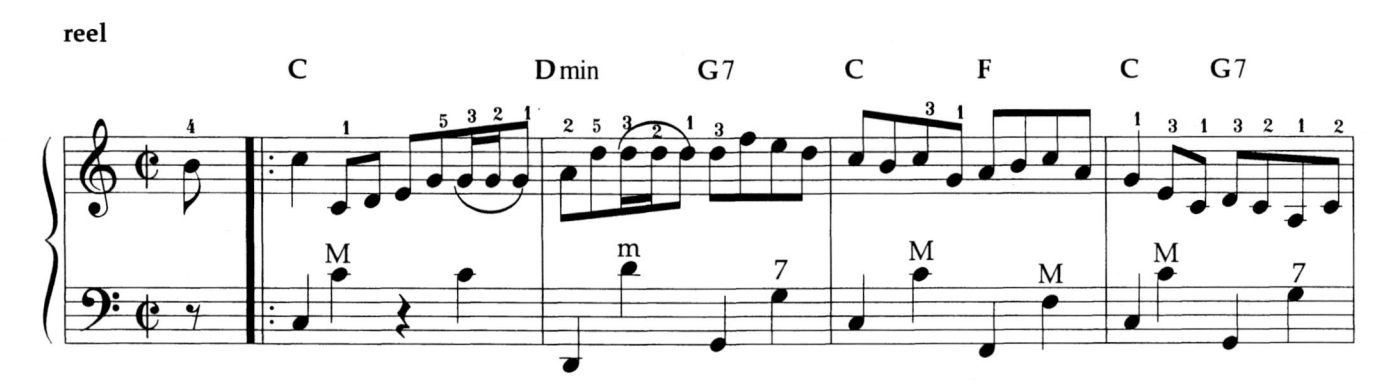

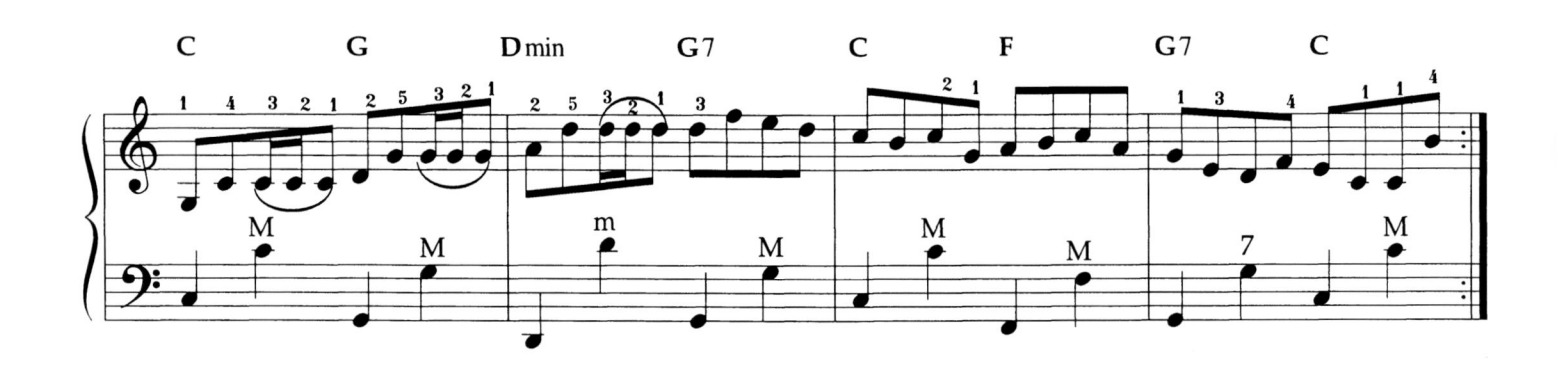

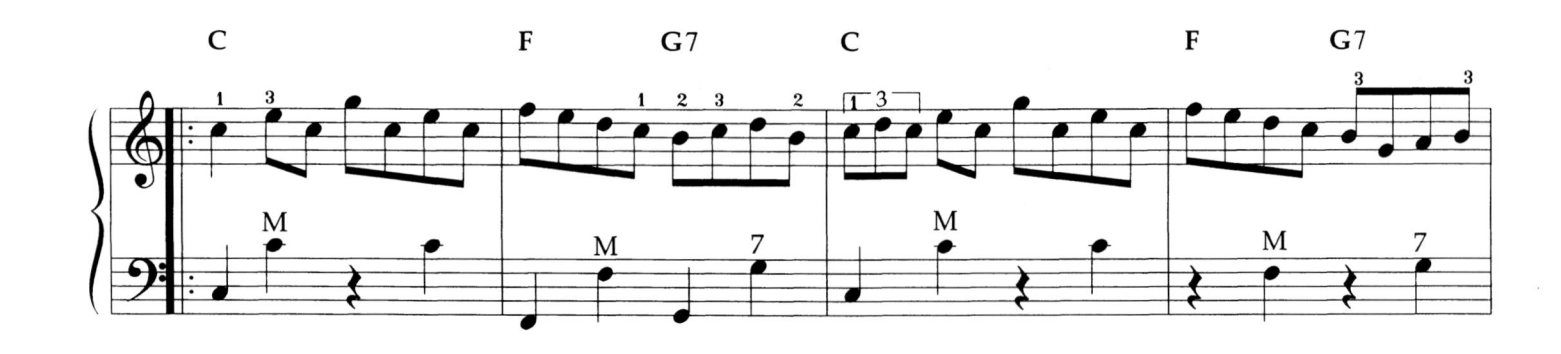

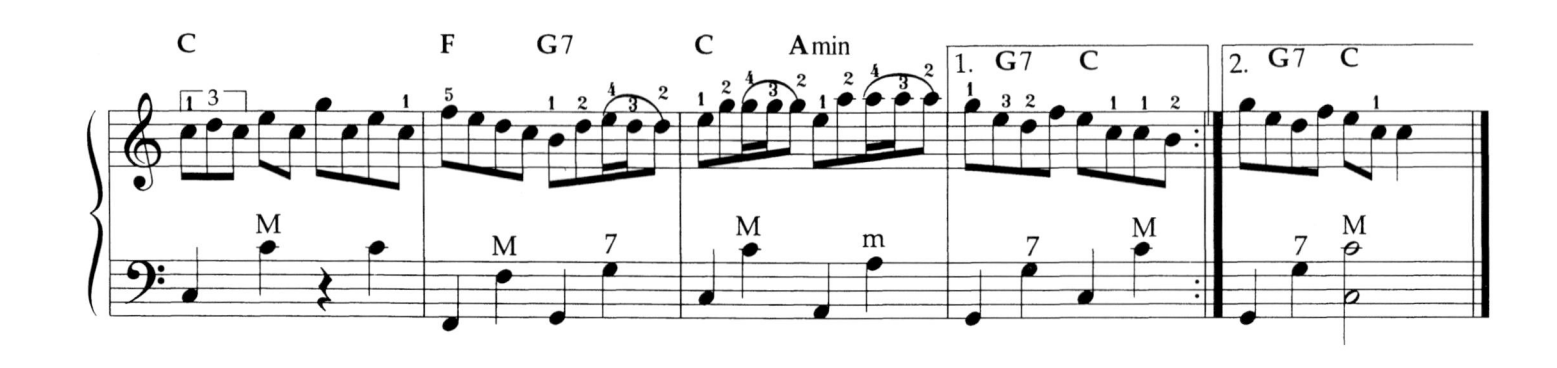

Sweet Cup of Tea

reel

arrangement by Tom Doherty

Chords based on piano playing of Felix Dolan.

arr. © Tom Doherty. All Rights Reserved. Used by Permission.

Tamlin

Tar Road to Sligo

Tatter Jack Walsh

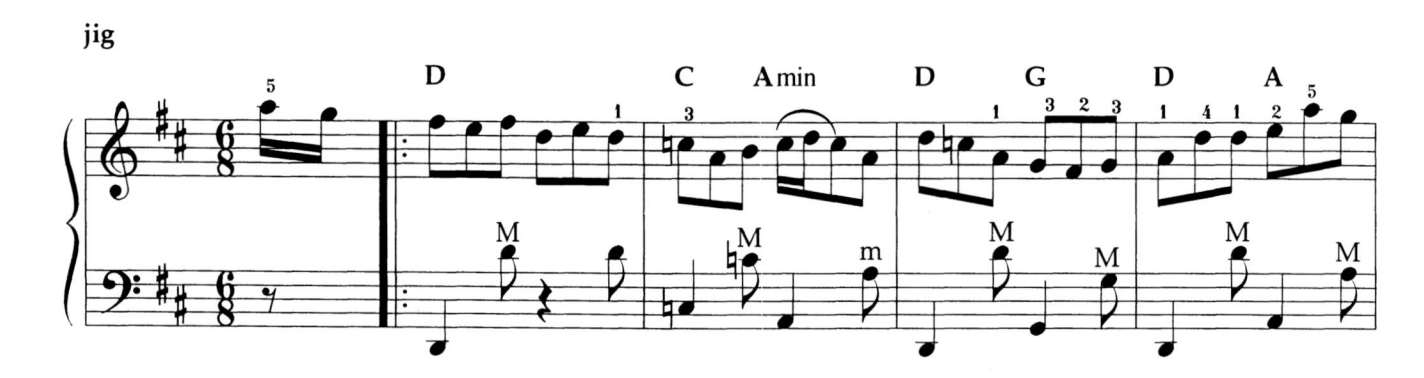

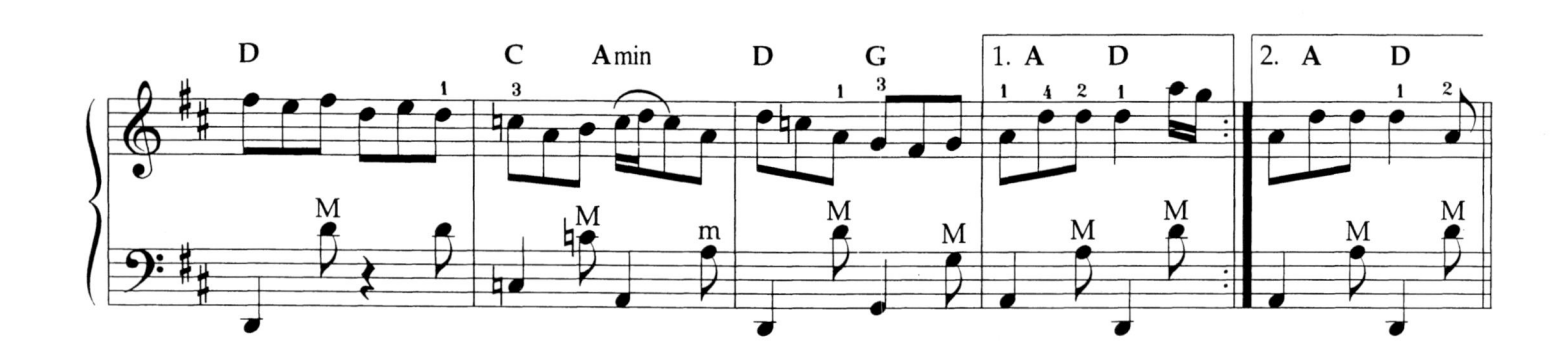

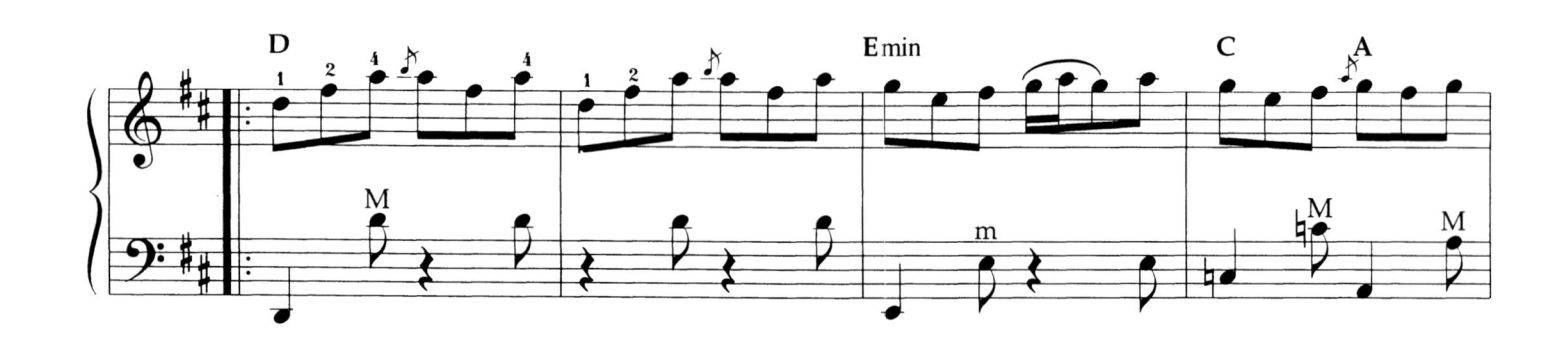

Tom Doherty's

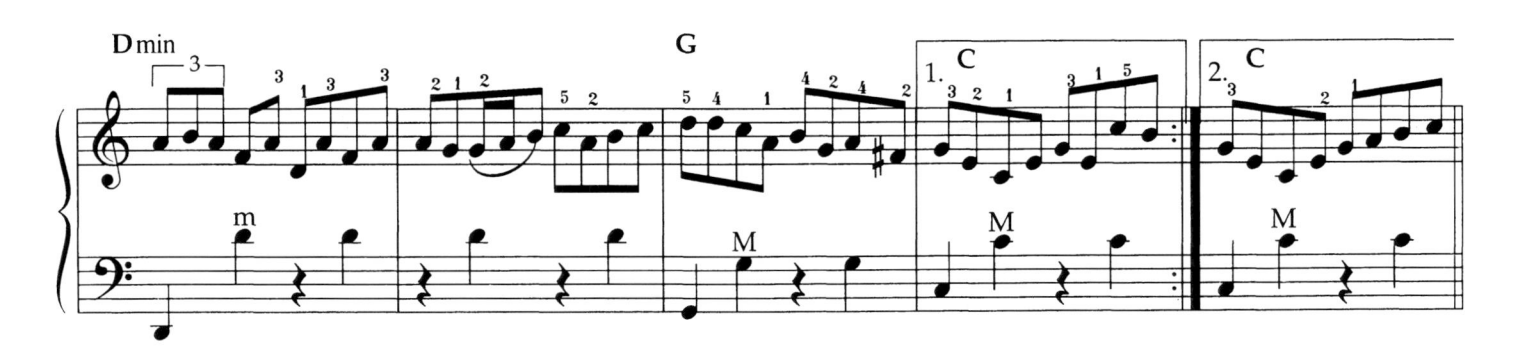

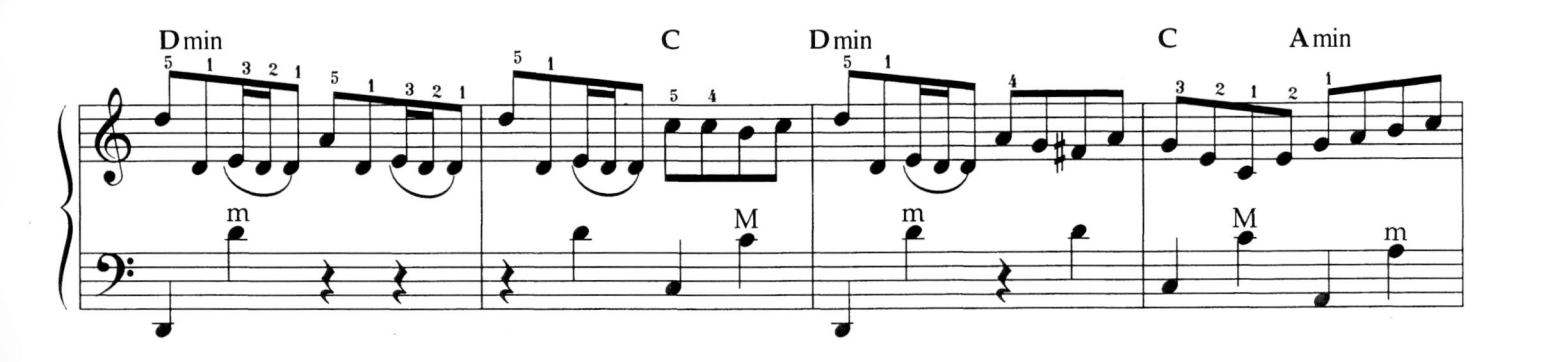

reel
arrangement by Billy McComiskey

Chords based on guitar playing of Daithi Sproul

arr. © Billy McComiskey. All Rights Reserved. Used by Permission.

Trip to Athlone

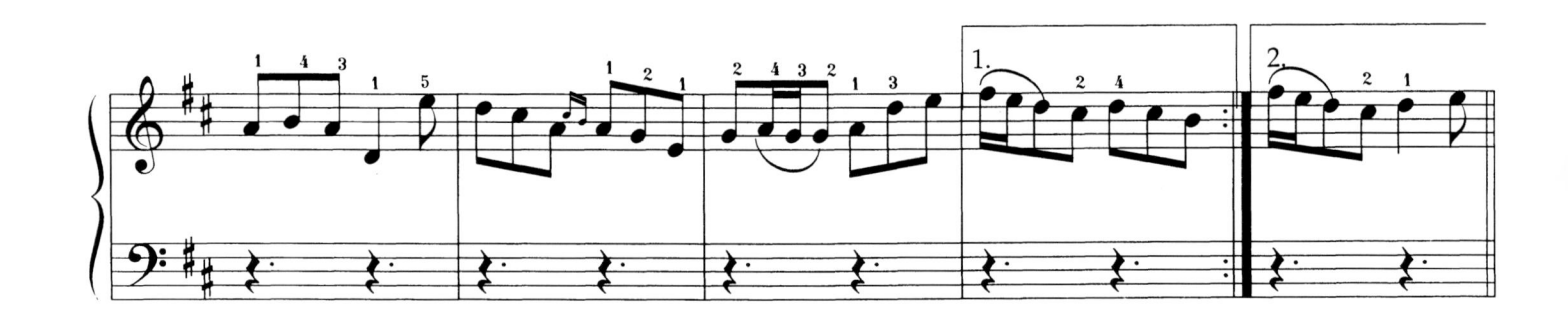

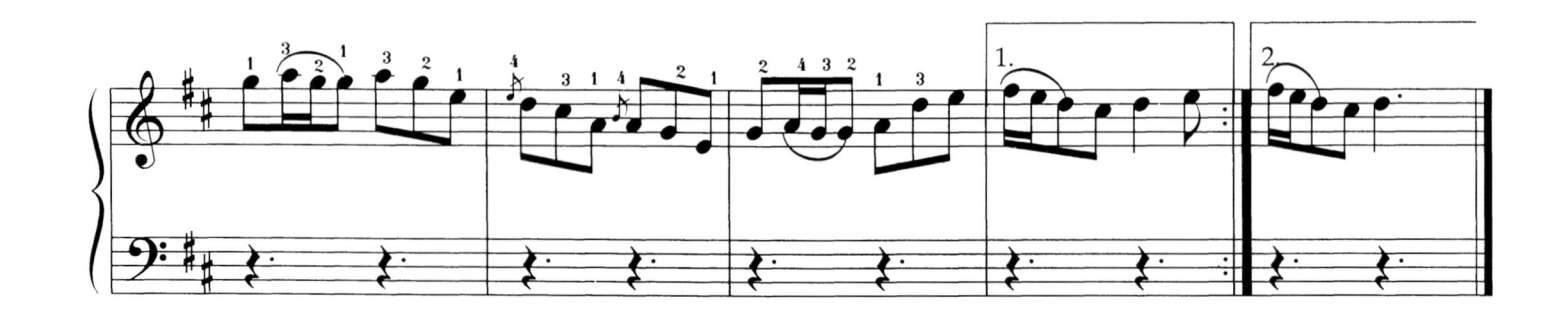

jig
arrangement by John Whelan

arr. © John Whelan. All Rights Reserved. Used by Permission.

Trip to Durrow

The White Petticoat

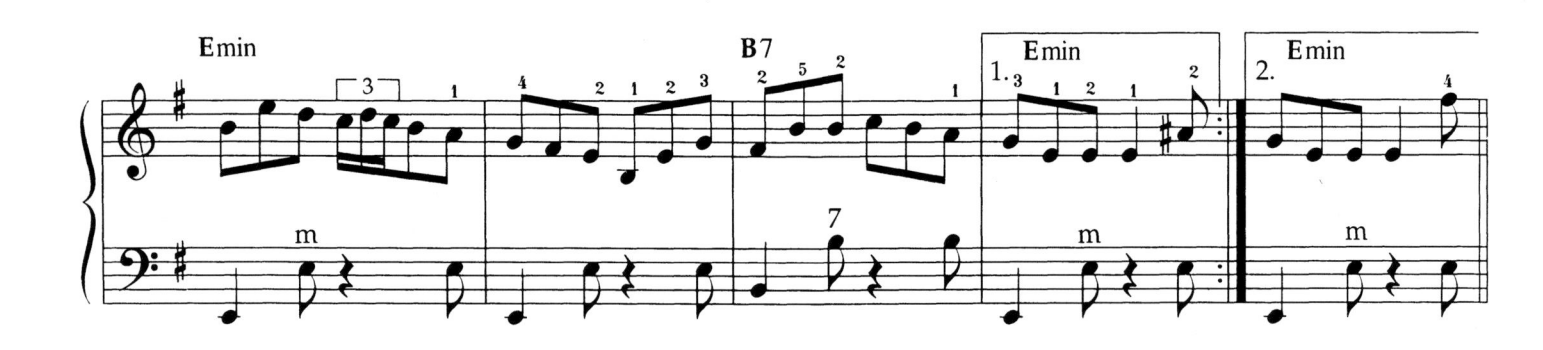

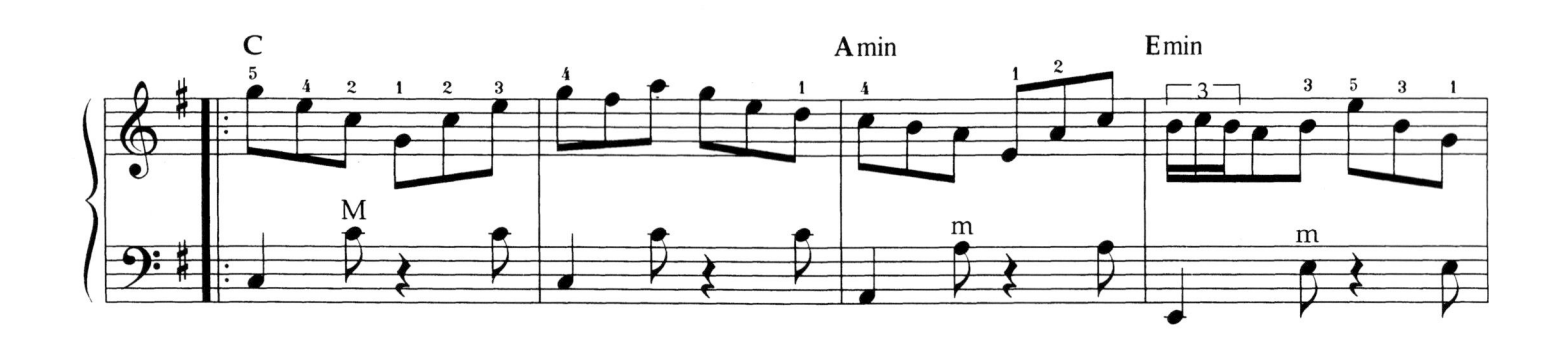

jig
arrangement by Joe Derrane

Chords based on piano playing of Felix Dolan.

arr. © Joe Derrane. All Rights Reserved. Used by Permission.

Willie Coleman's

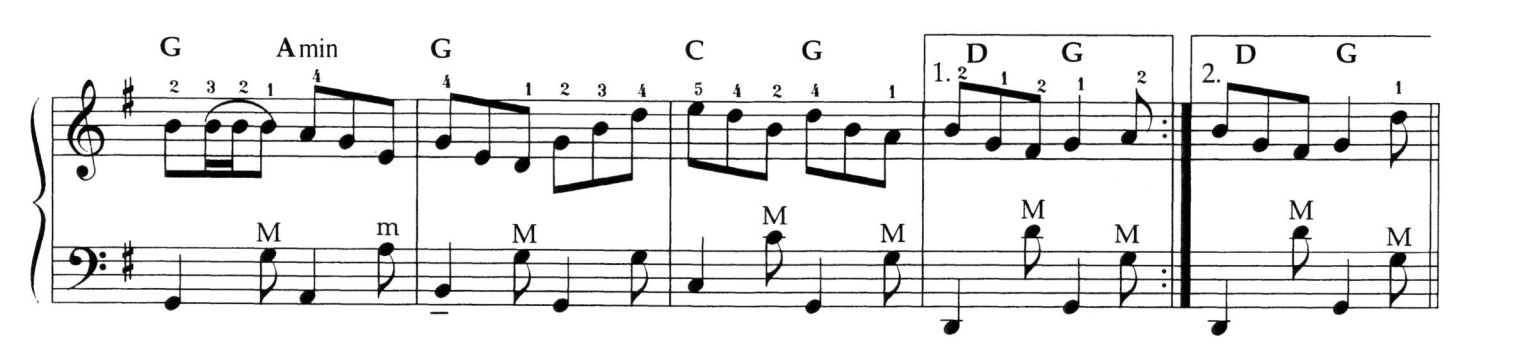

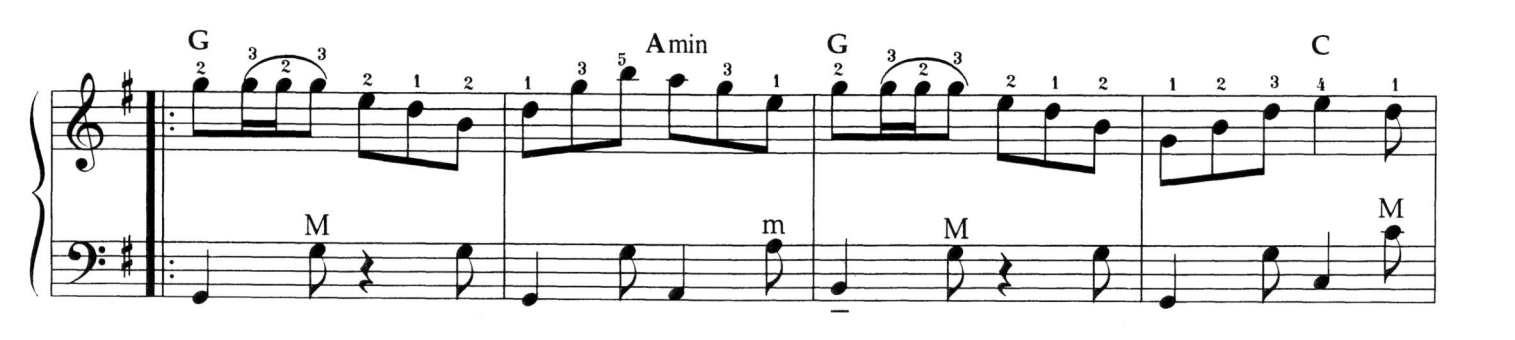

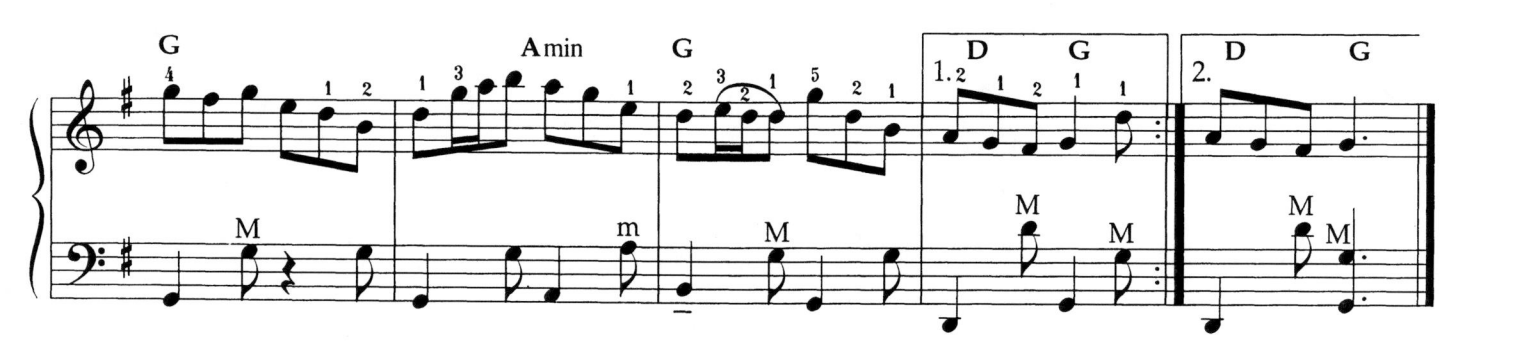

jig

Willie Coleman

The Wise Maid

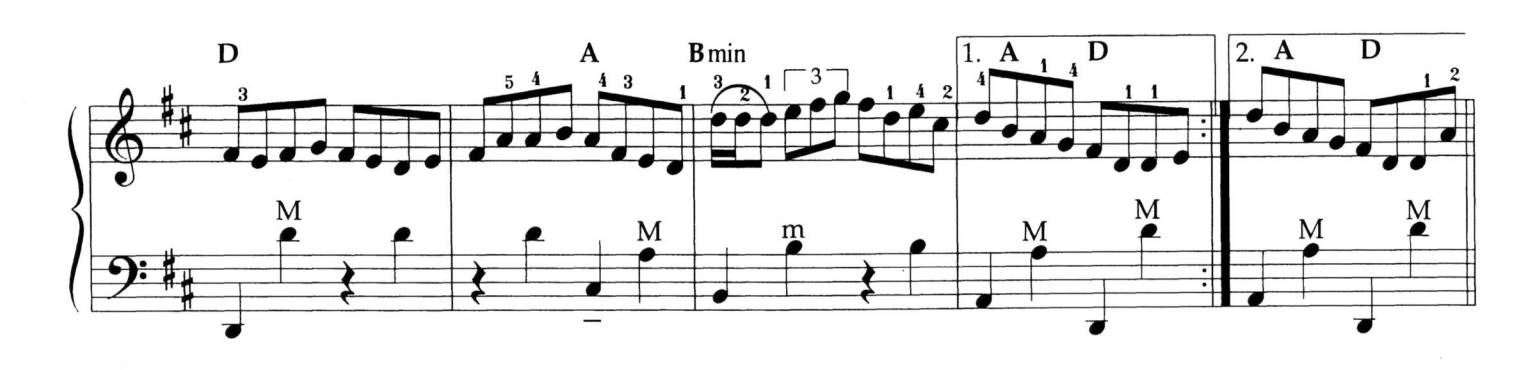

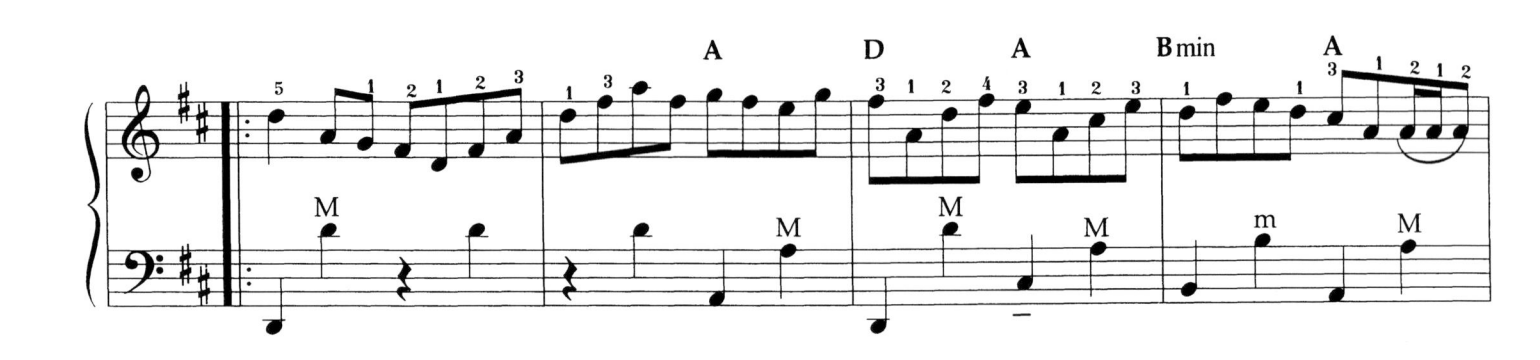

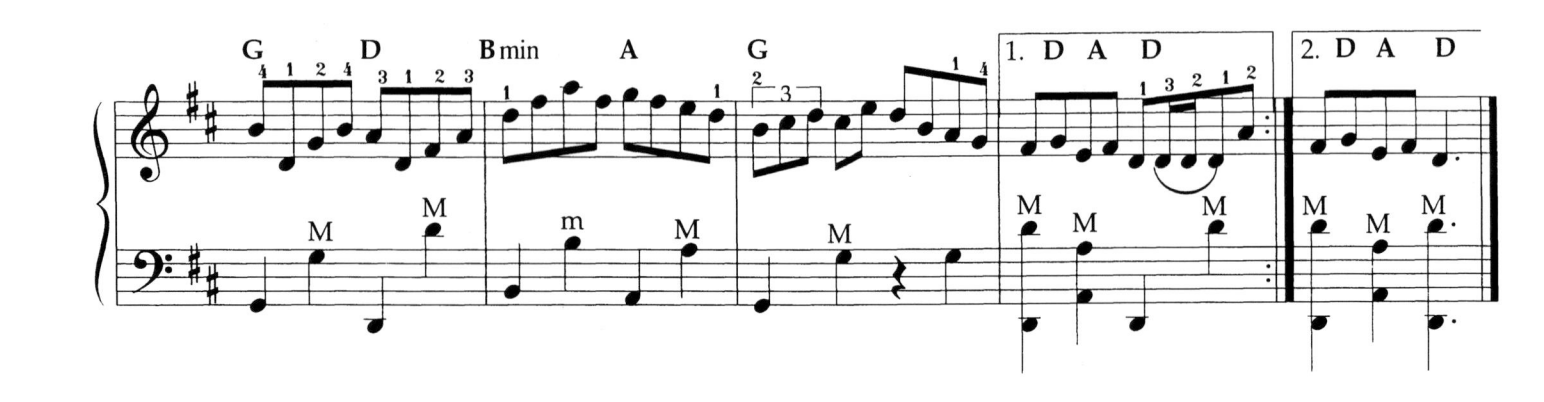

reel